LaFayette Wilbur

Early history of Vermont

LaFayette Wilbur

Early history of Vermont

ISBN/EAN: 9783742842428

Manufactured in Europe, USA, Canada, Australia, Japa

Cover: Foto ©ninafisch / pixelio.de

Manufactured and distributed by brebook publishing software (www.brebook.com)

LaFayette Wilbur

Early history of Vermont

EARLY HISTORY

—OF—

VERMONT.

BY LAFAYETTE WILBUR,

OF JERICHO, VT.

History maketh a young man to be old, without either wrinkles or gray hairs, privileging him with the experience of age, without either the infirmities or inconveniences thereof.—*Fuller.*

MIDDLEBURY COLLEGE LIBRARY.

JERICHO, VT.
ROSCOE PRINTING HOUSE.
1899.

Entered according to act of Congress, June 24th, 1899, by

LAFAYETTE WILBUR.

In the office of the Librarian of Congress at Washington, D. C.

A day, an hour of virtuous liberty
Is Worth a whole eternity of bondage —*Addisson*.

L. F. Wilbur

PREFACE.

This volume has been written to give to the public an accurate account of the early history of Vermont when it was called New Hampshire Grants and New Connecticut, and down to the time that the State was admitted into the Union in 1791. The writer has not created any fiction for the book, but facts have been related that are more interesting and useful than fiction, to Vermonters. It may lack the polish that some literary writers would give it. The most of it has been prepared for the press during the past year in bits of time that the writer has been able to snatch from pressing professional business. The reader will find accurately stated the action of the hardy pioneers that resulted in establishing the State amid the greatest difficulties in a dense wilderness, beset with dangers from hostile Indians, and bitter opposition from the people of neighboring territory, and the British army.

In drawing conclusions the proper data has been given, and exact dates given to historical events and transactions related, the absence of which is a serious lack with many historians.

PREFACE.

Ethan Allen's life was so prominently connected with the early history of Vermont, that one chapter has been devoted exclusively to his life. The Boorn Case given in Chapter fifteen was an early interesting case where innocent men were tried and convicted of murder and sentenced to be hung. The Chapter on Jericho may be of some local interest. The Charter or Grant of the township from Gov. Benning Wentworth was similar to those given in granting other towns by him. The chapters giving a list of the Members of the Windsor Convention of 1777, Council of Safety, Governors, Senators, and Judges of the Supreme Court, and giving the duration of their official service, will be useful as a handy reference. I have endeavored to give credit in quoting from other writers, and here express my acknowledgements to them.

This volume now given to the public takes up the History of Vermont and the doings of her people, only down to the time when she was admitted as the thirteenth State of the American Union. A more complete and continued history must be left for future volumes.

LaFayette Wilbur.

Jericho, July 4th. 1899.

History is Philosophy teaching by example.—*Dionysius.*

The greatest glory of a free born people, is to transmit that freedom to their children.—*Havard.*

CONTENTS.

CHAPTER I. (Page 1.)
HOW VERMONT BECAME A STATE, AND ITS EARLY HISTORY.

CHAPTER II. (Page 67.)
THE STRUGGLE OF THE NEW HAMPSHIRE GRANTS TO ESTABLISH A SEPARATE JURISDICTION BY THE NAME OF VERMONT, AND HER EARLY HISTORY.

CHAPTER III. (Page 127.)
EARLY HISTORY OF VERMONT—CONTINUED.

CHAPTER IV. (Page 134.)
EARLY HISTORY OF VERMONT—CONTINUED.

CHAPTER V. (Page 145.)
EARLY HISTORY OF VERMONT—CONTINUED.

CHAPTER VI. (Page 162.)
LEGISLATION AND INTERNAL AFFAIRS OF EARLY VERMONT.

CHAPTER VII. (Page 175.)
THE STRUGGLE OF VERMONT FOR ADMISSION INTO THE UNION.

CHAPTER VIII. Page 186.)
THE ACTION OF NEW HAMPSHIRE AND NEW YORK.

CHAPTER IX. (Page 193.)
EARLY HISTORY AND ADMISSION AS A STATE—CONTINUED.

CHAPTER X. (Page 196.)
LAND TITLES, BETTERMENT ACTS AND HARD TIMES.

CHAPTER XI. (Page 204.)
VERMONT ACTS OF SOVEREIGNTY.

CHAPTER XII. (Page 209.)
SETTLEMENT OF THE CONTROVERSY WITH NEW YORK AND ADMISSION OF VERMONT.

CHAPTER XIII. (Page 227.)
A RESUME AND EARLY HISTORY OF VERMONT—CONCLUDED.

CHAPTER XIV. (Page 240.)
GENERAL ETHAN ALLEN.

CHAPTER XV. (Page 281.)
THE TRIAL OF STEPHEN AND JESSE BOORN FOR THE ALLEGED MURDER OF RUSSEL COLVIN.

CHAPTER XVI. (Page 295.)
THE TOWN OF JERICHO.

CHAPTER XVII. (Page 330.)
MEMBERS OF THE WINDSOR CONVENTION, COUNCIL OF SAFETY, GOVERNORS AND SENATORS.

CHAPTER XVIII. (Page 236.)
LIST OF JUDGES OF THE SUPREME COURT FROM THE YEAR 1778 TO THE YEAR 1899, AND SHOWING THEIR TERM OF OFFICE.

WIT AND HUMOR. (Page 347.)

ERRATA.

Errors found in printing, so far as they are misleading, are corrected below.

On page 30 the verses should have been divided into five parts.

On page 34 in the 6th line from top it should read "about" instead of "go out."

The word "grants," wherever it occurs referring to the people or territory of New Hampshire Grants, should be "Grants."

On page 62, bottom line, word "no" should be inserted before the word "pains."

On page 150, in eighth line from bottom, the word "setting" should read "sitting."

On page 173, the name "Neshbe" should read "Neshobe," and the name "Mendon" should read "Minden."

On page 227, the words "this and," in first line, should be erased.

On page 304, the name "Brutt's" should read "Butts."

In the list of Judges for 1879, on page 344, the name of H. Henry Powers should follow that of Jonathan Ross.

PERSONNEL.

The Author makes his grateful acknowledgement for quotations taken from the Addresses of

Hon. Lucius E. Chittenden,	Pages 82, 230
Hon. John W. Stewart,	Page 225
Hon. Edward J. Phelps,	" 229
Hon. John N. Pomeroy,	" 279
Hon. Julius Converse,	" 280
Professor Joseph S. Cilley,	" 316

A Free State gathered in the Council should speak by all its citizens, each one claiming as of birthright a voice to aid his country: None should be excluded from the privilege, if grown to man's estate, unless he fail of intellect or lose his right through crime.

* * * * * *

Ancestors who won their way should shine in their descendants.—*Tupper.*

CHAPTER I.

HOW VERMONT BECAME A STATE, AND ITS EARLY HISTORY.

IT is interesting to study the history of any people who are struggling for existence, or who are striving to maintain their rights and to assert their liberties and establish their independence; and this must be especially so when that history relates to one's ancestors and their own land. How intensely did our feelings and sympathies reach out for the Hungarians under their leader Kossuth when they were struggling to be free; but their endeavors and aspirations were not more noble, and the difficulties that stood in the way of their freedom and independence were not greater than seem to environ the Green Mountain Boys. The hardships and the dangers with which the hardy sons of the territory now called Vermont were beset, grew largely out of the claims that different parties made to her lands, and the assumed right to govern her people. New Hampshire claimed her from the East, New York claimed her from the West, and Massachusetts would take a slice from the Southern border.

The first settlement, within the jurisdiction now known as Vermont, was made at Fort Dummer, in the present County of Windham, in the year 1724, under a grant from the Provincial

Government of Massachusetts. A controversy arose between the Provinces of Massachusetts and New Hampshire in reference to the line between the two Provinces. In the year 1740, the King of England in Council settled the line between the two jurisdictions, and located it in running West of Connecticut River, where the jurisdictional line now is between Massachusetts and Vermont, which brought the settlement at Fort Dummer within the jurisdiction of New Hampshire. This line between New Hampshire and Massachusetts as settled by the King and Council, was to extend West till it should meet with His Majesty's other governments.

In the year 1741, Benning Wentworth was commissioned as Governor of New Hampshire. It was understood at that time that the jurisdiction of New Hampshire was established as far West as Massachusetts, and Massachusetts claimed and exercised jurisdiction to within twenty miles of Hudson River. With this understanding, the Governor of New Hampshire, on the third day of January, 1749, made a grant of a township six miles square, situated twenty miles East of Hudson River, and called it Bennington. Numerous applications were made to Gov. Wentworth for grants in the vicinity of the Province of New York. Gov. Wentworth not feeling exactly certain how far West the jurisdiction of New Hampshire extended, opened a correspondence with the Governor of New York, Nov. 17th, 1749, with a view of ascertaining and settling the Western line of his jurisdiction; and in that correspondence informed him that people were daily applying for grants of land, some of which were in the neighborhood of the New York Province, and asking the Governor of the Province of New York in what manner these grants will affect the grants made by the New York Governors; also informing him by the same letter, that the surveyor who had run the line between Massachusetts and New Hampshire, had declared on oath that in running that line Westerly it would strike Hudson River about 80 poles North of where Mohawk's River comes into Hudson River, which he presumed is North of the City of Albany, and asked to be informed how far North of Albany the government of New York extends, and how many miles to the East of Hudson River. Governor Clinton of New York, April 9th, 1750, replied, "that the Province of New York is bounded Eastward by Connecticut River, and that letters patent from King Charles II. to the Duke of York, expressly granted all lands from the West side of Connecticut River to the East side of Delaware Bay. Governor Wentworth, the 25th of April, 1750, said, in his reply to that letter, to Gov. Clinton of New York, that the subject of his letter would have been entirely satisfactory had not the two charter-governments of Connecticut and Massachusetts Bay extended their bounds many miles Westward of Connecticut River, and that he was advised by His Majesty's Council that New Hampshire had an equal right to claim as far West as the charter-governments of Connecticut and Massachusetts Bay, but disclaimed any intention of interfering with his Government, and asked Gov. Clinton to inform him by what authority Connecticut and Massachusetts governments claimed so far to the Westward as they have settled. And on the 6th of June, 1750, Gov. Clinton informed Governor Wentworth by letter, that as to Connecticut their claim was founded upon an agreement with his government, in or about the year 1684; and afterwards confirmed by King William, and that the line was run and marked in 1725; and as to Massachusetts, she got possession at first by intrusion and were allowed to continue the intrusion by the negligence of New York, and complained to Gov. Wentworth for granting the township of Bennington, and asked him to recall the grant. But Gov. Wentworth, on the 22nd of June, 1750, wrote Gov. Clinton that he would represent the whole matter to the King His Majesty, and advised him to do the same, and that he would not enter into any controversy until his Majesty's pleasure should be further known, and declined to recall the grant.

Notwithstanding the claims of New York that their jurisdiction extended to Connecticut River, Gov. Wentworth continued to grant townships, and from Jan. 3d, 1749, till the 4th of Aug., 1763, granted 129 townships, 11 of which were in the County of Chittenden. Hinesburgh was granted June 21, 1762; Charlotte was granted June 24, 1762; Colchester, Bolton, Burlington, Williston, Huntington (called New Huntington), were granted June 7th, 1763, and Jericho, Milton,

Westford and Underhill, were granted June 8, 1763; St. George and Shelburne were granted Aug. 18th, 1763; and in 1764, 14,000 acres were granted to certain officers. To arrest these proceedings, Colden, Lieut.-Governor of New York, on the 28th Dec., 1763, issued his proclamation commanding the Sheriff of the County of Albany to make return of all names who had taken possession of lands under New Hampshire grants, and claiming jurisdiction as far East as Connecticut River, by virtue of the grant to the Duke of York.

On the 13th March, 1764, Governor Wentworth issued his proclamation assuring the people who had taken grants of land from New Hampshire, that the patent to the Duke of York was obsolete, and did not convey or give any certain boundary to New York, and encouraging his people not to be intimidated, hindered or obstructed in the improvement of the lands granted them, and to maintain the jurisdiction of His Majesty's government of New Hampshire as far Westward as to include the lands granted, and commanding all civil officers to deal with any persons that may presume to interrupt the settlers on said lands as to law and justice appertains.

New York not willing to rely for their claims to the land as far East as Connecticut River, on the grant to the Duke of York, made application to the Crown for a confirmation of their claim. And on the 20th day of July, 1764, at the Court of St. James, the King in Council took the matter of the application into consideration, ordered and declared the Western bank of the Connecticut River, from where it enters the Province of Massachusetts Bay, as far North as the 45th degree of North Latitude, to be the boundary line between the said two Provinces of New Hampshire and New York. Although New Hampshire grants were surprised at this order, they were willing to submit, as they did not suppose it would affect the title to their lands, their land titles having come from the Crown through the grants made by the Governor of New Hampshire. The Governor of New Hampshire after remonstrating against the change of jurisdiction, for a while abandoned the contest, and recommended the settlers to due obedience to the authorities and laws of the Colony of New York.

Soon, however, a controversy arose between New Hampshire grants and the government of New York as to the effect and construction of that order. The government of New York contended that the order had a retrospective operation and that all the grants made by the Governor of New Hampshire were void, while the New Hampshire grants held that the effect of the King's order in Council was only to operate from the date of the order, and that the title to their lands, granted before the date of that order and before the change of jurisdiction, would remain good. The government of New York insisting that their construction of the order should prevail, extended their jurisdiction over the New Hampshire grants; divided their territory into four counties, Albany, Charlotte, Cumberland, and Gloucester, and established in each courts of justice, and called upon the settlers to surrender their grants obtained of New Hampshire, and purchase again under grants from New York, and thus pay for their lands twice.

This the Grants refused to do, and New York proceeded to grant their lands to others, who brought actions of ejectments in the courts at Albany, and obtained judgments against the grants; but the officers of New York, while attempting to execute those judgments, and deprive the Grants of their lands, met with determined resistance. Associations among the Grants were formed for their protection: there was organized an obstinate resistance to the New York authorities. A convention at length was called of representatives from several towns of the West side of the mountain, which appointed Samuel Robinson agent to represent them at the Court in England, and set forth to the King and Council their grievances and obtain a confirmation of their grants from New Hampshire. He went to London on his mission, the result of which was, the King in Council on the 24th day of July, 1767, commanded the Governor of New York for the time being, "do not, upon pain of His Majesty's highest displeasure, presume to make any grant whatsoever covered by the New Hampshire grants;" but notwithstanding this order, the Governor of New York continued to make grants, and continued to bring actions of ejectments against those who held land under the grants made by New Hampshire. The courts at Albany decided not to receive in evidence duly authenticated copies of the royal orders to the Governor of New Hampshire, giving the Governor of New Hampshire, as they claimed, the right to grant the lands to the defendants, which made the trial, jug-handle like, all on one side.

Let us look at the surroundings of this people then called New Hampshire Grants. The government of New Hampshire had acquiesced in the order that their jurisdiction should not extend West of Connecticut River. New York had got an order allowing their jurisdiction to extend to Connecticut River, and the New York courts had decided all the cases affecting the title to the land granted against the New Hampshire Grants. The Governor of New Hampshire had withdrawn their authority and protection from the settlers. New York was a powerful Province, and its people selfish and unrelenting. The New Hampshire Grants were few in number. Any people thus situated, less hardy, bold and brave than the Green Mountain Boys, would have shrunk from a contest with the government of New York. The course of the government of New York had stung the Grants to madness, and they were driven to the last resort. A convention of the people assembled at Bennington and resolved to support their rights and protect their property against the usurpation and unjust claims of the Governor and Council of New York by force. The contest commenced. Several of the Grants were indicted as rioters by the New York courts. The officers of New York sent to arrest the persons indicted, were chastised with the "twigs" of the wilderness. A military association was formed with Ethan

Allen as commander. Committees of safety were formed in several towns west of the Green Mountains. On the other hand, the sheriff of Albany County was directed to raise the *Posse comitatus* to assist in the execution of his office. The Governor of New York offered a reward of 150 pounds for the apprehension of Ethan Allen, and 50 pounds for each of five others. And in retaliation, Ethan Allen and the other five proscribed persons issued a proclamation offering five pounds for the apprehension and delivery to any officer of the Green Mountain Boys, the Attorney General of the Colony of New York. On the 19th of May, 1772, Gov. Tryon of New York addressed a letter to Rev. Mr. Dewey and the inhabitants of Bennington and the adjacent country, telling them he had heard of their violent and illegal acts which could not fail of being highly offensive to their Sovereign, and that if they persevered in their disobedience it would bring against them the exertions of the powers of government, but claimed he was willing to examine into the grounds of their complaints, and asked them to lay before him and His Majesty's Council the cause of their behavior and discontent, and promised to give relief, and promised protection to any one they saw fit to send to represent them, except Robert Cochran, Ethan Allen, Remember Baker, Seth Warner, and a Mr. Sevil, persons for whose apprehension he had offered rewards; and closed his letter by saying "they might not be deceived by a persuasion that part of the country that you inhabit will ever be annexed to the government of New Hampshire." Rev. Dewey answered, in short, stating some of the causes of discontent, setting forth that, "they held the fee of the land that they had settled on by virtue of grants from the King of England and was reputed to be within the Province of New Hampshire, and that by some means they had got the jurisdictional line changed; and that grants of land had been made by New York government covering the same lands granted by New Hampshire, and that repeated efforts were made by writs of ejectment to dispossess the settlers, who had titles under grants from New Hampshire, and who had been deprived of the right to show their defense by the courts of New York; they, the Yorkers, had violently broken open the settlers' houses to get possession, and to arrest the settlers; and had fired upon and injured innocent women and children; and closed by supplicating the Governor to assist in quieting his people in the possession of their lands, till the controversy should be settled by the King.

At the same date, Ethan Allen, Warner, Baker, and Cochran addressed a long communication to Governor Tryon, in which they stated that "no tyrannical exertions of the powers of government can deter us from asserting and vindicating our undoubted right and privileges as Englishmen," and informed him, "that since their misfortune of being annexed to the Province of New York, the law has been rather used as a tool (than a rule of equity) to cheat them out of their country that they had made valuable by labor and expense." "And if they did not oppose the New York sheriff and posse, they would take immediate possession of their houses and farms; and if they did oppose them they were indicted as rioters, and all assisting, are indicted as rioters so long as they act the bold and manly part and stand by their liberties." They told the Governor it had come to this, at least, that "we must tamely be dispossessed of our rights and property or oppose officers in taking possession; and as a necessary step, oppose taking rioters, so called, or run away like so many cowards, and quit our country to a number of cringing, polite gentlemen who have ideally possessed themselves of it already;" and informed the Governor that changing the jurisdiction from New Hampshire to New York did not and could not deprive them of their lands and property; and moreover, the King in Council had ordered the government of New York not to disturb the settlers till they had decided the whole controversy, and therefore it was the Yorkers that were rioters and land robbers; and that every act they had done to compass their doings, though under the pretense of law, was violation of law and an insult on the Constitution, and authority of the Crown, as well as to us; and informed him, if he did not know before, that "Right and wrong are eternally the same, to all periods of time, places and nations;" the taking away their rights under the specious pretense of law, only adds to the criminality of it. They closed their letter by assuring the Governor that their acts were not against his government, but looked upon him as their political father, but it was oppression that was the ground of their discontent, and entreated the Governor to aid in quieting the settlers in their possessions, and if he should do this there would be an end to riots, so called, and their tongues would express their gratitude for such protection. While negotiations were pending, the Green Mountain Boys dispossessed certain settlers, on Otter Creek, who claimed lands under New York, by reason of which Governor Tryon addressed a highly seasoned letter to the inhabitants of Bennington, the 11th of August, 1772, charging them with breach of faith and honor; on the 25th of August, 1772, the people of the grants replied and stated to the Governor that the dispossessing certain persons from certain lands and a saw-mill on Otter Creek, was but a repossession of property previously taken from the New Hampshire Grants by the Yorkers.

This controversy continued to engage the attention of the British Cabinet, and on Dec. 3d, 1772, they seemed to have declared that grants made under New Hampshire ought to be confirmed and the settlers hold title to their lands under their original grants, though their lands were within the Province of New York.

We have come now to an interesting period of our early history, when the New Hampshire Grants were to declare themselves independent of New York. New Hampshire had withdrawn their claim from all territory west of Connecticut River and consequently all protection to its people. The mass of settlers on the New Hampshire grants consisted of a brave, hardy race of men. Their minds had been aroused to the exercise of their highest energies in a controversy involving everything that was dear to them, property, liberty, and life. Foremost among the Grants stood Ethan Allen. He was bold, ardent, and unyielding, and was peculiarly fitted to become their leader. During the progress of this controversy, several pamphlets were written by him well suited to stir up public feeling against the injustice of the New York claims. At this period, the people in what are now the Counties of Bennington and Rutland, called a convention by committees from the several towns. This body declared among other things, that no persons should take grants, or confirmation of grants, under the government of New York, and they forbade all inhabitants in the district of New Hampshire grants, to hold, take, or accept any office of honor or profit under the Colony of New York, and all officers, either civil or military, who had acted under the authority of New York, were required to suspend their functions on pain of being viewed. The word "viewed" had a peculiar signification. These decrees were frequently enforced by the application of the "beech seal." At this day we might feel inclined to censure the Green Mountain Boys for the severity of the punishment they were called upon to inflict, but we must remember there was no choice left them. It was an entire surrender of their farms, or a determined resistance by force. Necessity and force drove them to resistance. Benjamin Hough, who accepted and officiated as a justice of the peace under the authority of New York, was brought before the Committee of Safety, composed of Green Mountain Boys, for trial. In his defense he claimed and plead he was acting under the authority of New York, but it was replied that a convention of Grants decreed and forbade all persons holding any office, civil or military, under New York. He was adjudged guilty and sentenced, "that he be taken from the bar of the Committee of Safety, tied to a tree, and there on his naked back receive 200 stripes; his back being dressed, he should depart out of the district, and on return, without special leave of the convention, to suffer death. New York regarded this conduct as treasonable, and proceeded to legislate against the Grants in the most despotic manner. These persons thus interviewed, and others, made complaints to the New York government, and claimed its protection. A New York committee passed resolves Feb. 25th, 1774, declaring that many acts of outrage and cruelty had been perpetrated by lawless persons, calling themselves the Bennington mob, and have seized, insulted and terrified magistrates and other civil officers so that they dare not exercise their functions; have rescued prisoners for debt, assumed to themselves military commands, and judicial power, burned and demolished houses and property, beat and abused the persons of his Majesty's subjects," and many other acts. And they resolved they would not countenance such conduct, and prayed their Governor to issue a proclamation, offering a reward of 50 pounds for the apprehending the leaders of the Green Mountain Boys, among whom were Ethan Allen, Seth Warner and Remember Baker, and committing them to the jail at Albany; and recommended that a law be passed to suppress such proceedings, and "to maintain the free course of justice, and for bringing the offenders to condign punishment. This act did not seem to intimidate the Grants against whom such action was taken, for at a meeting held in Manchester, in March, 1774, they declared in substance, that the New York Committee had passed over in silence the great bone of discontent, the Green Mountain Boys' right and title to the lands granted them by New Hampshire, and how the Yorkers had attempted, through the New York courts and other means, to deprive them of their land and their improvements thereon, and declared "we are determined to maintain those grants against all opposition, until His Majesty's Royal pleasure shall be known in the premises."

On the 9th of March, 1774, the General Assembly of New York enacted, among other things, that if any number of persons, to the number of three, being unlawfully, riotously and tumultuously assembled in the Counties of Albany and Charlotte, do not disperse at the command of a justice of the peace or sheriff, they should, on conviction, suffer twelve months' imprisonment, without bail, and such other imprisonment as the court should see fit to impose, not extending to life or limb; and that if any person should knowingly hinder such justice or sheriff in making proclamation to disperse, should, on proof, be adjudged a felon and suffer death without the benefit of the clergy. And if any person should in said counties assume judicial powers as judge or justice, and should try, fine, sentence or condemn, unless having authority under the Province of New York, or should seize, detain or assault and beat any civil officer in the exercise of his office in order to compel him to resign, or should terrify, hinder or prevent him from exercising his authority under New York, he should be adjudged a felon and suffer death without benefit of clergy. And that special provision were made for bringing the ringleaders of the Green Mountain Boys to trial and punishment, that they might be committed to the prison at New York City or Albany, without the right of bail; and that they should voluntarily surrender themselves for commitment and trial; and if they fail to do so, should suffer death without trial; and if any person receive, harbor or succor, any such person, knowing they had been required to surrender themselves, they should suffer imprisonment; and if any person committed any of the offences specified they might be taken to Albany for trial. So you see that the provisions were of the most sweeping character, intended to awe the people into abject submission and to crush out the spirit of liberty and independence. With the passage of this law, terminated every prospect of peace or to the submission to the claims of New York. The Grants regarded it as originating solely in the avarice of a set of speculators who coveted their lands and their valuable improvements thereon. The great body of the people of New York did not sympathize with those acts or the course of the New York authorities. The threatenings of the New York government were regarded with utter contempt by the Green Mountain Boys; they had been educated in the school of adversity and inured to hardship and danger, and they met the shock with a firm, unbroken spirit. The spirit and determination of the people calling themselves the New Hampshire Grants, were clearly set forth in a remonstrance issued by Ethan Allen and others the 26th day of April, 1774, against the enactment of such cruel laws and against the course of the New York authorities. After setting forth, in substance, that the object of those laws was greed, declared that they were conscious that their cause was good and equitable in the sight of God and all unprejudiced and honest men, that the spring and the moving cause of their opposition to the government of New York, was self preservation, and to preserve and maintain their property and defend their lives. They told the Yorkers in that remonstrance "that they had gained as well as merited the disapprobation and abhorrence of their neighbors; that the innocent blood they had already shed, called for Heaven's vengeance on their guilty heads; and said, "that if they should come forthwith against us, thousands of their injured and dissatisfied neighbors, in the several governments, will join with us, to cut off and extirpate such an execrable race from the face of the earth." They described to the Yorkers the character of their laws in this remarkable statement, viz.,: "If we oppose civil officers, in taking possession of our farms, we are, by those laws, denominated felons; if we defend our neighbors who have been indicted as rioters only for defending our property, we are likewise adjudged felon. In fine, every opposition to their monarchial government is deemed felony, and at the end of every such sentence, there is the word death." But the Green Mountain Boys said, "there was one matter of consolation for us, viz., that printed sentences of death will not kill us when we are at a distance, and if the executioners approach us, they will be as likely to fall victims to death as we." And in the same document, addressed themselves to the people of the Counties of Albany and Charlotte, as Gentlemen, Friends and Neighbors, and after stating to them that they cannot but be sensible that the title to their lands is in reality the bone of contention, and that they were industrious and honestly disposed, paid their debts, and were friends of good order, they warned all officers who might be induced to apprehend any of their people under the so-called laws of New York, that they were "resolved to inflict immediate death on whomsoever may attempt the same; and that they would kill and destroy any person or persons whomsoever, that should presume to be accessory, aiding or assisting in taking any of them. They declared that all such "officers or persons had license under the laws of New York to kill us, and an indemnification for such murder from the same authority, yet, they have no such indemnification from the Green Mountain Boys."

The New Hampshire Grants known as the Green Mountain Boys were fully persuaded that the laws referred to, directed against their property, liberty and lives, were not only oppressive and cruel, but unconstitutional and void, and asked in their address, "can the public censure us for exerting ourselves nervously to preserve our lives in so critical a situation? For in the Provinces of New York into which we are unfortunately fallen, we cannot be protected in either property or life, except we give up the former to secure the latter; so we are resolved to maintain both, or to hazard or lose both." This address bears date the 26th April, 1774, and attached to it were the following lines composed by Thomas Rowley, to wit:—

> When Cæsar reigned King of Rome
> St. Paul was sent to hear his doom ;
> But Roman laws in a criminal case.
> Must have the accusor face to face.
> Or Cæsar gives a flat denial—
> But here is a law now made of late.
> Which destines men to awful fate.
> And hangs and damns without a trial ;
> Which made men view all nature through,
> To find a law where men were tried
> By legal act which doth exact
> Men's lives before they're tried.
> Then down I took the sacred Book.
> And turned the pages o'er,
> > But could not find one of this kind.
> > By God or man before."

At this stage of the controversy, while the matters between the New Hampshire Grants and New York had advanced near to a general war, the contest between Great Britain and her American Colonies had reached an alarming crisis. Measures had been taken for convening a Continental

Congress, which was held at Philadelphia on the 5th of Sept., 1774.

The meeting of this congress was followed by a general suspension of the royal authorities in the Colonies, and many of the courts of justice were shut up or adjourned without doing business. In the New Hampshire Grants at this time there were three parties. There was the Tory party that were loyal to Great Britain and did not sympathize with the action of the Continental Congress which was looking to a final separation from the British government; there was a party that was loyal to New York, and who were doing what they could to cause the New Hampshire Grants to submit to the laws of New York; and the third and the most powerful party that had determined to resist the authority of New York at all hazards. The latter party also sympathized with the action and purpose of the Continental Congress. It is difficult to say what would have been the result of the controversy between the Green Mountain Boys and New York, had not the controversy been arrested by the commencement of the revolutionary war. That war called forth all the energies of the united Colonies. Although New York did not entirely forget the Green Mountain Boys, still the NATIONAL contest demanded and received their greatest attention. The Green Mountain Boys profited by this change in affairs. There was opposition in the County of Cumberland to the court being convened and held at Westminster under the royal authority and the Province of New York, but those in authority whose feelings were enlisted in favor of New York, as against the New Hampshire grants, and who were supporters of the royal authority of Great Britain, persisted in forcing their way into the court house, being armed with guns, shot one man, William French, and wounded others. This massacre, as it was called, so aroused the people of Cumberland County and the people of New Hampshire, that two hundred armed men from New Hampshire came over to the assistance of the people, and they, with the others from the Grants, arrested and confined those of the royal party that were concerned in the massacre, and the leaders were sent under strong guard to jail at North Hampton. This transaction served to arouse the people on the east side of the Green Mountains against New York.

Previous to this, the opposition to the claims of New York had been confined, principally, to the inhabitants on the western side of the mountains. Indeed some of those on the eastern side of the mountains had surrendered their charters to their lands received from New Hampshire, and taken new grants under the authority of New York, and stood unconcerned spectators of the controversy in which the settlers on the western side of the mountain were so deeply involved. Twenty towns east of the mountain had been granted under New York. But their people were fired with a commendable zeal in favor of the course taken by the Continental Congress. This fact, and the massacre of the 13th of March, 1775, at Westminster, referred to above, stirred the people throughout the County of Cumberland, and gave new impulse to the opposition to New York, in that part of the country. And at a meeting of the inhabitants in that quarter held at Westminster on the 11th of April, 1775, the opposition to New York took a more definite shape. At that meeting it was voted, "That it is the duty of said inhabitants, as predicated on the eternal and immutable law of self-preservation, to wholly renounce and resist the administration of the government of New York, until such time as the lives and property of those inhabitants may be secured by it, or till they could lay their grievances before His Majesty's Council, with a petition to be taken out of so oppressive a jurisdiction, and either annexed to some other government or erected or incorporated into a NEW ONE."

The conflict with Great Britain overshadowed every cause or duty, and seemingly the New York controversy came to a standstill. But the New Hampshire Grants did not fail to profit from this state of things, and never, for a moment, lost sight of the object for which they had so long contended; "they improved the delay in the cultivation of a more perfect Union, and in better organization, and they settled down into a more deliberate, but not less decided, hostility to the claims of New York. On the 9th day of May, 1775, Ethan Allen, with his valiant band of Green Mountain Boys, surprised and captured the Fort of Ticonderoga—demanded its surrender "in the name of the Great Jehovah and the Continental Congress." This signal exploit brought the Green Mountain Boys into prominence and gave them influence in the country, and they were treated with more consideration; and the inhabitants on the grants began to feel their importance, but were determined to have no immediate connection with New York, even in the common defense. On the 17th day of January, 1776, the Grants sent a petition to Hon. John Hancock, the President of the Continental Congress, then assembled at Philadelphia, setting forth therein in substance, their controversy with New York, and asking that their controversy might lay dormant till the contest with Great Britain should end; and asked that they might do military duty in the Continental service as inhabitants of New Hampshire grants, and not as inhabitants of the Province of New York, and that commissions be granted accordingly. But Congress recommended that they, for the present, submit to the government of New York, and gave them the encouraging assurance that "the submission ought not to prejudice their right to the land in controversy," and when their present troubles were at an end the final determination of their rights may be mutually referred to proper judges. Up to this time the Grants had not enjoyed the benefit of a regular organization as a Colony, and had no bond of union, save a common interest to resist the claims of New York. And thus matters stood on the 4th day of July, 1776, when the American Declaration of Independence was published to the world. The American Colonies had declared themselves independent of Great Britain, so that in theory, at least, she had no authority to settle the dispute with New York. Congress, then in its infancy, and with its uncertain right and power, had no disposition to interfere. There existed no earthly power, recognized as superior, having the right to decide the controversy. This state of things suggested to the settlers the expediency of declaring themselves independent. Therefore measures were taken to call a convention of the people. Delegates were appointed in different towns, who met at Dorset on the 24th of July, 1776. There were 58 delegates coming, from 26 towns from the west side of the mountain, and from eight towns from the east side of the mountain. At an adjourned meeting of this convention, held on the 25th of Sept., 1776, it was resolved, "to take suitable measures, as soon as may be, to declare the New Hampshire Grants a free and separate district. And also declared their attachment to the common cause against Great Britain. And the convention on the 15th of Jan., 1777, declared the New Hampshire Grants a free and an independent State. It was voted at that convention to ascertain how many were for a new State. The committee reported that "We find by examination that more than three-fourths of the people in Cumberland and Gloucester Counties, that have acted, are for a new State; the rest we view as neuters."

A committee of that convention reported, and the convention adopted, among other things, a declaration that they "do proclaim and publicly declare that the district of territory, comprehending and usually known by the name and description of New Hampshire Grants, of right ought to be, and is hereby declared hereafter, to be called, known and distinguished by the name of New Connecticut, *alias* Vermont." While these events were transpiring, the Green Mountain Boys held themselvs ready to meet any calls that were made upon them to sustain the common cause against Great Britain, and to repel any attempt that New York should make to encroach upon her domain. On the 6th of Jan., 1776, Gen. Worcester, commanding the Colonial troops in Canada, called for help from the Green Mountain Boys, till the regular forces could be sent him. They responded at once. Warner and his men were in Canada in a very short time. Their promptness and alacrity elicited the notice and approval of both Gen. Washington and Schuyler. At first the different towns were like separate and independent governments. Those towns that were granted under New Hampshire, had by their respective charters, the right of self government in March meeting, by the election of town officers and ordering town affairs. And, as has been intimated, New York repudiated these charters and any action taken by the people under them. It was for the mutual protection of the people of these different organizations, and to maintain their common rights against New York, that led the different towns to act in concert. It was a matter of necessity. They learned to act on the old maxim, "that in union there is strength." These people were hardy, brave, and true to each other. These several towns appointed Committees of Safety; and these Committees met in convention as occasion required, to consult and adopt measures for their common protection. Then as the exigencies of the people demanded, and especially to prepare to bear their part in the war of the Revolution, there was a call made for a GENERAL CONVENTION, the proceedings of one of which have already been alluded to. The first regular organized regiment was voted at a meeting held at the Inn of Cephas Kent in Dorset, July 26th, 1775, on the west side of the mountain. At that meeting they proceeded to choose officers of the regiment, according to the wishes of the Provincial Congress and the directions of Gen. Schuyler. Ethan Allen and Seth Warner were candidates for the office of Lieut.-Colonel. Allen was defeated, and greatly mortified by his defeat. He charged his defeat to the old farmers, who, he said, "did not incline to go to war."

The 7th Company of the regiment was raised, in part, from the towns near Onion River. Perley Sunderland was made Captain of one of the Companies, and it was said of him, "he was a mighty hunter of both beasts and Tories." When the Colonies declared themselves independent of Great Britain, there was quite a sprinkling that adhered to the government of their mother country—remained loyal to her. Such persons were called Tories. The property of many Tories was confiscated and used to pay the expenses of the war. Many of such persons joined the British. On the 26th day of Feb., 1779, this State passed an act, that if any such persons should return and should be found guilty, they should "be ordered to be whipped on the naked back, not more than forty, nor less than twenty stripes which shall be inflicted. And the delinquent shall be ordered to quit the State immediately;" and if such return without leave from the Governor's Council and General Assembly, and be found guilty, he should be put to death; and if any one should harbor such person, he should pay a fine of 500 pounds. Col. and Daniel Marsh fled to Canada at the time that Gen. Burgoyne swept along the western border of the State, and was reported to be marching to the valley of the Connecticut. They afterwards returned, and were allowed to remain. Daniel Marsh, in 1784 to 1789, represented his town, Clarendon, in the General Assembly. In 1778, James Rogers of Londonderry joined the King's troops, and his property was confiscated; and in 1797, his son petitioned the General Assembly for the restoration of his property, and all that remained unsold was restored to him.

The people were determined to root out Toreyism, and various measures were passed by General Convention looking to that end. The General Convention held on the 25th of Sept., 1776, at Dorset, "voted to erect a jail in the town of Manchester, 20 ft. by 30 inside; said jail to be built of logs and earth; and for the confinement of Tories and other offenders that may be adjudged to be confined." At this meeting twelve persons were chosen to be a committee to attend the next meeting of the Convention. The office of this committee was to act advisory and prepare business for the Convention. This was the commencement of the body afterwards called the Council. And after that, the delegates that were chosen to the Convention, was called the House.

Separate from these bodies was a Committee of Safety, the origin of the Council of Safety. The original number composing that body, and just the manner of the election or appointment at first, is involved in some doubt, but enough is known of it to show it was an extraordinary body with extraordinary powers. It exercised a combination of legislative, judicial, and executive powers. The government administered by it was, in principle, nothing short of absolute despotism. It is stated in the 1st volume of Governor and Council, that the Council of Safety was appointed July 8th, 1777, as a temporary substitute for a State government in time of war. In power it was limited only by the exigencies of the times. Its acts and orders had the force of laws, and it was the executors of them; it exercised judicial powers; it served as a board of war; it punished public enemies or reprimanded them; it transacted business, civil and military, with other States and with Congress; it prepared business for the General Assembly—in short it was the State. Its President, Vice-President, and Secretary were its executive officers, and performed what the Governor, Lieutenant-Governor and Secretary did, after the organization of the State government. The officers of the first Council, in 1777, were Thomas Chittenden,

President; Jonas Fay, Vice-President; and Ira Allen, Secretary.

An allusion to the Allen family will not be out of place here. It was the most remarkable family that ever inhabited Vermont. From Samuel Allen of Chelmsford descended Joseph Allen, the father of six sons; to wit,—Ethan, Heman, Heber, Levi, Zimri, and Ira. Allens, Bakers, and Warners were related either by affinity or consanguinity, and thus the most distinguished of the early heroes and statesmen of Vermont were closely allied, and were a great power for many years. It was said of Ethan Allen that he was not a devoted Christian, but there was evidence that he believed in a God. The monumental inscription for his wife, Mary Brownson, was composed and run as follows :—

"Farewell, my friends, this fleeting world adieu,
My residence is no longer with you.
My children I commend to heaven's care,
And humbly raise my hopes above despair;
And conscious of a virtuous transient strife.
Anticipate the joys of the next life;
Yet such celestial and ecstatic bliss--
Is but in part conferred on this.
Confiding in the powers of God most high,
His wisdom and goodness, and infinity,
Display'd, securely I resign my breath
To the cold, unrelenting stroke of death ;
Trusting that God who gave me life before,
Will still preserve me in a state much more
Exalted mentally, beyond decay,
In the blest regions of eternal day."

Levi Allen resided in the State but a short time. He left the State, became a Tory, and continued to be one to the end of the Revolutionary war. He was a man of ability, but eccentric and unstable, and was said to be as the "rolling stone that gathers no moss." Somewhat of an ill feeling grew up between him and his brothers Ethan and Ira. While smarting under the loss of his property, which he attributed to Ira, he wrote the five following verses. The first represents Ethan speaking; the 2nd, Ira; the 3d, Levi; the 4th, Ethan and Ira; and the 5th, Levi—to wit:—

> Old Ethan once said over a full bowl of grog,
> Though I believe not Jesus, I hold to a God;
> There is also a Devil—you will see him one day
> In a whirlwind of fire to take Levi away.
>
> Says Ira to Ethan, it plain doth appear
> That you are inclined to banter and jeer —
> I think for myself and freely declare
> Our Levi's too stout for the prince of the air;
>
> If ever you see them engaged in affray,
> 'Tis our Levi who'll take the Devil away.
> Says Levi, your speeches make it perfectly clear
> That you both seem to banter and jeer;
> Though through all the world my name stands enrolled
>
> For tricks sly and crafty, ingenious and bold,
> There is one consolation which none can deny,
> That there is one greater rogue in this world than I.
> Who's that? they both cry with equal surprise.
>   'Tis Ira! 'tis Ira! yield him the prize."

Ira Allen was 21 years of age when he came to Vermont. He became distinguished both in civil and military service. He arose to the position of Major General of militia. He was busy with his pen in defending the interests of the State, assisting Gov. Chittenden in his correspondence, preparing documents for the Convention, and in conducting the diplomatic correspondence with the enemy hereafter referred to. He was a member of the Council of Safty and of the board of war, member of the legislature two years, and of the Governor's Council nine years. State treasurer nine years, and a leading man in conducting the affairs of the State till she was admitted into the Union. Hon. E. P. Walton, remarking upon him and Ethan Allen, said in his 1st volume of the "Governor and Council," "That the State of Vermont has just provided munificently for a statue of Ethan Allen to stand in the old Representative Hall of Congress till it shall crumble by the breath of time, a mute but an eloquent witness of the bravery and patriotism of her sons; but the record of the service of Ira Allen in her struggle and history —of his skill, as statesman and diplomatist—of his grand designs for the promotion of her learning and the development of the material resources of the State, will forever stand, a monument more brilliant than brass and more lasting than marble."

It would be interesting to follow the career of the prominent men intimately connected with the early history of Vermont, and especially that of Gov. Chittenden, who was Governor from March, 1778, till Aug. 25, 1797, except one year. The territory known as the New Hampshire Grants took on the name, and was called, down to the 4th of June, 1777, New Connecticut, but was changed at that date to Vermont, in accordance with a suggestion of a Dr. Young of Pennsylvania. By order of the Convention, held on the 4th of June, 1777, the Committees of Safety in the Counties of Cumberland and Gloucester were forbidden acting under any authority derived from New York. Many persons who continued to act in the interests of New York were summarily dealt with.

The first record of the doings of the Council of Safety, appointed under the Constitution, that have been preserved, were the records of its proceedings the day before the battle of Bennington, and is as follows: "Bennington, in Council of Safety, Aug. 15, 1777. Sir, You are hereby desired to forward to this place, by express, all the lead you can possibly collect in your vicinity, as it is expected, every minute, an action will commence between our troops and the enemy, within 4 or 5 miles of this place—and the lead will be positively wanted.—By order of the Council, Paul Spooner, D. Sec'y."

The orders of the Council of Safety were of the most peremptory kind, and some of them were not a little amusing. One to Capt. John Fassette was this: "You are requested to take a potash kettle, for the Hessian troops to cook in,—give your receipt for the same and bring the same to the meeting house in this place (Bennington)." Some of their orders were humane in their nature, as appears from one dated Aug. 27, 1777, which says "that the Council had received information that our scouts had taken all the stock of every kind, from Auger Hawley's wife, of Rupert, and she made application to him for a cow, as her children were in a suffering condition. These are therefore, to require you to let her have one cow, for the time being, out of the first cows you take from any disaffected person. By order of Council, Ira Allen, Sec'y." One order was to Mr. Harris, directing him to employ some one to harvest Mr. Brackenridge's wheat and put the same into his barn; to pay the expenses out of the wheat, and what is not wanted for the use of the family, you will keep until further orders from this Council.

The Council did not hesitate to order the taking of anybody's private property for the public service. On the 27th of Aug., 1777, they ordered four horses to be taken belonging to John Munroe, Esq., and convey them to the Council; but on the same day gave Mrs. Munroe the following permission: "By sending to Bennington to-morrow, you can have one of your riding horses to use, until we send for him." The Council did not seem to spare the Tories or their property, as it appears from the following order of the Council of Safety, to wit: "Aug. 28, 1777. To David Fassette—Sir, You will proceed to Mr. James Brackenridge's, and if you find any stock or other effects, which you have reason to expect belongs to any enemical person within this State, you will seize the same and cause it to be brought to this Council." Benjamin Fassette, on Aug. 29, 1777, was ordered to "proceed to Pownal and bring from some of the Tories, that are gone to the enemy, or otherwise proved themselves to be enemy to their country, a load of sauce for the use of wounded prisoners here." One Tory was permitted to return home "and remain on his father's home farm (and if found off, to expect 39 lashes of the beech seal)."

The Tories were closely watched in all their movements, and were required to obtain passes from the Council to go out of the State, as the following show. One was permitted to go to Arlington to see his wife as she was sick, and to return again in 36 hours. One was permitted to pass the guards from Bennington to Manchester, and remain on his farm, during his good behavior or the pleasure of the Council. One was allowed to go to his farm in Manchester, there to remain unmolested, "he behaving as becometh a friend to his country, as he has taken the oath of allegiance to the States of America."

Anybody's property was used or pressed into the service if the public needs demanded it. One order to Captain Nathan Smith was "to march with the men under his command to Pawlet, on horse back, where you will apply to Colonel Simonds for a horse load of flour to each man and horse, who will furnish sufficient for that purpose." One order was to Capt. John Simonds, giving him power to "let or lease the estate, both real and personal, of a certain Colonel late of Kent, now with the King's troops; and all real estate, except so much as humanity requires for the comfortable support of the family left behind, you will sell at public vendue, and return the money raised on such sale, after the cost is paid, to the treasurer of this State. You will return to this Council an account of all the estate, both real and personal, that you shall seize." The property of loyal people was, of course, returned to them when the necessity for its use had passed. One certificate from the Secretary of the Council was as follows: "This may certify that we, pursuant to Gen. Gates' orders, employed Mr. Moses Cleaveland to ride post from this to Sheffield, and to impress fresh horses when he should find it necessary." One certificate from the Council as to a certain Tory was, "That it was their opinion that he return to his farm in Castleton, whenever he shall procure a certificate from under the hands of his several neighbors in that vicinity, that they are severally satisfied to receive him into their friendship."

Whenever any were ready to return and remain loyal to the State, mercy and pardon was extended to them. On Nov. 16, 1777, the Council "recommended to the respective Committees of Safety in this State, to be ever mindful of the worthy and laudable example set by His Excellency Gen. Washington, and the good people, inhabitants of New Jersey—always bear in mind to consider the weak capacities of many who have been affrightened into submission to Gen. Burgoyne, after which, seeing their error, confess their faults, and are willing to defend their country's cause at the risk of life and fortune.

Many acts of favor were extended to the women. One order was, "Mary Reynolds is permitted to send for her gray horse, and keep him in her possession until further orders from this Council." Andrew Hawley was permitted to take his gun, first obtaining liberty of the Committe of Safety, and return it to the Committee within six weeks from the date of the order. Capt. John Fassette was commissioned to sequester Tory effects. John Wood and Benjamin Fay were appointed assistants to Capt. Samuel Robinson, as overseers of Tories. When crops were scarce people were forbidden transporting them out of this State. On Jan. 14, 1778, in Council, it was resolved, that no wheat, rye, Indian corn, flour, or meal be transported out of this State, except they have a permit from this Council, and if found guilty of violating the order, the property was forfeited and three-fold value thereof in money.

The first license law was passed by the Council Jan. 24, 1778, which provides that those who sold any kind of spirituous liquors in any less quantity than one quart, or in any quantity to be drank on or about the premises, should forfeit and pay the sum of six pounds.

It has already been stated that the Convention held at Westminster Jan. 15, 1777, had declared the district an independent jurisdiction or State, and christened it New Connecticut. At the same Convention a report of a committee was adopted, recommending that proper information be given to Congress of the reasons why the New Hampshire Grants have been declared a free State, and praying Congress that the State be granted representation in that Honorable body. Jonas Fay, Thomas Chittenden, Heman Allen and Reuben Jones were appointed a committee to convey the information and prayer to the Honorable Continental Congress of the U. S. A. The authorities of New York learning of this, Ten Broeck, President of the Convention of New York, Jan. 20, 1777, made a bitter complaint to Congress and protested against the dismemberment of their State. He claimed the action of the New Hampshire Grants was brought about by the arts and influences of certain designing men, and that it was a misfortune to be wounded so soon, sensibly, while they were making their utmost exertions in the common cause. And he found fault with Congress for allowing Col. Warner and other officers to receive commissions independent of New York, and closed his letter by saying, "If the State is to be rent asunder, and its jurisdiction subverted, to gratify the deluded and disorderly subjects, it is a folly to hazard their lives and fortunes in a contest which in every event, must terminate in their ruin."

As the New York authorities learned that the then so-called State of Vermont had friends scattered all through the Colonies, both in and out of Congress, they became thoroughly alarmed, and again addressed John Hancock, the President of Congress, endeavoring to stay any action of that body favorable to Vermont. Thomas Young of Philadelphia, heretofore alluded to, a friend of the Grants, had written several communications, encouraging the Grants to take action towards becoming a State, and asking to be represented in Congress. These communications reached the New York authorities. New York, on the 23d of

June, 1777, got Congress to take action on these complaints; and among other things, it resolved, "That the independent government attempted to be established by the people styling themselves inhabitants of New Hampshire grants, can derive no countenance or justification from the act of Congress; and that the petition of Jonas Fay, Thomas Chittenden, Heman Allen, and Reuben Jones, be dismissed; and that Congress, by raising and officering the regiment commanded by Col. Warner, never meant to give any encouragement to the people aforesaid, to be considered an independent State; and certain paragraphs in the letters of Thomas Young, addressed to the people of the grants, were derogatory to the honor of Congress, and tended to deceive and mislead the people to whom they were addressed."

This was throwing cold water on the movement of the people in Vermont to become independent and free. While Congress was passing these resolves, the people of Vermont, in convention assembled, were forming a constitution and perfecting a system of civil government. While the Convention was at work at Windsor, their attention was called to the more exciting scenes of war. News arrived of the evacuation of Ticonderoga. Gen. Burgoyne was sweeping up Lake Champlain, across the western border of the grants, and towards Albany, creating consternation and alarm. The Green Mountain Boys, for a time, forgetting everything but the common cause and the enemy, gathered with the New Hampshire soldiers under Gen. Stark, and met the British forces under Gen. Baum, fought and won the battle of Bennington on the memorable 16th of Aug., 1777, and which led to the surrender of Gen. Burgoyne a few days after. The bravery and success of the Green Mountain Boys on this occasion won for them and the people of the grants a respect and a standing that they had not before gained.

The New Hampshire Grants had declared themselves an independent State. No sooner had they done this than they were met with new difficulties. The territory of New Hampshire was made up of several grants from the Council of New England to John Mason, between the years of 1621 and 1635, and their western boundary was 60 miles from the sea. The land between Mason's grant and Connecticut River, was granted by virtue of a royal commission to the Governors of New Hampshire. The people of this last grant, as soon as Vermont had organized its government, showed a disposition to dissolve its connection with New Hampshire and unite with the people of Vermont. They put their claim on the ground that inasmuch as the Colonies had dissolved their connection with the mother country, they had reverted to a state of nature, and were at liberty to form a separate government, or connect with another, as they thought best. Consequently 16 towns on the east side of Connecticut River petitioned the Legislature of Vermont, praying to be admitted into its union. This proposition was referred to the people of Vermont, and a majority of the towns voted "that the union take place;—the vote standing 37 in the affirmative and 12 in the negative. These 16 towns announced their withdrawal to the Governor of New Hampshire, and asked for a divisional line to be drawn. You may imagine the just alarm it created in New Hampshire. Governor Weare of New Hampshire, Aug. 19, 1778, addressed their delegates in Congress, informing them of the situation, and asking them to advise with other members of Congress concerning the situation; and giving it as his opinion, that if they did not, it was "very probable the sword would decide the controversy, as the minority in those 16 towns were claiming protection from this (New Hampshire) State, and he thought they were bound by every tie to afford it.

On the 22nd day of Aug., 1778, Gov. Weare addressed Gov. Chittenden, and stated to him, among other things, that the idea that those 16 towns did not belong to any State and were at liberty to form another union with Vermont, was "an idle phantom, a mere chimera, without the least shadow of reason for its support." He told Gov. Chittenden, the people of Vermont were furnishing her enemies, to her becoming a separate State, with arguments against her. And he besought him for the sake of the people he presided over and for the sake of future peace, to relinquish every connection, as a political body, with the towns on the east side of the Connecticut River. Gov. Chittenden, on the receipt of this letter, convened the Council and sent Ethan Allen to Philadelphia to ascertain in what light the proceedings of Vermont in this matter, were viewed. Ethan Allen performed this service and reported back to the Council, October 10, 1778, that it was his "opinion, that unless this State recede from such union immediately, the whole power of the Confederacy of the United States of America will join to annihilate the State of Vermont and vindicate the right of New Hampshire. The whole matter was taken into the consideration by the Vermont Assembly for a long time, and finally it began to hesitate to go any further with the hazardous experiment of claiming to hold the 16 towns against the wishes of New Hampshire.

The seceding 16 towns struggled hard to continue their union with Vermont, but the people of Vermont had become aware of the danger of attempting to continue the union, and by a vote of the General Assembly, Feb'y 12, 1779, voted that the union of the 16 towns with Vermont ought to be considered as being null from the beginning. About this time there had been a convention called, of those who were favorable to uniting with the 16 towns, that met at Cornish; and a petition was presented by that convention to the House of Representatives of New Hampshire, asking that all towns west of the Mason line, might go together—either all be allowed to go with Vermont, or all the grants, including the 16 towns, be allowed to unite with New Hampshire, and thus annihilate Vermont; and the House of Representatives of New Hampshire, by a committee, reported that "New Hampshire should lay claim to all of New Hampshire grants (so-called) lying west of Connecticut River, but, if the Continental Congress shall allow the towns west of

Connecticut River to become a separate State, they would acquiesce therein," which report was adopted June 24, 1779, by the House. This idea of being swallowed up by New Hampshire was opposed by the leading men of Vermont.

At this critical moment, when the State was threatened with annihilation, events took place in the County of Cumberland, which gave a new impulse to the controversy with New York. There was a party that had always existed in the County of Cumberland that was opposed to the independence of Vermont, and had up to that time reluctantly submitted to its authority. A convention was organized by these disaffected ones, which met at Brattleboro on the 4th of May, of 1779. This convention petitioned Gov. Geo. Clinton of New York for relief from their unhappy situation, setting forth in their petition that those who did not yield obedience to the pretended Vermont authorities, had to suffer the loss of their property both real and personal, and that they were compelled to pay taxes to the authorities that be, that they did not recognize as legal, and called earnestly for protection from the New York government, and if that protection was not speedily granted they should have to obey a government which they viewed as usurpation, and add their strength to oppose the government of New York. About this time a military association was formed in the County of Cumberland to oppose Vermont authorities. Ethan Allen was directed by the Governor to suppress it. Col. Patterson, who headed the opposition to Vermont authorities, asked aid from New York, which was promised by Gov. Clinton of New York, who assured the opposition party that the authority of Vermont should in no instance be acknowledged, except in the alternative of submission or inevitable ruin; and also addressed Congress, stating in that address, that he daily expected to be obliged to order out a force for the defence of those who adhered to New York.

Congress took the matter into consideration June 1, 1779, and appointed a committee to repair to the New Hampshire Grants and inquire the reasons why they refuse to continue citizens of the States that before that time exercised jurisdiction over them, and to take prudent means to effect an amicable settlement of the difficulty. A committee of five was appointed. While these matters were transpiring in Congress, Col. Ethan Allen marched with an armed force and arrested the militia officers that were acting in Vermont under the authority of New York. This was made known to Congress by Gov. Clinton, and Congress authorized said committee to take this matter also into their consideration. Only two of this committee appeared in Vermont, and on the 24th of Sept., 1779, the committee was by Congress discharged.

At this time the Vermont authorities were pained and surprised to learn that Massachusetts was laying claim to a part of her territory. And Gov. Chittenden addressed a letter Oct. 28, 1779, to Samuel Adams, President of the Council of Massachusetts, and sent the same by Brig.-Gen.

Ethan Allen, asking him to state "what part of this State they meant to extend their claim over, and how far they meant to carry such pretension into execution. At this time Congress had passed a resolve to take the claims of New Hampshire, New York, and Vermont into their consideration, with a view of settling them in some way. On the 28th of October, 1779, Adams replied to Chittenden, "that Massachusetts had an ancient and a just claim to all the territory between Connecticut and Hudson Rivers—that their territory was bounded easterly by Connecticut River, westerly, by the eastern line of New York, and northerly by the northern boundary of Massachusetts Bay; and this includes a part of that territory which you call the State of Vermont, and over this tract they meant to extend their claim." This shows that Massachusetts was not bashful. After a partial hearing of these disputes in Congress, they were postponed.

Previous to this, on the 24th of Sept., 1779, and on Oct. 2, 1779, Congress unanimously passed resolutions recommending to New York, Massachusetts Bay, and New Hampshire to pass laws authorizing Congress to hear and determine the controversy as to their respective boundaries and the dispute with the Grants, and then Congress would, on the first day of Feb., 1780, hear and determine said controversy and dispute, and pledged their faith to carry into execution their decision. And also resolved that it was the duty of those who were loyal to Vermont, to abstain from exercising any power over any of the inhabitants who profess to owe allegiance to either of the other States; and that the other States abstain from exercising authority over the loyal citizens of Vermont; and that no towns east of Connecticut River should be conceded within the jurisdiction of Vermont; and that any violation of the true intent and meaning of these resolutions of Congress should be considered as a breach of the peace of the confederacy. In short, Congress desired that all matters should remain as they then were till a determination should be made in Congress as to the matters of dispute. Congress sent a copy of these resolutions to Gov. Chittenden.

On the 29th of October, 1779, the Governor, Council, and House of Representatives of Vermont resolved unanimously "that this State ought to support their rights to independence, at Congress, and to the world, in the character of a free and independent State," and chose Ethan Allen, John Fay, Paul Spooner, Stephen R. Bradley and Moses Robinson "to vindicate their rights to independence, at Congress, and to transact all other political affairs of this State at Congress, as a free and independent State." Congress did not proceed to a final determination of said dispute on the 1st of February 1780, but the matter was postponed from time to time, and on the 2nd of June, 1780, it passed a resolve requiring the authorities of Vermont to abstain from all acts of authority, civil or military, over the inhabitants who hold themselves to be subject to any other State.

Vermont now was literally struggling for existence. Had she not had men of extraordinary wisdom and firmness, she would have gone down. Gov. Chittenden, July 25, 1780, addressed the President of Congress, setting forth their rights and determination in a bold and firm manner. He told him, that "the people of this State viewed the resolutions of Congress in their nature subversive of the natural rights which the people have to liberty and independence," and had a "direct tendency to endanger the liberties of America; and denied the power of Congress to decide that Vermont, a free and independent State, belonged to any other jurisdiction; and being an independent State, Congress had no business to legislate over Vermont." He told him, "there may, in future, be a trial at Congress, as to which of the United States shall possess this territory, or how it shall be divided between them; but this does not concern Vermont." He told him, "that the cloud that has hovered over Vermont since the ungenerous claims of New Hampshire and Massachusetts Bay were made, has been seen, and its motions carefully observed by this government, who expected that Congress would have averted the storm; but disappointed in this, and unjustly treated, as the people over whom I preside concieve themselves to be, in this affair, yet blessed by heaven with constancy of mind, and connections abroad, as an honest, valiant and brave people, are necessitated to declare to your Excellency, to Congress, and to the world, that as life, liberty, and rights of the people, intrusted them by God, are responsible, so they do not expect to be justified in the sight of heaven, or that posterity would call them blessed, if they should, tamely, surrender any part." And he closed his letter to him by saying, that "they were induced once more, to offer union with the United States of America,—should that be denied, this State will propose the same to the legislatures of the United States, separately, and take such other measures as self preservation may justify.

On the 10th of Dec., 1779, Vermont issued an appeal (written by Stephen R. Bradley) to the candid and impartial world, stating the claims of New York, and New Hampshire, and Massachusetts, and the right of Vermont to her independence, and an address to Congress. It was grand, bold, logical, and convincing. I only have time to refer to one or two passages in it: "Again," he said, "the State of Vermont has merited an indisputable right to independence, in the esteem of every true Whig, by her brave and noble conduct, in the gloomy struggle of America with Great Britain. First in America were the Green Mountain Boys (to their immortal honor be it written) that commenced an aggressive war against British tyranny. Under every disadvantage in being a frontier, they nevertheless, with their lives in their hands, took Ticonderoga and other important garrisons in the north, so early that New York as a government, was called as a dead weight in the continental scale. The Green Mountain Boys, like men, determined to obtain liberty or death, pursued the war into Canada, and many fell fighting in the glorious cause of American liberty and freedom. Let the brave, immortal Gates, and the deathless Stark, tell posterity that they, in the year 1777, assisted by the militia of the State of Vermont, humbled the long boasted pride of Great Britain, and brought the towering Gen. Burgoyne, with his chosen legions, to ask mercy at their feet. In a word, Vermont, by her blood and treasure, at the point of the sword, has fairly merited liberty; and by the eternal rule of reason has a right of independence from every consideration; she has received it from God, as being created with equal liberties in the scale of human beings; in nature, from the formation of territories and from her victorious struggles with Great Britain." And in short, they had promised protection to all the loyal citizens, and, therefore, were under the necessity of supporting their independence.

The letter of Gov. Chittenden and the appeal referred to, had a great impression on the small States, who were found favoring Vermont, and Congress hesitated; but the subject of admitting her into the Union was postponed. Gov. Chittenden addressed a letter to John Hancock, Governor of Massachusetts, the 15th of Dec., 1780, and made a powerful appeal to him, setting forth among other things, that, "Vermont labored under many great evils—Congress claiming jurisdiction over them, three of the States claiming their territory, in whole or in part, and exposed to British invasion from Canada; and in one event they might be under the disagreeable necessity of making the best terms with the British that may be in their power; and that it was out of the power of Vermont to be further serviceable to the United States unless they were admitted into the Union. And that it was high time that Vermont had better assurances from the several States now in the Union, whether at the conclusion of the present war, she may without molestation enjoy her independence, or whether she is only struggling in a bloody war to establish neighboring States in their independence, to overthrow or swallow up her own, and deprive her citizens of her landed estates."

This letter had the desired effect on Massachusetts. On the 8th of March 1781, the Governor of Massachusetts replied "that when Vermont should be recognized as an independent State, that they would relinquish all claim to her jurisdiction."

Vermont did not cheerfully yield to the policy that resulted in the indefinite postponement of the decision that they hoped would make Vermont one of the States of the Union. Nor did it produce the best of feelings toward the three States that had been putting forth their best efforts to rob Vermonters of their lands and deprive them of their independence.

At this time a new effort was made to unite the towns in New Hampshire west of the Mason line, with the towns west of Connecticut River. And at a convention held at Walpole, N. H., on the 15th of November, 1780, in which several of the towns in the County of Cheshire were represented, action was taken favoring the union, and it took measures to call a convention of the

Grants, from both sides of the river, to be held at Charleston on the third Tuesday of January, 1781, at which convention 43 towns were represented; and on the 10th of February, 1781, an application was made by the Charleston convention to the Legislature of Vermont for the union of the grants on both sides of Connecticut River.

The Legislature of Vermont, on receiving that application, adopted a report that set forth, in substance, that the State of New Hampshire had receded from her former position acknowledging the independence of Vermont, and had made attempts to unite the whole of the grants to New Hampshire, and that some people from New Hampshire had endeavored to support internal broils in the eastern part of Vermont; and on the 10th day of February, 1781, recommended that the Legislature of Vermont lay jurisdictional claim to all lands east of Connecticut River, north of Massachusetts, and south of latitude of 45 degrees. Then the Legislature set forth a declaration that New York for many years had undertaken to usurp the rights and the property of the people of Vermont, and, therefore, the committee recommended the Legislature to lay jurisdictional claim to all lands north of the north line of Massachusetts, and extending the same to Hudson River, "but not to exercise jurisdiction, for the time being." The Legislature adopted the recommendations; and in April, 1781, the union of the towns east of Connecticut River, west of the Mason line, was consumated, and 35 representatives from the Grants east of Connecticut River took their seats in the General Assembly of Vermont. This union being accomplished, the General Assembly turned their attention to taking in a part of the State of New York east of Hudson River. And on the 11th of April, 1781, the Legislature appointed a committee to meet with a convention to be held at Cambridge, N. Y., in May, 1781, to take into consideration the subject of the defense of the frontier, and the union of the towns east of the Hudson. This report was adopted by a vote of 48 yeas to 39 nays. Representatives from 12 towns met at Cambridge and adopted the recommendations of the Legislature of Vermont, and declared that the territory as far west as the Hudson, pursuant to the recommendations, be considered as a part of the State of Vermont.

And they further declared that the whole military force of Vermont shall be exerted in their defence; and that the independence of the State of Vermont shall be held sacred. These recommendations were approved by the Vermont Assembly, June 16th, 1781, by a vote of 53 yeas to 24 nays. Ten members were chosen from the New York towns, and eight of them took their seats in the Vermont Assembly.

Vermont was now placed in an interesting and a critical position. By the bold and decisive policy that she had followed, she had augmented her resources, compelled the respect of her enemies, gained upon the confidence of her friends, quieted disaffection in her own borders, invited immigration and laid the foundation of a large and powerful State. Up to this time no people were more firmly attached to the cause of American independence than the people of Vermont, and none had more successfully contributed to sustain it; and this, too, in face of difficulties and discouragements with which the people of other States of the confederacy did not have to contend.

After all their efforts to maintain the common cause, they were denied by Congress a just participation in the blessings they had done so much to secure. Their claim to independence had been treated with indifference, they were threatened a dismemberment of her territory, and annihilation of her sovereignty; and were left to contend single handed against the common enemy. Their lands bordered on that of the enemy on the north, and if the British invaded the American States from the north, the Vermonters must first stand the shock of battle, and not till they should be overpowered could the other States be harmed.

It seemed to the Green Mountain Boys that they had got to take this terrible burden or enter into some arrangement with the British enemy, whereby they might delay the conflict and better their condition. Their right to independence had been denied by Congress, and as much as they loved the cause of their country, attested by their deeds, they saw every step taken to support it, rendered their condition more hopeless. It was of no importance to them that the American arms should be successful, while they were threatened with subjugation by the States, and her existence as a State blotted out. She could make better terms than that with the enemy; and entered into negotiations with the British.

These negotiations were carried on with great secrecy by the leading men of Vermont. The British were aware that a warm contest had been carried on between New York and Vermont, and that Congress had denied Vermont an independent existence, and that the people of Vermont were dissatisfied with the course that Congress had taken in refusing Vermont admission into the confederacy of the States; and, therefore, took advantage of this state of things and made an attempt to induce Vermont to remain loyal to Great Britain. This correspondence was conducted mainly on the part of the British by Frederick Haldimand, a British General in Canada, and is called the Haldimand correspondence. On March 3d, 1779, Lord Geo. Germaine, the British Secretary for colonial affairs, wrote to Gen. Haldimand, that the British Minister could see no objection to giving the people of Vermont reason to expect that the King will erect their country into a separate province.

On the 30th of March, 1780, Beverly Robinson, an adherent of the British at New York, (the same man who made the successful attempt to corrupt Benedict Arnold) addressed a letter to Ethan Allen. This letter was delivered to Allen in the streets of Arlington by a British soldier in the habit of an American farmer. The letter was quite artfully drawn, setting forth that he had been informed that he, Allen, and most of the inhabitants of Vermont, were opposed to the wild and chimerical scheme in attempting to separate the continent from Great Britain; that he would willingly assist in restoring America again to Great Britain; and if those were his sentiments, begged him to communicate what proposals he had to make to him, said Robinson, or to Sir Henry Clinton, the British Commander-in-Chief at New York City; and assured Allen that upon his taking an active part in restoring the people of Vermont in favor of the Crown of England, Vermont might obtain a separate government under the King and the constitution of England. Robinson claimed he was an American himself, and felt much for the distressed situation his poor country was in, and was anxious to restore peace and the mild and good government they had lost; and said if Allen disapproved his hinting the things he had referred to, and did not choose to make any proposals to the government, he hoped he would not suffer any insult to be offered to the bearer of the letter. And if he should see fit to send proposals, and they should not be accepted or complied with, the matter should be buried in oblivion between them. And if he saw fit to send a friend with proposals he should be protected and well treated. This letter was not received by Allen till sometime in July, 1780. He immediately communicated it to Gov. Chittenden and to some other principal men of Vermont, who thought it best not to make any reply.

At this time some Vermonters had friends that were prisoners in the hands of the British in Canada, and negotiations were entered into by the Vermont authorities with Gen. Haldimand to settle a cartel for the exchange of prisoners. During the negotiations, Maj. Carleton, a British officer, promised not to commit any hostile acts on Vermont during the negotiations, and the Vermont authorities also agreed to cease hostilities during the same time, providing the truce should embrace the northern frontier of New York. This was agreed to. This truce was used by Gen. Haldimand as the opportunity for attempting to detach Vermont from the American cause. After this truce was agreed upon, Gen. Carleton ceased his hostile demonstrations both in New York and Vermont and returned to Canada.

The British had great hopes at this time of detaching Vermont from the American cause. Gen. Haldimand wrote to Gen. Lord Germaine Dec. 16, 1780, that he "had some reason to believe the offers he made to the chief of that district (Vermont) some time since have been or may be accepted." Commissioners had been appointed to carry out the matter of the exchange of prisoners, and the Vermont commissioners had entertained Gen. Haldimand's agents, with much political conversation, and exhibits of papers took place, from which the British concluded they were in a fair way to effect their purposes. The agents or commissioners appointed by Gen. Haldimand had full power to negotiate for the return of Vermont to their British allegiance. Gen. Haldimand, Dec. 20, 1780, in his instructions to his commissioners, said, "I authorize you to give these people the most positive assurance that their country will be erected into a separate province, independent and unconnected with every government in America, and will be entitled to every prerogative and immunity which is promised to other provinces in your proclamation of the King's commissioners."

On the 9th day of March, 1781, Ethan Allen addressed a letter to the President of Congress, and sent him the letter that he received from Beverly Robinson, and also informed him that Vermont had opened a truce with Gen. Haldimand in order to settle a cartel for the exchange of prisoners. Allen justified the course that Vermont had taken in negotiating with the enemy, and said "I am fully grounded in opinion that Vermont has an indubitable right to agree on terms of cessation of hostilities with Great Britain, provided the United States persist in rejecting her application for a union with them; for Vermont of all people would be the most miserable, were she obliged to defend the independence of the United States and they at the same time at full liberty to overturn and ruin the independence of Vermont," and closed the letter by saying, "I am as resolutely determined to defend the independence of Vermont as Congress is, that of the United States; and rather than fail, will retire with the hardy Green Mountain Boys into the desolate caverns of the mountains, and wage war with human nature at large."

Colonel Allen met the British commissioners, to agree on a cartel for the exchange of prisoners, and told the British commissioners that his authority did not extend to treat for a union with Great Britain; but from a history of the conference it is evident it was the main topic under consideration. Ira Allen told them, "that matters in Vermont were not yet ripe for any permanent proposals"—referring to the subject of the renewal of their allegiance with Great Britain,—and told them that, "some of the Council were anxious to bring about a neutrality, being convinced that Congress never intended to admit them as a State;" but for the time being desired to settle a cartel for the exchange of prisoners, and thereby keep open a door for negotiations."

From a memoranda of the conference held in May, 1781, it was evident that the British commissioners were willing to comply with all the demands of Allen, except allowing Vermont to choose her own Governor, if Vermont would return to her allegiance; but Allen plead for delay, and said it would be impossible to effect a union with Great Britain until the union with a part of New Hampshire and a part of New York, that had in a formal way taken part, had become more firmly united, and until they had better prepared their people for the change. Allen told them that when the western union was complete, Vermont could raise ten thousand fighting men. He said he, and Vermont in general, were inclined for the success of America, but interest and self-preservation (if Congress continued to oppress them) more strongly inclined them to wish for the success of Great Britain, and fight like devils against their oppressors, be they who they might.

Before Allen left them, he agreed with the British commissioners how they might in future keep each other informed of the progress of affairs. Signals were agreed upon for the messages that Allen might send; that if the British should send messengers they were to be men of trust; that the contents of the message should be a secret, to the messenger, written on a small piece of paper, which he should be directed to swallow, or otherwise destroy, if in danger of being taken by a scout from New York. These negotiations continued 17 days, during which time a cartel for the exchange of prisoners was completed; hostilities were to cease between the British and the Vermonters until after the then next session of the Legislature of Vermont, and in the meantime Vermont was to consolidate her unions to weaken Congress, permit letters to pass through Vermont to and from Canada, and take prudent measures to prepare the people for a change of government.

The course of Vermont was mysterious. Beverly Robinson wrote Gen. Haldimand, in May, 1781, that Vermont deserves our diligent attention, and that he had much to say respecting her mysterious conduct." In one letter, dated at Quebec, May 21, 1781, to Vermont authorities, it urged Vermont to take immediate and decisive steps to unite with Great Britain; it stated that, "there is from accounts from Europe great reason to think that a general negotiation for peace has commenced under the mediation of the Emperor at Vienna." Whatever the terms of peace may be, the people of Vermont must be left in the same unfavorable situation they were in before the present trouble, unless they accept the terms offered them by Great Britain, and "save themselves a separate government independent of the other States." Gen. Washington disapproved of the cartel for the exchange of prisoners made by Vermont with the British in Canada.

I think it very clear that Vermont had a double purpose in these negotiations. If the people of Vermont should become perfectly satisfied that they should not be recognized as an independent State by Congress, but that her territory should be divided between the States claiming her territory, many of the leading men had come to a determination to unite their fortunes with Great Britain, if they should be granted a separate existence. So, for the time being, it was with them "Good Lord, good devil," for they did not know whose hands they might fall into."

If the war should continue, it was evident that Vermont must become the battle ground between the British in Canada and the American forces, and, therefore, Vermont attempted to take the neutral position. It was a stroke of policy on the part of Vermont to make the British believe that they had no hope of being recognized as a separate State, and that, therefore, as soon as the Vermont authorities could get the Vermont people ripe for a union with Great Britain, it should be done. By this means they avoided the calamities of active war within their own borders. Without doubt the people of Vermont had rather unite their fortunes with the United States, and consequently made frequent endeavors to be admitted as the fourteenth State; but Congress dallied along without any decisive action for the fear of offending New York and New Hampshire, and during this state of affairs, the Vermont authorities gave the British to understand that they were preparing to cast in their fortunes with them.

As late as the 10th of July, 1781, Col. Ira Allen wrote to Gen. Haldimand, that "It is expected that Vermont's agents to Congress will make offers to Congress that will not be accepted, by which means those in favor of government will be able to evince to the people of this State that Congress means nothing more than to keep this State in suspense to the end of the war, and then divide the territory among the claiming States." " It is exceeding difficult and somewhat dangerous attempting to change the opinion of large and popular bodies. Therefore, carrying these matters somewhat under the rose until the next election, when in all probability a large majority of the then officers of the government will be well disposed, and then by the advantage of another denial from Congress, with the reins of government in their hands for one year, they will make a revolution so long wished for by many."

Sir Henry Clinton wrote to Gen. Haldimand from New York 23d July, 1781, that "if a reunion of Vermont with the mother country can be effected, it must be productive of happy consequences, but I confess I have my suspicions of those people." Lord George Germaine wrote from London to Gen. Haldimand the 26th of July, 1781, "I am sorry you have cause to doubt their sincerity, but I flatter myself that when they see a body of troops sufficient to protect them near at hand, they will readily yield to the force of the weighty arguments you will have it in your power to urge." And he urged him to appear in considerable force on the frontier, which he said would be the surest means to give efficacy to the negotiations with the Vermont people. And nothing should be omitted to attach them to His Majesty's government."

Gov. Chittenden on the 14th of November, 1781, addressed a letter to Gen. Washington, justifying their course in attempting to effect a union with a part of New Hampshire and a part of New York, and the agreement Vermont made with the British for a cartel for the exchange of prisoners and cessation of hostilities, thereby saving the shedding of blood and the State from invasion, by a stroke of policy that they could not have prevented by any military force they had at their command. And closed his letter on that subject by saying, "And in the month of October last, the enemy appeared in force at Crown Point, and Ticonderoga; but were maneuvered out of their expedition, and they returned into winter quarters in Canada, with great safety, that it might be fulfilled which was spoken by the prophet, 'I will put my hook in their nose and turn them back by the way which they came, and they shall not come into this city (alias Vermont,) saith the Lord.'"

Gen. Washington, in his reply by letter dated Jan. 1, 1782, said, "Your late extension of claim has rather diminished than increased the number of your friends, and that if the extension should be persisted in, it will be made a common cause." and it must involve the ruin of that (Vermont) State against which the resentment of the others is pointed." And said, "I will only add a few words upon the subject of the negotiations which have been carried on between you and the enemy in Canada and in New York. It has this certain bad tendency; it has served to give some ground to the delusive opinion of the enemy, upon which they in a great measure found their hopes of success;" and gives Gov. Chittenden a hint that if Vermont releases her claim to any part of New Hampshire and New York, Congress would be more likely to admit her as a State into the Federal Union.

New York sought the aid of Federal troops to enforce their demand against Vermont. But as Congress was prevented from using United States troops against Vermont, by the intervention of Geo. Washington in February, 1783, New York had no means to a resort to force, except by her own troops. To this the sixth article of confederation interposed an obstacle which could not be removed without the consent of Congress. New York repeatedly and persistently urged Congress to give their consent till May, 1784, but did not succeed in getting consent of Congress.

One of the British agents, speaking of Ira Allen's letters in the carrying on of the negotiations referred to, said, "the apparent studied style of Allen's letters does not appear to us like the undisguised sentiments of an honest heart." And in speaking of Mr. Fay, a Vermont agent, he said, "we have spared pains, the short time Mr. Fay has been with us, to endeavor him out. He professes so much honesty, accompanied with so many gestures of sincerity, that he seems to over act his part. He is perfectly honest, or a perfect Jesuit. We have too much reason to fear and believe the latter; however, it appears plain that he wishes to continue the negotiations till next November, for what reason it is uncertain. He declares solemnly that they will be then able to join us. Allen declared the same would happen in July; —to us it appears they wish to have two strings to their bow, that they may choose the strongest, which they cannot determine till Mr. Washington's success shall be known. We do not believe that Vermont expects by procrastinating to strengthen herself as a State, but we believe sincerely they design to secure themselves in this campaign from invasion of King or Congress by spinning out the summer and autumn in truces, cartles and negotiations, by the expiration of which they expect to hear the result of the negotiation at Vienna, and other matters, by which they may be enabled to judge of the strongest side, the only motive (we believe) by which they are influenced."

There were eight persons on the part of Vermont that were engaged in carrying on these negotiations. Samuel Williams, one of Vermont's early authors, put the matter in its true light. He said, "But whatever may be thought respecting the propriety of such policy (as was pursued by Vermont) the event showed that the gentlemen of Vermont had formed a sound judgement with regard to the effect. The British, flattered with the prospect that they should draw off a considerable part of the continent to their government, therefore carefully avoided hostilities against Vermont, restored her persons, forbade her troops to enter or attack her territory, and considered her people rather in the light of friends than enemies. Thus, while the British generals were freely imagining that they were deceiving, corrupting and seducing the people of Vermont, by their superior arts, addresses and intrigues, the wise policy of eight honest farmers, in the most uncultivated part of America, disarmed their northern troops, and kept them quiet and inoffensive through their campaigns, assisted in subduing Cornwallis, and finally saved the State.

While these negotiations were going on Vermont made application to be admitted as a State, and let Congress settle the boundaries between New Hampshire and New York, as to whether the East and West Unions should constitute a part of Vermont, but no decisive action was taken by Congress. Vermont also proposed to New York and New Hampshire to adopt some measures to settle the boundary between Vermont and their respective States, but not much was accomplished in that line. New Hampshire would not agree to surrender any claim east of the Connecticut River, and New York would not surrender anything, and would take measures that indicated that they should exercise their jurisdiction by force over the towns that had formerly united with Vermont. The warlike spirit ran high both in New Hampshire and in New York, and that aroused the people of Vermont. The following verse was composed at that time, showing the spirit of the Vermonters, namely:—

> "Come York, or come Hampshire—come Traitors and Knaves,
> If you rule over our lands, ye shall rule over our graves;
> Our vow is recorded—our banner unfurled,
> In the name of Vermont we defy all the world."

Actual conflict for a time was imminent between the forces of Vermont and New York on the one side, and the forces of Vermont and New Hampshire on the other side, but it was avoided by negotiation. But the right of existence of Vermont, and if an existence, whether she had a separate jurisdiction, and the extent of that jurisdiction, continued to be a matter of controversy between the respective claiming States and before Congress. On the 20th February, 1782, the Legislature of Vermont passed a resolution to the effect that the west bank of the Connecticut should be the east line; and a line running from the north corner of Massachusetts northward, twenty miles east of Hudson River, the west line of Vermont, and relinquished all claim over any district of territory outside of those lines; and this was done with the expectation, that if they did so, Vermont would have a speedy admission into the Federal Union as a State. And they appointed Jonas Fay, Moses Robinson, Paul Spooner and Isaac Tichenor agents to negotiate her admission into the Union. The friends of Vermont were again disappointed, but through all the disappointments, and the indifference manifested by Congress, the hostility of

Vermont to New York never abated. They never for one moment contemplated submitting to New York, but were determined either to be an independent State or a member of the Federal Union.

On the 7th of October, 1790, commissioners from New York and Vermont settled the controversy between the two States. The line between them was to be "the west line of the most western towns which had been granted by New Hampshire, and the middle channel of Lake Champlain, and Vermont was to pay New York $80,000." This agreement was ratified by both States, and thus terminated a controversy which had been carried on with great animosity for twenty-six years. Vermont approved and ratified the constitution of the United States, and by act of Congress passed the 18th of February, 1791, Vermont, on the 4th of March, 1791, was received and admitted into the Union "as a new and entire member of the United States of America."

Vermont may be small in a geographical sense; it may be rough and rugged in physical contour, and may not possess the wealth, or resources from which to obtain it, which some States and Territories have; yet it is rich in heroic history, in grand and sublime scenery, a favorite climate, and the full freedom of hand and thought, which makes noble men and women. This is her glory and her pride, and she can never be robbed of these.

CHAPTER II.

THE STRUGGLE OF THE NEW HAMPSHIRE GRANTS TO ESTABLISH A SEPARATE JURISDICTION BY THE NAME OF VERMONT, AND HER EARLY HISTORY.

The former chapter was an address prepared by the writer of this volume, a few years ago, and is inserted without adding to it so as to make it a complete history of the times it purports to cover. It will be my endeavor in the present and following chapters to supply much that was omitted in the first chapter, so as to give the reader a more complete idea of early Vermont and the sturdy character of her people. And in doing so it has become necessary to state more in detail, what has been said in a general way in the former chapter. And this is my apology for any repetition that may, in some instances, occur.

It is stated in the 26th Vol. of New Hampshire State Papers, by A. S. Batcheldor, the editor, that an acquaintance with the contentions between the provincial or colonial governments of New York, Massachusetts and New Hampshire is necessary to a fair conception of the legal and political status of the grants made by those States in the first period of their history. At an early period

Massachusetts claimed, from the language of its charter, that the north line of that State was three miles north of the outlet of Lake Winnipiseogee. But the King in Council in 1739, determined the line to be governed by the river Monomack, alias Merrimack, so far as that followed a westerly course, but when it turned to the north, the line should continue "thence due west across said river till it meets with His Majesty's other governments." This determination was favorable to New Hampshire. A joint commission of the two States fixed the boundary line. In running this line westerly Fort Dummer fell within the limits of the province of New Hampshire and within the limits of the present town of Brattleboro, Vt. The western terminus of this line and the western boundary of New Hampshire would depend upon where the eastern boundaries of the other governments should be determined to be. The general understanding was, at that day, that the easterly boundary of New York was not on Connecticut River. The question had been previously raised. The Hartford treaty of 1656, between the United Colonies of New England on the one part, and the Dutch Colonies of New Netherlands on the other, fixed a line of division, between New Netherlands and New England, to begin at the west side of Greenwich Bay, and to run a northerly course up into the country, and after, as it should be agreed by the two governments of the Dutch and of New Haven, provided the line should not come within ten miles of Hudson River. From this time till 1664, the Dutch did not claim as belonging to them, any territory or lands, except in Hartford, east of Connecticut River; and it was believed that the Dutch possessions would not extend easterly of the extension, northerly of the twenty mile line, providing it did not come within ten miles of the Hudson River. In 1664, a charter was granted to the Duke of York, by King Charles, to confirm his purchase of Long Island and other territory from the Earl of Stirling, to whom they had been conveyed by the Council of Plymouth on the surrender of their charter to the Crown in 1635. In the charter to the Plymouth Colony, to which the Duke of York succeeded, the language used in describing the eastern boundary of the territory was as follows, "and all the lands, from the west side of Connecticut River to the east side of Delaware Bay."

Contention arose, between the Duke of York as one party, and Connecticut and Massachusetts successively as the other party, the foundation of which was the construction of said charter. The controversy resulted in fixing the boundary line between the last two named Provinces and that of New York at twenty miles east of and parallel with Hudson River. It was understood after this period to 1740, that the western boundary of Massachusetts, against New York, extended northerly to the line of Canada. The region now called Vermont was then, for the most part, a wilderness, and the relations existing between the English and the French and their Indian allies, rendered the settlement of that part of New England extremely hazardous, and the persons who undertook its settlement were subjected to many hardships. The claims of New York to territorial jurisdiction to the Connecticut River, if not practically abandoned, were for a long time held in abeyance.

Under these circumstances Governor Wentworth might well apply the practical test of actual land grants on the west side of Connecticut River as far west as the west line of Massachusetts, with a reasonable expectation of being sustained in the movement.

The early town organizations of the New Hampshire Grants within the present limits of Vermont, that were granted by the Governor of New Hampshire, had the right of self-government in March meeting in the election of all town officers and in the management of town affairs. As early as the year of 1770, the New York courts repudiated the town charters granted by the Governor of New Hampshire, but those towns, with great unanimity, resolved to support their rights and protect their property under the grants against the unjust claims of the Governor and Council of New York, *by force*. These towns appointed Committees of Safety to attend to their defence. These committees met, from time to time, to take measures for the common protection. A General Convention was called to meet on the 16th of January, 1776, by a warrant issued Dec. 10, 1775, by a committee appointed for the purpose. It is not known by what authority it was called, but the Convention was composed of town Committees. In January, 1777, a Convention composed of committees or delegates, assumed jurisdiction of the whole territory, and declared it to be a separate and independent State. The resolves of the Convention were executed by committees or agents appointed by the Convention. This simple arrangement stood in stead of a formally constituted State government. This body exercised supreme legislative and executive power. It was elected by the people, expressed their will, and was answerable to them. New York claimed that the whole territory, now called Vermont, was within their jurisdiction. The contest between the two jurisdictions was earnest and unyielding. The Grants made application to the King to settle the controversy in their favor, insisting that their territory was not within the boundary of New York. The commencement of the Revolutionary War, and the news of the battle of Lexington, fired the hearts of most of the people. A body of troops was raised for the common defense from among the New Hampshire Grants, by the request of Congress, who were called the Green Mountain Boys, and who chose their own officers. A part of this regiment was raised from the towns near Onion River. Peleg Sunderland, who was called a "mighty hunter of both wild beasts and Tories," was recommended as one of their captains. At a meeting of the representatives of the several towns in the New Hampshire Grants, on the west side of the Green Mountains, held at the Inn of Cephas Kent in Dorset, Jan. 17th, 1776, it was voted that, "the inhabited towns in the Grants be allowed votes in the meetings or conventions in proportion to the number such deputed member or members shall represent." Committees were appointed at said meeting to warn General Meetings of the committees on the Grants when they should judge necessary from southern or northern intelligence.

On the 20th day of July, A. D. 1764, the King of England with the advice of his Council, on petition from the authorities from New York, annexed all the territory west of Connecticut River, south of Canada line, and north of Massachusetts, to New York Province. To this action the Grants remonstrated and reported to the King the situation, and on the 24th day of July, 1767, the King and his Council took the report into consideration and commanded the New York authorities, that they, for the time being, make no grants in the territory of the New Hampshire Grants.

A petition was drawn, to present to the Continental Congress, setting forth the condition of the Grants, the action that the King and his Council had taken, and the course of conduct of New York, and praying Congress to take their cause into their wise consideration, and order that the Grants do duty in the Continental service as inhabitants of New Hampshire Grants, and not as inhabitants of the Province of New York. This petition was presented at the adjourned meeting held at the Inn of Cephas Kent the 17th of January, A. D. 1776, and was agreed to. Lieut. James Breakenridge and Capt. Heman Allen were chosen to prepare said petition to Congress.

The Grants were willing to do all in their power

in the common cause, but not as Yorkers. It was the wish of the Grants, as expressed in the petition, to have the dispute between them and New York lie dormant till the contest with Great Britain was over, when there would be a better opportunity to get an equitable decision in the disputes with New York.

On the death of Gen. Montgomery the command of the Colonial forces in Canada devolved upon Gen. Wooster who was left in charge of the troops at Montreal, and he wrote Col. Warner a pressing letter for reinforcements. This was after the defeat of the Colonial forces at Quebec. He said the safety of the Colonies, and especially the frontiers, depended upon keeping possession of Canada, and said, "I am confident I shall see you here with your men in a very short time." Gen. Wooster was not disappointed. His promptness in rendering aid elicited the approval of both Gen. Washington and Gen. Schuyler. The alacrity with which the Green Mountain Boys furnished aid showed their readiness to serve the common cause, and defend their rights against the arbitrary power of King George III., as well as the usurpation of New York. The stand that the hardy Green Mountain Boys took educated the people of their territory to become brave, independent and self-reliant.

Said petition to Congress was presented to that body by the committee chosen for that purpose, but it was opposed by New York, and ordered to lie on the table for consideration. A motion was made to withdraw the petition that it might not be acted on when the Grants were not properly represented in the absence of the Committee. Congress passed a resolution that the petitioners, for the present, submit to the government of New York till the contest with Great Britain was over, without prejudice to their rights to their lands, and that the controversy with New York, in the end, be submitted to proper judges, and that the Committee have leave to withdraw their petition. The Grants were willing to aid the common cause as the resolutions required, but they never yielded allegiance to the government of New York.

Many persons residing in the New Hampshire Grants joined the enemy of the United States, and on the 26th day of February, 1776, the Grants passed an act to prevent such persons returning to the State, and if any violated the act they were to be arrested and tried in the courts, and if found guilty were to be whipped on the naked back, not more than forty, and not less than twenty, stripes, and ordered to quit the State; and if he returned again to the State, he was to be put to death; and if any one harbored such persons they should forfeit and pay five hundred pounds. There was a list of one hundred and eight names incorporated in the act to which the first part of said act applied. At the adjourned session of the Convention held on the 17th day of January, 1777, it was voted that "the district or territory is hereby declared forever hereafter to be considered as a separate, free and independent jurisdiction or State."

At an adjourned Convention, held at Dorset on

the 25th of Septenber, 1776, where towns from both sides of the Mountain were represented, it was resolved that, "no laws, direction or directions" from the State of New York, would be accepted by them.

James Rogers came from New Hampshire to Londonderry, Vt. That town had been granted by New York (by the name of Kent) to said Rogers Feb. 13th, 1770. He held a commission as justice of the peace and as assistant justice of an inferior court in 1766, and 1772. In 1775, his political situation and views were doubtful, both parties supposing him to be a friend of their party, probably for want of accurate information as to his position. But on Burgoyne's invasion he joined the King's troops, and on Oct. 3d, 1777, the Council of Safety took control of his property and confiscated it in 1778. But in 1795, and 1797, on a petition of his son James, so much of his property as had not been disposed of was returned to him by the General Assembly. The property of Tories and enemies was from time to time confiscated by the authority of the State.

The government of New York continued to keep up a semblance of authority over the Grants, and to commission various persons residing in the Grants to carry out the will of New York government. All such commissions and appointments to office, they thought, would serve to keep the people loyal to the government of New York. But it is evident that the people of the Grants were too determined to maintain and guard their liberties and rights, and to establish their absolute independence as a separate power or as a separate State of the Union, to be easily dissuaded by flattery, or by the gift of emoluments, or a little brief authority under the government of New York. The Vermont Council of Safety and the Conventions composed of committees, or representatives, or delegates, from the different towns, acted independent of New York in all of their deliberations, and in appointing officers in their military force.

Jails were voted to be built, by the Convention, of logs and earth, in Manchester, for the confinement of Tories and other offenders. It was voted by the Convention Sept. 28th, 1776, that, "as it appears that the town of Arlington are principally Tories, yet the friends of liberty are ordered to warn a meeting and choose a Committee of Safety and Conduct, as other towns." And at the same meeting, voted to appoint Col. Seth Warner, Capt. Heman Allen and four others a committe "to prepare a citation to send to the State of New York, to know if they have any objection to our being a separate State from them." On January 15, 1777, a committee reported to the Convention that, "we find by examination that more than three-fourths of the people in Cumberland and Gloucester Counties, that have acted, are for a new State; the rest we view as *neuters*." And at the same meeting it was voted that a committee (naming them) prepare a draught for a declaration for a new and separate State.

The next day the committee reported, viz.: "Right 1st, That whenever protection is withheld, no allegiance is due, or can of right be demanded;"

and secondly, they set forth fully their grievances against New York and their monopolizing land traders, and declared that the New Hampshire Grants of right ought to be, and is hereby declared forever hereafter a separate, free and independent jurisdiction or State, by the name, and forever hereafter to be called, known and distinghished by the name of New Connecticut. On the 4th of June, 1777, the name was changed to Vermont. Down to the 17th day of January, 1777, certain delegates from the New Hampshire Grants had served as delegates in the New York Convention, and on the last named date the Vermont Convention directed that a letter be drawn directed to them, that they would "on sight hereof withdraw themselves from the Convention of the State of New York and appear there no more in the character of representatives for the County of Cumberland." That County was not represented in New York after 1784. The people of the New Hamp-Grants, who were endeavoring to throw off all allegiance to New York, were not only severe on all New York sympathizers, but the deacons of the churches were severe with their members whose conduct was not strictly in accordance with the fourth commandment.

An anecdote is related about Dea. Session of Westminister. A member of Parson Buelin's church had shot a bear in his cornfield on Sunday, and for this, excommunication was voted. When the Parson attempted to read this document in church, the accused, fully armed, rose to his feet and brought his musket to bear on the Parson.

This so shocked the nerves of the Parson he handed the document to Dea. Sessions to read. The deacon declined, saying, "all things are lawful unto me but all things are not expedient." The New York sympathizers in Cumberland County had appointed Dea. Sessions to represent them in New York, and he found it also not expedient to continue to represent them in New York. The Convention of the New Hampshire Grants under the name of New Connecticut, on the 17th day of March, 1777, published to the world their declaration as a free and independent State.

The first proclamation for a fast was issued the 7th day of June, 1777, by Joseph Bowker, President of the Convention, and by its order. It was set forth in the proclamation that, "since God has been pleased in his wisdom to visit the inhabitants of this land with his judgements by suffering our unnatural enemies to wage war against us, the pestilence to prevail," etc., as a just reward for the many prevailing sins, it called upon the people for solemn fasting and prayer. I suppose this was an old theological view of God's dealings with the children of men; that it was a world of special providences. But how different is this from the more reasonable idea that everything is worked out by God's natural laws according to the principles of evolution.

On the 4th day of June, 1777, the Convention passed resolves as a sovereign body, and took exclusive jurisdiction of the territory under the new name of Vermont, and soon after, in July, 1777, proceeded to frame and adopt a Constitution for the State. At this time the Convention was very much disturbed by reason of a dispatch from Col. Seth Warner announcing the advance of Burgoyne upon Ticonderoga, and calling for assistance. And as a further soveringn act the convention asserted its right, as against New York, to the County jail at Westminister, and issued orders to a sergeant and six men to guard it.

Many of the militia of Vermont at this time were with a part of the Continental army defending Ticonderoga under General St. Clair, but the pressing needs of that General for assistance, and at the earnest request of Col. Seth Warner, the Convention took further measures to aid the common cause by furnishing more men and stores. While the Convention at Windsor was in session, a dispatch from General St. Clair was received, announcing the evacuation of Ticonderoga on the morning of the 6th of July, 1777, and the pursuit of the retreating Americans by the British, and the attack upon the forces of Col. Warner at Hubbardton on the morning of the 7th of July.

The Convention received a letter from General St. Clair bearing date at Col. Mead's at Otter Creek, July 7th, 1777, stating, among other things, that, "Finding that the enemy were ready to attack, and that it was morally impossible to maintain the Post with the handful of troops, and at the same time considering how necessary to the States it was to perserve our army, small as it is, it was determined in a council of general officers, that the Post on Ticonderoga and Mount Independence, should be evacuated and a retreat attemped to Skeensborough by the way of Castleton," on his march to Bennington.

Before the Convention adjourned, a Council of Safety was appointed to administer the affairs of the State until some other provision in that regard should be made. This was the first Council appointed under the Constitution. Thomas Chittenden, Ira Allen, Moses Robinson, Jonas Fay, Joseph Fay, Paul Spooner, Nathan Clark, and Jacob Bayley were of the number of that Council of Safety. The whole number was twelve, but it is not certain who all the other four were. The duties of this Council were onerous, delicate, and confidential, and owing to the fact that the people of Vermont had declared their position as an independent and sovereign State, and had to contend against a powerful enemy on the north, and as New Hampshire on the east, Massachusetts on the south, and New York on the west were striving to extend their jurisdiction over Vermont lands, it required men of the best talent and of reliable character, imbued with the most exalted patriotism, to discharge the duties of the Vermont Council.

This Council, and those they selected to aid them, were vigilant and thorough in their work in suppressing all action that was intended to favor New York. Their faithful service was shown in the case of Benjamin Spencer of Durham, now called Clarendon. Spencer had held the office of justice of the peace and assistant judge of the court of common pleas under the jurisdiction of New York. He and other New York officers in the neighborhood persisted in issuing writs against New Hampshire grantees, and conveying lands under New York title; and they were charged with seducing and inveigling the people to be subject to the laws and government of New York. Ira Allen said he was "an artful, intriguing and designing man." The Vermont leaders visited him with a large body of men in the autumn of 1773, and warned him to desist on penalty of suffering violence, which he did not greatly heed. They made a second visit to him, and Spencer was arrested. The people assembled when Ethan Allen announced that "the proprietors of New Hampshire Grants had appointed himself, Seth Warner, Remember Baker, and Robert Cochran to inspect and set things in order, and to see that there should be no intruders on the Grants, and said that Durham had become a hornet's nest which must be broken up." Spencer's trial immediately commenced and he was required to stand up with uncovered head. He was charged with the above mentioned offences; in short with cudling with the land jobbers of New York. He was found guilty of all the charges, his house declared to be a nuisance and must be burnt; and he was required to promise that he would no longer act as a New York magistrate. Spencer objected to the destruction of his house and property, as it would be cruelty to his wife and children. The committee modified the order and simply required the roof of the house to be taken off, to be replaced when Spencer would accept it under the New Hampshire title. This was agreed to, and

Spencer promised to no longer act under New York, and he afterwards became a delegate in the Convention at Windsor, pledging to stand by the new State.

Other Yorkers were visited in like manner, with salutary effect. When Burgoyne's army advanced into the country, Spencer sought personal safety with the enemy at Ticonderoga, where he died a few weeks afterwards.

There has been considerable criticism of the conduct of General St. Clair in not defending Ticonderoga, and evacuating the place, and exposing the country south, and western Vermont to the ravages of the enemy. And it has been asserted by many that his conduct was not consistent with loyalty to the American cause. On this question I here insert an address delivered by Hon. Lucius E. Chittenden of New York, but formerly of Burlington, Vt., before the Soldiers' re-union at Bennington, Vt., on Nov. 5th, 1897. Mr. Chittenden, as a writer on the early history of Vermont, is eminently qualified to accurately state the facts, and his address can be treated as good authority on the historical facts related by him. The address is worthy of being preserved in a substantial form, and is as follows:—

"I come to address you when my life has "fallen into the sere and yellow leaf," and whatever of ability to interest you I once had has left me, because I hope still to be competent to perform an act of justice to one of the founders of independent Vermont and to correct another chapter of the false history written about her before she had fought her way into the Federal Union. Of the events with which you were personally connected it would be presumptuous for me to speak. Of these, you have your own historians who have written with the bayonet and sabre as well as with the pens of ready writers. Without further preface, then, let me come at once to the event which forms my subject and which ushered in upon this theatre the battle summer of 1777. It is the second capture of Ticonderoga, and its historian, Ira Allen.

"With the current history of this capture, you are familiar. It runs after this wise. Gen. Schuyler was in command of the continental army at Saratoga; Gen. St. Clair held the twin posts of Ticonderoga, and Mount Independence on the Vermont shore, the two being connected by a bridge. The army of Burgoyne was approaching by the lake and along the west shore. St. Clair, who was perfectly aware of Burgoyne's advance, had given out that his force was quite sufficient to hold these forts, if attacked, until he could be reinforced from Schuyler's army or from the militia of Vermont and Massachusetts.

"But on the morning after Burgoyne appeared, St. Clair was surprised to find that the British had a battery on the top of Mount Defiance which commanded the interior of Fort Ticonderoga. This position St. Clair supposed was impregnable. Finding that the British had taken it and placed a battery upon its top which commanded every square foot inside the fort, there seemed to be no alternative between retreat and surrender. He therefore summond a council of war, which with equal haste decided to withdraw the army, partly in boats to Skenesborough, now Whitehall, and partly on land, via. Hubbardton, Castleton and a round-about circuit through the woods, to Saratoga.

"This retreat was attended with disaster. That by water had scarcely commenced before the whole region was lighted up by the burning buildings on Mount Independence. The boats exposed were attacked by the British and many of them were captured. Only an insignificant remnant reached Skenesborough.

"The retreat by land was more disastrous. What became of Gen. St. Clair does not appear in the current accounts. But it does appear that the British pursuit under Gen. Fraser was immediate; that within the first ten miles the retreat of the continentals had become a rout, and that the regiments of Francis and Warner, which held the rear, were the only regiments which undertook to preserve their formation, and that these regiments protected the retreat from destruction. At Hubbardton they halted.

"The continentals scattered, and a few of them afterwards came in at Castleton and other southern towns. Warner and Francis were attacked the next morning by an overwhelming force of British and Indians, and after a fierce resistance in which over 300 of the British were killed, Francis fell and Warner directed his regiment to retire and make their way as best they could to Manchester. There they remained until the great day of Bennington, when Major Safford led them by that night march through the mud to this town, and brought them to their colonel in the field in time to defeat the second column of British and Hessians, and to turn a great battle into a great victory.

"It has been impossible for anyone to read even the most partisan account of the loss and retreat from Ticonderoga and to suppress his suspicions of the loyalty of Gen. St. Clair. These suspicions were rife at the time. Warner did not hesitate to denounce him, and to declare that his treachery caused the loss of the battle of Hubbardton and the other calamities of that disastrous retreat. There was a court of inquiry, but it was conducted at a time when the country was rejoicing over great victories; Warner was a soldier who had no love for the role of a prosecutor; the inquiry was very superficial and resulted in St. Clair's acquittal. The account which I have sketched has therefore become the accepted history of the second capture of and the retreat from Ticonderoga.

"I propose to-night to inquire into the historical accuracy of this version. It is a subject in which Vermonters are interested, for it concerns the only defeat that has ever occurred on her soil. It concerns also the reputation of her soldiers and at least one of the founders of independent Vermont who had much to do with bringing her into the Federal Union.

My principal witness will be Ira Allen. As the weight of his evidence depends upon the character of the witness, you will ask:

Who was Ira Allen?

I answer that he was one of the founders of Vermont. The first governor, assailed for his alleged favoritism to Ira Allen when he fell into pecuniary difficulties, is reported to have exclaimed with an indignation that he seldom exhibited, that he "would not be the governor of a people who found fault with him for helping Ira Allen. For!" he said, "there would have been no Vermont if there had not been an Ira Allen." When, in 1774, the governor settled upon his Williston farm, Ira Allen was making a survey of the Colchester lands, of which he became the owner. It is quite possible that he knew Ira Allen in Connecticut. Ira was the brother of Ethan, and the youngest of a family of nine children. We know almost nothing about him until he came to the New Hampshire Grants. There, he became one of the most energetic of the leaders, always working in close connection with Thomas Chittenden. He was a born diplomatist and writer. He was the author or editor of all the Allen pamphlets, which are now so rare and so indispensable to Vermont history. Vermont had no newspaper until 1778. When it became necessary to make public some new phase of the controversy with New York, Ethan Allen would write it out and Ira would revise it; or Ira himself would prepare a pamphlet, procure a small edition printed in Hartford, Connecticut, and distribute it. In this way the case of Vermont in all its changes, was kept before the Continental Congress and the public. He was Thomas Chittenden's most able lieutenant. They were present in all the conventions of the Grants, either as delegates or officers. Both were delegates to the convention at Windsor on the second of July, 1777, when the first constitution was adopted, and the members hastened home to resist the advance of Burgoyne.

"The last act of the Windsor convention was to name a Council of Safety to govern the new State until the State government went into operation. Of that council of eight members, Thomas Chittenden was made president and Ira Allen secretary. It was agreed that the council should meet at Manchester as soon as Allen could return from Hartford, where he went to have the constitution printed for distribution.

"What time Allen reached Manchester, we do not know, for there is no record of the council meeting there. It was probably about the middle of July. In the meantime, disastrous events had occurred. Ticonderoga had been evacuated; the battle of Hubbardton had been lost; St. Clair, with the remnant of his continentals, was retreating toward Saratoga, and Burgoyne was pursuing his triumphal march southward and the whole frontier was open to the enemy.

"Warner, who was now satisfied with the treachery of St. Clair, had directed the men of his regiment to separate and make their way as best they could to Manchester, where he would meet them. They obeyed his orders and about 150 of them reached Manchester, where they remained while Warner went with Gen. Stark to Bennington.

"Ira Allen then not only met Col. Warner at

Manchester, but he was there when Warner's men, fresh from the retreat and the defeat at Hubbardton, arrived there. He must have had means of knowledge of the facts of that retreat almost equal to that of having been personally present. When, within a few years afterwards, he wrote out the story, we may, I think, accept it as the true history of the events in the order of their occurrence.

"Before I lay this interesting document before you, I should explain how it came to be written. After the war was over, Ira Allen purchased of the French directory 15,000 muskets and 21 brass cannon for arming the militia of Vermont. They were shipped from a French port in the 'Olive Branch,' which was captured on the high seas by a British ship and proceeded against in Admiralty on an unfounded claim that the cargo was intended for use in Ireland.

"The case of the 'Olive Branch' is too dark a chapter in English judicial history to be presented in the time at my command. It began in December, 1796, when Gen. Allen was probably the wealthiest man in Vermont. It ended in February, 1804, when he was a ruined man who could not return to Vermont without being imprisoned for debt. The ship and cargo was discharged because no syllable of evidence against them was ever produced. There was no justification or apology for the capture, and yet Gen. Allen was condemned to pay the captor's costs, amounting to some four thousand dollars.

"To anyone desiring to understand the scientific process of the ruining a man by litigation, where the party is a nation having one of its own judges at command, I recommend the study of Ira Allen's account of the 'Olive Branch,' published in 1805. It comprises 550 closely written pages and is a history of judicial oppression and tyranny which would be incredible were it not supported by documentary proof. It accomplished its intended purposes, for it crushed the most patriotic, brilliant and deserving of the early Vermonters, and drove him to his death in exile and in poverty. It is not agreeable to me to be compelled to make the admission that we do not even know where his body lies buried.

"The 'Olive Branch' is the first reported case in the British Court of Admiralty. Ira Allen determined that such an exhibition from the English judicial bench should not be lost to posterity. He paid for the report, and the case now stands at the head of a long list of reported cases in which no parallel to it can be found. I will give you one example from the report.

"Sir James Marriot was an irritable old man long past his usefulness, if that condition ever existed. Mr. Pitt had offered him a pension for life and an Irish peerage if he would resign. But he would not be tempted. The 'Olive Branch,' however, was his last judicial appearance. He was succeeded by that able judge, Sir Walter Scott, who was one of the counsel for the captors of the 'Olive Branch.'

"On a motion for the discharge of the 'Olive Branch,' while the counsel for the claimant was pointing out that there was not one syllable of proof to sustain the allegation of the captors, Judge Marriot burst in upon him with this fulmination:

"'Why, Doctor Nicholl! I am surprised that you will attempt to support such' a cause. What! the State of Vermont want 20,000 stands of arms? No such thing; 400 or 500 would be enough for them. Why, they are a young, sucking State. The people are a banditti, transported for crimes from France and England; not well settled in government. These arms may be intended for use against Mr. Washington. The claimant is like Romulous and Remus who sucked the wolf, full of fight and revolution. I knew he was a military man by his step on the floor and his name (Ira), which denotes rage, revenge and madness.' The lawyer who reads this paragraph will not be surprised that Judge Marriot condemned the cargo of the 'Olive Branch.' True, it was held on appeal that there was not a particle of evidence to sustain the finding, but Judge Marriot was not embarrassed by a little fact like that. He would probably have condemned the ship if the captors had not consented to her discharge.

"Why was Ira Allen dogged to his ruin by British emissaries? Unfounded suits for hundreds of thousands of dollars were commenced against him by London traders, in which he had to give bail. They pursued him to Paris, had him arrested and confined, without fire or light, in the cold of winter, in the prisons of the Temple and St. Pelagie. And when finally he compelled a decision in his favor, it was with the singular condition that he must pay the captor's costs of three thousand three hundred pounds. For Ira Allen was a fighter. Through these seven years he had stood as the vindicator of Vermont in London. There he wrote his history in her defence. There he compelled even Judge Marriot to retract his libels on the people by showing that Vermont was settled by the best emigrants from Connecticut and other New England States, and he never gave up the fight until though ruined in fortune, he was vindicated as a Vermonter.

"The treatment of Ira Allen is so contrary to British notions of fair play, is apparently so causeless and inexcusable, that many have long believed in and looking for a secret and deep-seated cause for it. I have been one of their number, and I now believe that cause is susceptible of explanation. I shall make no apology for attempting to explain it, for if I succeed I shall have made a valuable contribution to our early history.

"The Allens' were a family of fighters. Ethan had captured Ticonderoga, invaded Canada, and when captured and made a show in England, had never failed to beard the British lion and show his contempt for him at every opportunity. Ira was not a soldier, but he was the most adroit and skilful of the early leaders. It was largely through his influence that Vermont, when rejected by Congress and opposed by the surrounding States, instead of yielding to the apparently inevitable, became independent and stood upon her own resources.

"And there came a time when it seemed that the Vermonters must yield. It was after the winter at Valley Forge. The military strength of Vermont of males from 16 to 45 was over 7000 men, and they were almost all in the army. Warner's regiment of Vermonters was withdrawn from the State and put under continental authority. Every gun, even the spades and pick axes, had been ordered out of the State for the use of the 'army. Then it was that Governor Chittenden made a statement of the facts to General Washington and showed that the whole frontier was open to British invasion, and asked him what the Vermonters were to do. Washington replied in substance, admitting the truth of the governor's statement, and stating that the fate of the war depended upon keeping his army together; that there was no other way to do it, and that the Vermonters must be left to take care of themselves.

"And this occurred just at the time when the British agents were tempting our generals with bribes of money and place. Arnold yielded, but he was the only traitor. The same agent, Beverly Robinson, made similar offers to Ethan Allen, and his response to the tempting offer was to send the letters which made it, to Congress.

"It was then that Ira Allen preformed the great act of his life—an act for which Vermonters should honor his name and defend his memory. The famous Haldimand negotiation for a truce and an exchange of prisioners was opened and its management was entrusted to Ira Allen. I cannot here go into details. I can only speak of its results.

The whole Northern frontier was open and undefended. On one side of it lay Vermont and a part of New York; on the other were ten thousand disciplined British regulars, and there they lay all through the years 1780 and 1781, and until the capture of Cornwallis and his army put an end to the war and secured the independence of the United States of America. And the entire negotiations were conducted with such diplomatic ability and skill that no accusation was ever made of the slightest deception, misrepresentation or unfairness on the part of Ira Allen or his associates.

"Until the logic of facts convinced him of his error, Allen relied confidently upon the impartiality of the Court of Admiralty, and with Sir Thomas Erskine, one of his council, referred to his services in the Revolution as not discreditable to his standing in a British court. When confined in the Temple prison in Paris in November, 1791, he had addressed a letter to the French Directory showing that himself and his family had been influential in ripening and bringing about the Revolution, in the capture of Ticonderoga, in cutting off the right wing of Burgoyne's army, and in keeping the British in Canada, inactive in 1780 and 1781. This letter was before Judge Marriot's court, and there are powerful reasons for supposing that had much to do with influencing Judge Marriot's decision. In fact, it is impossible to account for the temper and partiality of that decision in any other way. If the purpose existed to ruin Allen in return for his success in the Haldimand negotiation, Judge Marriot proved to be a very willing instrument in carrying that purpose into execution.

"That Allen believed that the court was influenced by the prejudices excited against him is evident from his own comments upon the case. On page 390 of the report, he says: 'In the course of events that took place in the Revolutionary War, British gold was repeatedly offered to my deceased brother, Col. Ethan Allen, the late Col. Joseph Fay and the claimant.'

"If the exertions of the Council of Safety in Vermont disconcerted any mysterious plans of the British cabinet and their generals and thereby contributed to the capture of Burgoyne and his army, it might have been the means of raising greater prejudices against the claimant in the Court of Admiralty. If these early exertions in defense o his native country, (for he was an active member of the Council) furnished ground for a judge of the Court of Admiralty to impeach his character and condemn his property, taken on the high seas, it must be a hard case if it does not furnish some support of his character and rights in the United States against the speculators there, engaged in a conspiracy against him.

"I think as Allen's countrymen we may ask if it was not intended to punish Allen for defeating the projects of the British in Canada. Why does Judge Marriot, after being driven from the first ground stated in his sentence of condemnation, at this late period in the trial in the Court of Appeals abandon these suggestions about Ireland, and then raise suspicions without one syllable of evidence, after near two years diligent inquiry respecting hostile designs against the Canadians?

"After the decision in his favor, which, at the end of eight years of litigation had ruined him, was too late to be of any value, Allen made some attempts to secure indemnity for his losses from the British government which he believed was responsible for Judge Marriot's conduct. In this he failed; and then for his own vindication he wrote and published the history of the litigation and the matters connected with it. The volume is now of great rarity, and most indispensible to the early history of Vermont. In it occurs the document to which I have already called your attention. It is entitled 'Ticonderoga Evacuated.' I can only give it in a condensed form as follows:—

"On the 6th day of July, 1777, while it was yet dark, the Americans evacuated the garrison of Ticonderoga and its dependencies, previous to which the commandant had requested assistance from the militia of Vermont in virtue of which about nine hundred and fifty militia men had assembled at said garrison; some officers that were members of a convention to form a constitution for said State had been excused that service on the frontier and gone to Windsor. The militia of Vermont were united in one regiment under the command of Col. Moses Robinson and Major Heber Allen as field officer; Joseph Fay, as adjutant; James Brooklings, as quartermaster.

"'This regiment was quartered within the fort in the barracks, and, as the continental troops were without and around them, it was said by an old aid-de-camp of the general that it was not necessary to keep out guards, and when they were wanted to man the lines they would be notified. In this situation, said regiment remained from their arrival on Thursday until Saturday evening, when they received orders to lie on their arms as they might be called on to man the lines before daylight. Towards day, Col. Robinson, being unwell, called on Adjutant Fay to get him some water. On his going out, he saw the general's house on fire, by the light of which he discovered that all the tents were struck and removed, and not a man to be seen on the ground. He immediately returned to Col. Robinson with this information; the regiment was ordered to parade, when Col. Robinson ordered Major Allen to take the front and march, quick time, to Mount Independence, and brought up the rear himself. Just as the front entered on the bridge to pass from Ticonderoga to said Mount, the British arrived at the outposts, as appeared by their firing and shouting for success. As the rear left the bridge, the British shipping in the lake were bearing down under a press of sail.

"'I pause here to ask: If this account is true, what becomes of the discovery of the battery on Mount Defiance and the council of war, in the St. Clair version, which advises the evacuation?'

"Allen's account continues that when the regiment had marched about a half mile to the top of the Mount, Major Allen found two regiments of continentals there and ordered his own to halt. The vessels had then reached the bridge and commenced firing.

"'But for the providence that led Col. Robinson for water,' continues Ira Allen, 'in twenty minutes more, nearly 1000 Vermonters would have been prisoners to Gen. Burgoyne. For neither Gen. St. Clair, or any of his officers, had given Col. Robinson the least information of the intended evacuation, although Robinson's regiment comprised nearly one-fourth of St. Clair's army, and every man but that regiment had crossed the bridge, or gone by water toward Skenesboro, a considerable time before.'

"On the top of Mount Independence, Major Allen found Gen. St. Clair and two regiments of continentals. St. Clair seeing the Vermonters halted, asked: 'What regiment is that?' 'Col. Robinson's', was the answer. 'What!' exclaimed St. Clair in a tone of surprise. 'Of the militia?' 'Yes,' replied Major Allen, 'of the militia.'

"I remark here, as Ira Allen implies in a note, there were good reasons for St. Clair's surprise. He had stolen away in the silence of the night, leaving his regiment to be made prisoners to Burgoyne, and now they were here, under their own officers, in no temper to be trifled with by the traitor who had intended to betray them.

"According to Allen's account, St. Clair undertook to assume the command just as though nothing had happened. He ordered the Vermonters to remain where they were until all the continentals had passed and then to bring up and protect the rear, thus exposing them to all the danger of the actual pursuit of the enemy, which he knew was inevitable.

"Major Hebar Allen was sufficiently convinced of St. Clair's treachery to Vermonters to justify him in repudiating his authority and disobeying his orders. Ira Allen's account states that the major told St. Clair to his face, and with emphasis that the regiment did not come there to guard the continentals but to assist them; and turning to the regiment gave it the order to march.

"St. Clair then ordered Warner to guard the road of the retreating continentals. Warner replied that 'by the rules of war, his place was in the front and not in the rear, but he could only obey orders.'

"The retreat then began by the road to Castleton. Within the first mile it become a panic-stricken rout. The continentals did not attempt to preserve their formation and broke up in the utmost confusion. The panic was increased when St. Clair and his staff, on horseback, dashed through and rode down the crowd until they reached the front.

"Within the first five miles, Warner repeatedly sent to the front to halt until some order could be restored. No attention was paid to him. Then Warner himself rode through the crowd until he overtook St. Clair and demanded 'What in the name of God' he meant by such confusion? said that there was neither front, rear or flank guards, nor one regiment or company together; that no officer knew his men nor men their officer; and that a small party of the enemy would capture the whole body. St. Clair then ordered Warner to stop and see that the men passed in files, and then to take the rear. St. Clair and his aids kept the front to Lacey's camp, fifteen miles from Mount Independence. He then ordered the men to halt and sit down on each side of the road. Major Allen with about 200 men of the Vermonters, apprehensive that parties of the enemy were by this time distressing their families, were marching with trailed arms until they came up with St. Clair, who ordered them to halt. No attention was paid to his orders; he then gave peremptory orders for them to halt or he would order the continentals to fire on them. 'Fire and be damned, if you dare,' was the indignant reply of Major Allen. His men cocked their guns and marched past St. Clair. In about a mile they discovered the trail made by a party of the enemy, which they crossed and marched rapidly to Castleton Mills, which they found in possession of the enemy. Robinson's men were then ordered to disperse, and each man was directed to go to the defence of his family and home, for these men all lived in the frontier towns.

"At Hubbardton, Warner found the regiments of Francis and Hale, and with them decided to wait for the attack of the pursuing enemy. The next morning they were attacked by the British under Colonel Fraser and a force of nearly twice their number. The regiments of Warner and Francis defended themselves with their usual courage, inflicted a loss on the British of over three hundred, and would have defeated them had not Francis mistaken a movement of Warner to a less exposed position for a retreat. Francis was killed, and Warner ordered his men to disperse and make their way to Manchester. St. Clair had reached Castleton when he heard the guns of the battle at Hubbardton. Several of his officers wished to go to the assistance of the Vermonters, but St. Clair forbid them. Capt. Fletcher of the militia ordered his company to leave their packs with the guard and follow him. St. Clair ordered them to stop. But Fletcher and his men went on until they were met with the news of the defeat. Then the brave St. Clair with the guns of Hubbardton booming in his rear, continued his flight to Rutland, Clarendon, Wallingford, Hardwick, Manchester, Sunderland, Arlington, White Creek or Salem to General Schuyler's headquarters at Saratoga.

"This was a circuit of thirty miles and left this part of Vermont exposed to the ravages of the enemy. Warner's men gave the people some assistance in saving their cattle and goods; Capt. Gid Brownson made a stand with his company at Pawlet until Warner collected his men at Manchester.

"Ira Allen further says that St. Clair was a citizen of Pennsylvania, that the grants of that State covered lands previously granted by the Colony of Connecticut to the Delaware and Susquehanna companies; that disputes existed between the claimants and blood had been repeatedly shed; that in 1778 a great part of the settlers under said companies had been killed by the common enemy, and that St. Clair participated in the prejudices of Pennsylvania against Vermonters and other men of New England origin.

"The remaining portions of Allen's article, while they are not pertinent to the loyalty of St. Clair, are of great interest to Vermonters. He said that circumstances in 1780 led the Vermonters to believe that their frontiers were left exposed to the enemies through the influence of the land claimants of New York. But the negotiations and truce between the British in Canada and the Vermonters protected her alike against the British and the intrigues of the land claimants of New York.

"The capture of General Burgoyne and his army (continues Allen) was of the first consequence to the cause of the United States from its more than threefold effect; first in uniting and strengthening the people and their armies; second, in discouraging the British, Hessian and Loyalist troops in America, strengthening the minority and opposers of the war in England; thirdly, it enabled the United States to make a treaty with the French nation in 1778 which brought the French fleets and armies to their assistance and opened the French ports to the cruisers of the United States; and, finally, the truce between Vermont and the British in Canada, kept 10,000 troops inactive in 1780 and 1781, and enabled General Washington to recall his forces from the north and concert measures with the French Admiral and General for the capture of Cornwallis and his army.

"There is much more of interest to Vermonters in this record of Ira Allen's, but I must not further trespass upon your time by its presentation. You have done great things for the honor of Vermont; you may yet do one more. You may advocate until you secure a history of early Vermont which shall do full justice to the members of the Vermont Council of Safety. Then will the story of the battle summer be remembered as long as the defeat of Pickett's charge, and the name of Ira Allen and George J. Stannard shine in her annals with equal and undiminishing lustre.

"Comrades: You are standing on consecrated ground. Bennington, like the field of Gettysburg, has been enriched by the blood and hallowed by the devotion of brave men. Our fathers have made it renowned while the bronze monument of Catamount Tavern stands. If you would know of what metal they are made, come here and see.

"It is July of the battle summer of 1777. The Green Mountain Boys have captured Ticonderoga, swept the British from the lake, pursued them into Canada, and everywhere been swift to answer every call of the Revolution. But every adjoining colony is against them now, and is waiting to pounce upon its share of dismembered Vermont. Congress has shut the doors of the Union in their face and advised them to make new terms with New York, which they have defied for fourteen years. Their answer to such gratuitous advice was to declare Vermont independent, with the Windsor constitution as their charter, and then they disperse to defend their homes.

"For now, a new peril threatens them. The undefended frontier is fringed with the invading hosts of Burgoyne, swooping down like Goths upon Roman Italy to burn, plunder and slay. Their able-bodied men with their arms, and even their axes, picks and shovels, are far away with the Continental army, and this year boys and women will gather the harvests. The need of the hour is armed men; and they must be had or Vermont must fall. Ticonderoga has been abandoned; the battle of Hubbardton has been lost, and the traitor St. Clair is swinging around a great circle as far as possible from Vermont and from danger. The Coucil of Safety has met in Manchester, and as that is now a frontier town, had adjourned to meet at the house of Joseph Bradley in Sunderland.

"That meeting was not unlike that other on the day of Pentecost. The apostles were not more faithful to their risen Lord than these men to Independent Vermont. We can almost see the cloven tongues, like as of fire, that sat upon each one of them, so filled were they with the spirit of liberty. Like the apostles, too, they had their Judas. His name was Spencer, of Clarendon, who had on that day deserted to Burgoyne, and with St. Clair became the only traitors who disgraced our history.

"These councillors lacked neither faith nor courage, but they could not achieve impossibilities. They could not bring gold for brass nor silver for iron, nor could they sow dragon's teeth and have them spring up armed men. All that long day they debated and consulted until the going down of the sun, but they had accomplished nothing. Then they agreed to adjourn to meet at sunrise next morning.

"Before the adjournment the president rose, (not to make a speech) Daniel Chipman said he was never known to make a speech, and the nearest he came to it was to make a suggestion. He made a suggestion now, in his ordinary tone, free from excitement but full of determination. 'The men must be enlisted,' he said, 'a full regiment, and armed ready for the field, and fed and paid. We will put that proposition behind us. It is not open to discussion.' 'I agree to the necessity,' said one, 'but how can it be done when we have neither the money nor the means of raising it?' 'I don't know how we are to get it,' said the president, 'but my wife has a string of gold beads and I have ten head of fat cattle. We will begin with the beads and the cattle, and trust the Lord to show us what then to do.'

"From this point I read from Record: 'We adjourned to meet at sunrise. One member of the Council who had spent the night alone concerting plans to raise the money, early in the morning proposed that the Council appoint Commissioners of Sequestration, who should seize on all the property of those who had joined the enemy, sell it at auction, and pay the money to a treasurer, to be appointed, for the use of the State. The plan was adopted which, it is supposed, confiscated the first property of the kind in the United States. The treasury was well supplied with money to defray the expenses of the government and to pay bounty, wages, and equip a regiment fit for service, under the command of Colonel Samuel Herrick, in about fifteen days.' I need scarcely add that the member who walked his room all that night; who devised the plan, and who wrote this modest record in which his name does not appear, was the youngest member of the Council, Colonel Ira Allen."

A Convention was summoned by the Council of Safety to meet at Windsor on the 24th of December, 1777. They met and revised the Constitution which had been framed, but postponed the election under it until the first Tuesday of March, 1778, and the sitting of the Assembly till the second Thursday of the same month. At this time there was no printing press establishment in Vermont, and Ira Allen procured the printing of the revised Constitution at Hartford in Connecticut. The Convention was fearful that if the ratification of the Constitution was submitted anew to the people it would be rejected. They, therefore, concluded to keep the ratification of it within as small a circle as possible, and keep its ratification away from the voice of the people further than was vested in the Convention by the delegates who were authorized to form the Constitution. The Constitution was so framed that legal means might be taken to alter or amend it once in seven years, agreeable to the will of a majority of the freemen of the State.

It has been noticed that the influence of Congress had been rather against the formation of the new State. And the intrigues of New York to divide the people would endanger the ratification of the Constitution if it was submitted to the voice of the people; so but little time and opportunity were given the people to discuss the merits of the document, or to stir up opposition to it. Allen returned with the printed Constitution from Hartford, Conn., only a few days before the general election. The friends of the Constitution were induced to attend the meetings in the several localities for the election of representatives, and to take the freeman's oath. By this means representatives were chosen to the Assembly that was to meet at Windsor on the 12th of March, 1778. The representatives met, and the votes of the freemen that had voted for Governor, Lieutenant-Governor, Treasurer, and twelve Councilors, were sorted and counted, and those who had a majority of votes for the respective offices were declared elected. Bennington was the only town that objected to the Constitution for want of a proper ratification of it, but as the Assembly approved of it, the objection died away, and the people of the State were satisfied.

The Constitution was, in the main, a copy of that of Pennsylvania, which was recommended as a model by Dr. Thomas Young, the early friend of Vermont; and who was influential in adopting the name *Vermont* for the State. The Constitution had the approval of Benjamin Franklin. There was added to the declaration of rights that was not in the Pennsylvania declaration, viz.: "Therefore, no male person born in this country, or brought from over sea, ought to be holden by law to serve any person as a servant, slave or apprentice, after he arives to the age of 21 years, nor female in like manner, after she arrives to the age of 18 years, unless they are bound by their own consent after they arrive to such age, or bound by law for the payment of debts, damages, fines, costs and the like." Vermont was thus the first of the States to prohibit slavery by constitutional provision, a fact of which Vermonters may well be proud.

The legislative power was vested in a single Assembly of members chosen annually by ballot by the several towns in the State; each town was entitled to one representative only, unless it had more than eighty taxable inhabitants, when they were entitled to two.

The executive authority was vested in a Governor, Lieutenant-Governor and twelve Councilors, elected annually by ballot of the whole freemen of the State. The legislative powers of the Councilors was simply advisory, but bills were allowed to originate in the Council. The judges of superior courts were elected annually by joint ballot of the Council and Assembly.

The people of the State were so completely set against any kind of slavery that the Assembly at its October session enacted, "that if any person shall hereafter make sale of any subject of this State, or shall convey or attempt to convey any subject out of this State, with the intent to hold or sell such person as a slave," and should be convicted thereof, they should forfeit and pay to the person injured 500 pounds and costs of suit. In Novemember, 1777, one Dinah Mattis, a negro woman, with Nancy, her child, who were in custody of the British army, were taken prisoners, with some soldiers. Ebenezer Allen, a captain in the Vermont service, immediately gave her and her child a deed of manumission.

The Allen family were most closely identified with the early history of the State, and were descendants of Samuel Allen, who resided at Chelmsford about 1632. Joseph Allen of Litchfield and Coventry, Conn., married Mary Baker, daughter of John Baker, March 11, 1737. From this marriage sprang Gen. Ethan Allen, who was born at Litchfield, Conn., Jan. 10, 1738, also, later, Heman, Lydia, Heber, Levi, Lucy, Zimri and Ira. Col. Ira Allen died at Philadelphia, Jan. 7th, 1814, in the 62d year of his age.

Ethan, Heman, Zimri and Ira Allen and Remember Baker constituted the "Onion River Land Co.," and became extensive proprietors of land in the State. Their lands were estimated to be worth from one to one and a half millions of dollars. The controversy with New York involved the title to their lands, and undoubtedly the great value of which stimulated their zeal, courage, persistent and successful efforts for the independence of the State.

The character and fate of the sons of Joseph Allen were different. Heber and Zimri did not become very prominent. The time of General Ethan Allen, when he might have been of the most use to his country, was spent in a British prison, and he died at the age of 51. Heman died in the 29th year of his age, but his life opened with promise. Levi was brilliant and daring, but "unstable as water," and his life was a failure. Ira attained the greatest age and rendered the most numerous and valuable service, but his great wealth was wasted through protracted litigation; he was forced to leave the State to preserve his personal liberty from exacting creditors, and died in poverty. In a letter to Eleazer Keyes, July 3d, 1810, after stating he had failed to obtain justice in Great Britain and Vermont, and the injury to his health by British, French and Vermont prisons, said, "he left Burlington in 1803: 'skin for skin, yea all that a man hath will he give for his life,'" and wanted to know if these were the rewards for exertions for the independence of Vermont and the United States? He came to Vermont when 21 years of age, and rose to the position of Major-General of militia, and was busy with his pen in the interest of Vermont, and conducted the diplomatic correspondence with Gen. Haldimand; he was one of the commissioners who amicably settled the long and violent controversy with New York that insured the admission of Vermont to the Union, and was the founder of the University of Vermont.

Thomas Chittenden, who was born at East Guilford, Conn., Jan. 6, 1730, was one of the most remarkable and important men that figured in the early history of Vermont. He was Colonel of militia and a justice of the peace. In 1774, he settled in the valley of the Winooski at Williston, from whence he was driven by the invasion of the British in 1776; and dwelt in Pownal and Arlington till 1787, when he returned to his homestead in Williston. He was a member of the Vermont Convention, President of the Council of Safety, and was Governor from March, 1778, with the exception of one year, until he resigned a short time before his death, which occurred August 25, 1797. He had but a common school education, and in his youth was not devoted to books and study so much as to athletic sports, but he had an intuitive insight into all men with whom he came in contact and into all questions he had to decide. Ethan Allen said, "he was the only man I ever knew who was sure to be right in all, even the most difficult and complex cases, and yet could not tell or seem to know why it was so."

When the Convention at Windsor adjourned, July 8th, 1777, Ticonderoga was in the hands of the enemy, Warner had been defeated at Hubbardton, Burgoyne was rapidly advancing into New York on the western border of Vermont, and General Howe with another British army was moving up North River to enable General John Burgoyne to join him. General Schuyler, in command of the Continental troops, was lying with his army between the two British forces. One part of Burgoyne's forces were threatening the American stores at Bennington. Under this state of affairs active measures must be immediately taken by the Vermont Council of Safety against the invasion of her territory by the Army under Burgoyne.

Ira Allen, Secretary of the Council, on the 15th of July, 1777, addressed a letter to the New Hampshire Council, urging their assistance, and said to them that, "unless we can obtain the assistance of our friends so as to put it immediately in our power to make a sufficient stand against such strength as they may send, it appears that it will soon be out of the power of this State to maintain a frontier," and New Hampshire would become the frontier. Meshech Weare, President of the

New Hampshire Council, replied in substance that three battallions under command of Brigadier-General Stark would be forthwith sent into the State to oppose the ravages and the coming forward of the enemy. Allen also communicated the alarming rumors to Gen. Philip Schuyler, who replied by letter dated at Fort Edward, July 16th, 1777, that, "As an officer of the Honorable the Congress, who represents the 13 United States of America, I cannot with propriety take notice of the 14th State, unknown in their Confederacy," but urged the Vermonters and the New Hampshire forces to co-operate in repelling the invasion of the British.

Stark came on with the New Hampshire forces, but refused to act under the Continental officers. A party of militia came on from Massachusetts to the aid of Vermont, and a regiment was raised in Vermont, and Samuel Herrick appointed its Colonel. No sooner had Gen. Schuyler, a citizen of New York and commander in chief of the Northern army, heard of the raising and the presence of these forces in Vermont to oppose the British than he sent orders to the militia of Massachusetts and to Colonel Herrick's regiment to repair to Saratoga. The Massachusetts regiment had to obey, according to the regulation of Congress, but the Council of Safety superceded Gen. Schuyler and gave orders to Col. Herrick to remain within the State of Vermont.

This occasioned some sharp correspondence between Gen. Schuyler and the Council of Safety. On the 13th of August, 1777, the Council of Safety issued a circular to the Colonels of the State militia, ordering them to repair to Bennington with their men, as the Council had just been informed that the enemy were within twelve miles of that place and doubtless there would be an attack at or near that place within twenty-four hours, and that they had the assistance of Maj.-Gen. Stark with his brigade, and to hurry what Rangers were recruited forward with all speed, and said, "Now is the time, sir." And on the 15th of August, 1777, the Council issued an order to send by express all the lead they could collect, "as it is expected every moment an action will commence between our troops and the enemy's, within four or five miles of this place, and the lead will be positively wanted."

The battle of Bennington was fought on the 16th of August, 1777. During the engagement, Jonas Fay, the Vice-President of the Council, wrote the following letter and order:—

"State of Vermont, in Council of Safety,
Bennington, 16th August, 1777,
6 o'clock [P.M.]

"Gentlemen: Brig.-Gen. Stark from the State of New Hampshire, with his Brigade, together with the militia and company of Rangers raised by this State, with parts of Col. Symond's regiment of militia, are now in action, with a number of the enemy's troops assembled near this place, which has been for some time very severe. We have now in possession (taken from them this day) four brass field pieces, ordnance, stores, etc., and this minute four or five hundred prisoners have arrived. We have taken the ground, altho fortified by entrenchments, etc., but after being driven about one mile, the enemy being re-enforced, made a second stand, and still continue the action. The loss on each side is doubtless considerable. You are therefore in the most pressing terms requested by Gen. Stark and this Council to forward the whole of the militia under your several commands to this place without one minute's loss of time:— they will proceed on horseback with all ammunition that can be provided conveniently. On our present exertions depends the fate of thousands. I am, gentlemen, Your most obt. servant,

JONAS FAY, Vice-President

To the Gentlemen Officers nearest this place commanding Regiments of Militia in the several United States."

Notwithstanding the continuance of the war with Great Britain, the New Hampshire Grants insisted upon maintaining the title to their lands against the authorities of New York. After the New York authorities had granted lands in Vermont in violation of the order of the King in Council, July 24, 1767, and taken measures to enforce the Grants to yield to the claims of New York, an organization of the Green Mountain Boys was formed for resistance, in which Ethan Allen, Seth Warner, Remember Baker, Robert Cochran and Gideon Warren were captains. They resorted to chastising Yorkers who interferred offensively, "with twigs of the wilderness." Hugh Munro, an old offender, was lashed three times, each time till he fainted, when his wounds were dressed and he was banished from the State.

Others were dealt with in a similar manner, whereupon Gov. Tyron of New York issued a proclamation, Dec. 9th, 1771, offering a reward for the arrest of each of the captains. Said Munro gathered in New York a posse of ten or a dozen men and repaired to the house of Remember Baker of Arlington to arrest him under Gov. Tyron's proclamation, and about daylight on the morning of March 22, 1772, broke into the house, wounded Baker and his wife, maltreated his children, and retired into New York with Baker as a prisoner. Munro was pursued and Baker was rescued. In 1777, Munro fled to Burgoyne,s camp, and the Vermonters confiscated his property. He was forever proscribed, with other New York sympathizers, by the Vermont Act of Feb. 26, 1779.

Doctor Samuel Adams settled in Arlington in 1764, and he advised and urged the New Hampshire Grantees to purchase the New York titles to their lands, but such conduct was very offensive to the opponents of New York, and he was advised to be silent. At this he took offence and threatened to silence any man who interferred with him. He was arrested, tried and convicted as an enemy, and punished by being hoisted up to the Catamount signpost and suspended there two hours, to his own chagrin and the merriment of the beholders, which had a salutary effect on the Doctor; but in 1777 he became a violent Tory, and raised a company in Arlington and vicinity to co-operate with Burgoyne. His property was confiscated and his family sent within the enemy's lines in 1778.

It was voted in the Vermont Assembly in 1778, "that the style of the Governor of this State be, His Excellency,', and that the bill presented to the

House by the Governor and Council relating to jurisdiction, be altered, and in the place of "New Hampshire," insert "the west bank of Connecticut River," and thus fixing the eastern boundary of Vermont on the west bank of that river.

All western Vermont was at one time named Bennington County, and eastern Vermont Unity County, which was changed to Cumberland. In 1776, and for a long time after, the inhabitants on the west side of the mountain were kept in a constant state of alarm for fear of sudden attacks from Indians and the British.

In 1776, Moses Pierson had raised a large crop of wheat on the "Ezra Meach farm" which lies in Shelburne on the lake a few miles south of Burlington, which he was forced to leave in the autumn, for fear of the enemy, but returned in January, 1777, accompanied by Capt. Thomas Sawyer and fourteen soldiers who had marched through the trackless wilderness about ninety miles, strengthened the place, built a block house, made of large logs laid closely together. On the 12th of March, 1778, they were attacked by 57 Indians, commanded by a British officer. The fight was stubborn; twice the house was set on fire by the enemy, but the flames were extinguished, once by Lieut. Barnum of Monkton, who lost his life by the daring act. After a two hours' fight the enemy retreated, but they were pursued and two of them were captured. The loss of the Vermonters were three killed, while the enemy lost twelve killed, among whom were a British captain and an Indian chief.

The Council from time to time ordered the commanders of the Vermont military force to protect the inhabitants, situated in the sparsely settled districts, from the enemy.

The General Assembly empowered the Governor and Council to appoint a court to confiscate and order the sale of both real and personal property of estates belonging to the enemies of the United States, and to appoint commissioners to adjust and settle the accounts of creditors to said estates. And, accordingly, a Court and Commissioners were appointed for those purposes.

One David Redding had been sentenced to death, after having been convicted by a jury of six men as a public enemy. Application was made for his reprieve, June 4th, 1778, because he was not tried by a full jury. The reprieve was granted till the 11th of June. The people were greatly excited by reason of the delay in the execution. To appease them Ethan Allen mounted a stump and promised them that, "if Redding escaped he would be hung himself." Redding was tried on the 9th by a full jury, and executed on the 11th of June, 1778.

The first divorce granted in Vermont of which I have any information was decreed by the Governor and Council in June, 1778. Lurania McLane petitioned to be discharged from her late husband, John McLane. After considering the petition and evidence (the husband not appearing), the Council declared, that "the said Lurania be discharged from him the said John McLlane, and that she has a good and lawful right to marry to another man." The first Vermont Statute on divorce of which there is any record, is the Act of February, 1789.

The frame of government declared that the House of Representatives "shall be styled the General Assembly of the Representatives of the Freemen of Vermont," but later it became to include the House, and when both acted together they were called the Joint Assembly.

From 1778 till 1781 there was a great agitation among the people of both Vermont and New Hampshire, growing out of an attempted union of the towns in New Hampshire, near Connecticut River, with Vermont. A union was consumated and at one time the representatives of thirty-five New Hampshire towns took their seats in the General Assembly of Vermont. New Hampshire claimed that this action and attempted union was illegal, and growing out of this controversy war was imminent between Vermont and New Hampshire, but better counsel prevailed and the union of those towns with Vermont was dissolved.

Tories were sentenced to banishment from the State, but many returned without permission, and consequently on Feb. 26, 1779, one hundred and eight persons were, by name, banished by an act of the General Assemby; and the Assembly passed an act "that if any such person or persons which have been sentenced to banishment as aforesaid, shall be found in this State after the first day of May, next, (which have not obtained, or shall not obtain a pardon or reprieve from their crimes from the Governor and Council of this State) such person or persons shall be whipt not exceeding forty stripes, to be repeated once a week, by order of any assistant judge or justice of the peace, so long as they shall continue in this State."

By an act of Feb. 25, 1779, the Governor and Council were constituted a Board of War, with full power to raise men for the defence of the frontiers, and the Council were given power to liberate the Tories under the care of Captain Samuel Robinson, or, dispose of them according to their merit. And on the 24th of February, 1779, the Assembly resolved to raise $15,000 by a lottery fund for military defence. In Cumberland County there was opposition to the draft that had been ordered by the Board of War. The opposition had been stimulated by Col. William Patterson, who was commissioned by Gov. Clinton. Patterson had a regiment of about 500 men. Gov. Chittenden sent Ethan Allen with an armed force, who promptly arrested Patterson and others, in all forty-four, most of whom were indicted, convicted and fined. These rioters, as they were called, were tried at Westminster in May, 1779.

William French and Daniel Houghton were killed or died of their wounds at Westminster in the collision that took place between the adherents of New York and the Green Mountain Boys the 13th of March, 1775. Ira Allen characterized the affair as "that odious and never-to-be-forgotten *massacre*," and it was charged as the "*shedding innocent blood.*"

The next Vermont Convention was improved

as a means of turning public opinion against New York, whose officers, it was charged, were responsible for the affair. New York charged the blame upon the Whigs. The people that did not sympathize with New York were determined that the court that was run by officers of New York should not hold the session under the New York regime, as the rights and liberties of the people of the State were in danger and their lands taken from them. The Vermonters had an interview with Col. Chandler, the chief judge, to dissuade him from attending court, as the sheriff would have attendants with arms, and there would be blood shed; but the judge told them there should be no arms brought against them, and he would open court on the 13th of March, 1775. Judge Sabin, the other judge who was to sit that term, and other officials of the court, were anxious to go on with the court as usual.

The Vermonters heard the Court was going to take possession of the court-house, and were going to keep a strong guard at the door and prevent them from coming in. Thereupon the Vermonters thought best to get to court before the armed guard were placed there. About one hundred of them entered the court-house, about four o'clock in the afternoon. They had no sooner entered before a large number of men, armed with guns, swords, and pistols, appeared, but the Vermonters had no weapons. Patterson came up at the head of his armed company and commanded them to disperse, and caused the King's proclamation to be read, and told them, that if they did not disperse in 15 minutes he would blow a hole through them. The Vermonters replied that they should not disperse, but that the court party might come in if they would unarm themselves. —not without—and hold a parley. Mr. Gale, the Clerk of the Court, drew a pistol, held it up and said, "I will hold no parley with such d—d rascals but by this," referring to his pistol. The Vermonters returned to the house. Col. Chandler, one of the judges, came in. They told him that they had his word that there should not be any arms brought. He said the arms were brought without his consent, but he would go and take them away, and they should enjoy the house undisturbed until morning. But about midnight the New York sympathizers came. The alarm was given and the Vermonters were ordered to man the doors. The sheriff's party marched up within ten rods of the door. Three obeyed the sheriff's order to fire. The word "fire" was repeated; "G—d d—n you, fire. Send them to hell."

An eye witness described the rest of the scene in the following language: "Several men were wounded; one was shot with four bullets, one of which went through his brain, of which wound he died the next day. Then they rushed in with their guns, swords and clubs, and did most cruelly mammock several more; and took some that were not wounded, and those that were, and crowded them all into close prison together, and told them they should be in hell before the next night, and that they did wish there were forty more in the same case with that dying man; when they put him into prison, they took and dragged him as one would a dog, and would mock him as he lay gasping, and make sport for themselves at his dying motions."

The people in that County and in New Hampshire and Massachusetts were notified, and alarmed at such an aggravated murder, and came to the assistance of the inhabitants. This massacre was on the 13th of March, 1775. The next day at twelve o'clock nearly 200 men well armed came from New Hampshire, and they, with those who had gathered from Cumberland County, took up those who were engaged in the massacre and confined as many as they could find evidence against. They held an inquest, and the jury on their oath brought in "that W. Patterson did on the 13th of March, inst., by force and arms, make an assault on the body of William French, then and there lying dead, and shot him through the head with a bullet, of which wound he died, and not otherwise." The leaders of the massacre were sent to the North Hampton jail, and others were put under bonds. The sheriffs party claimed the sheriff was struck several blows before he ordered his *Posse* to fire, and that some of the *Posse* were wounded.

The convention held at Westminster, April 11th, 1775, while the facts of the massacre were fresh in their minds, "Voted, as our opinion, that it is the duty of the inhabitants, as predicated on the eternal and immutable law of self-preservation, to wholly renounce and resist the administration of the government of New

York," until they could be protected in life and property, or be annexed to some other government, or be incorporated into a new one.

There is another account of the Westminster affair, not inconsistent with the above, that recently appeared in the Burlington "Free Press," a newspaper published at Burlington, Vt. The article was called out on the occasion of an oaken gavel, made from a sill of the old court-house at Westminster, having been presented to the Brattleboro Chapter of the Daughters of the American Revolution. I here insert that account:—

"This sill was originally a part of the court-house at Westminster, the scene of the Westminster massacre, where the first blood of the American Revolution was shed. The prized wood was carefully turned to the required shape by Mr. Hines and it was trimmed with sterling silver appropriately engraved. It was then determined that the presentation should be attended with special exercises.

"The first court-house in Cumberland County, now Windham County, was a rudely constructed affair, built in Chester about 1768. Many were dissatisfied, however, with its location and they desired that its site be changed to Westminster. After much agitation and rioting, this was accomplished and Westminster was chosen as the shire town of the County at a meeting of the supervisors in Chester, May 26, 1772. The erection of a court-house was begun in Westminster in the fall of that year and by the close of the next summer it was ready for use. The location selected was on the brow of an elevation which has since been known as 'Court-house hill.' The court-house was about 40 feet square and was built of hewn oak timber and clapboarded. The roof was gambrel, surmounted by a square cupola open at the sides. An aisle 10 or 12 feet wide ran east and west through the middle of the lower floor, with double doors at each end. The building was intended for a jail and tavern as well as a court-house, and in the southeast corner was a kitchen occupied by the jailer and in the southwest corner was a bar-room in which the jailer served in the capacity of bar-tender. In each room was a large fireplace connecting with the huge chimney, which rose between the two rooms. Another door was cut in the south side of the building leading into an entry, on either side of which were doors to the kitchen and bar-room. In the north part was the jail, which comprised two prison rooms separated by a narrow aisle running north and south. This aisle communicated with the broad aisle by a door. Doors also opened from the prison rooms into the narrow aisle. Stairs led from the east entrance to the court room on the second floor.

"A session of the Cumberland County court was to be held in the 'old court-house' March 13, 1775. Much dissatisfaction prevailed in the County because New York had refused to adopt the resolves of the Continental Congress, and the whigs made exertions to dissuade the judges from holding the stated session. They were unable to obtain from Chief Judge Thomas Chandler the desired promise that no session would be held, so they resolved to prevent it by strategy. On the day set for court a party of from 80 to 100 whigs from Westminster and surrounding towns armed themselves with cudgels and took possession of the court-house about 4 o'clock in the afternoon. Soon afterward High Sheriff William Paterson, fearing trouble, came to Brattleboro and enlisted the services of 25 men. Others joined them on the way back and soon after the whigs had obtained possession of the court-house Paterson marched up to the house at the head of 60 or 70 armed Tories. The whigs heeded not the order to disperse and after much heated argument and exchange of threats Judge Chandler appeared and promised the whigs possession of the house without molestation until morning, when court would convene and hear their grievances. The Tories then departed and the whigs left the house, leaving a guard to give notice in case of an attack in the night. The sheriff increased his forces and after having drank to the honor of George III he marched, as he supposed unobserved, to the court-house about 11 o'clock. The moonlight reflected from their bayonets told the sentry of their coming, however, and the doors were quickly guarded. The sheriff attempted to enter the house, but was twice repulsed. He then ordered his men to shoot, but the volley passed over the heads of those in the house. The next volley was lower and the guards were driven from their posts. The house was soon filled with Tories and a hand-to-hand conflict followed in the darkness. The deadly weapons of the Tories and their superior numbers soon gave them the victory. Ten of the whigs were wounded, two of them mortally, and seven were taken prisoners. Two of the sheriff's posse were wounded. The whigs who escaped spread the alarm and by the dawn of day a large number had assembled at the scene of the massacre. The prisoners were released and the leaders of the assault were arrested and sent to jail at Northampton, in Massachusetts, "until they could have a fair trial." The whigs or liberty men who were mortally wounded were William French of Brattleboro and Daniel Houghton of Dummerston, but as French died early on the following morning and Houghton lived for nine days, their names have not often been coupled as martyrs in the cause of freedom."

The inscription on the monument of William French was as follows, viz.:—

EPITAPH.

In Memory to William French Son to Mr Nathaniel French Who Was Shot at Westminster March ye 13th 1775 by the hands of Cruel Ministereal tools of Georg ye 3^d in the Corthouse at a 11 a Clock at Night in the 22^d year of his Age——

Here William French his Body lies
For Murder his blood for Vengance cries
King Georg the third his Tory crew
tha with a bawl his head Shot threw
For Liberty and his Countrys Good
he Lost   his Life his Dearest blood

CHAPTER III.

THE EARLY HISTORY OF VERMONT CONTINUED.

A County Committee of Safety that had been chosen by the New York Convention to look after matters in Cumberland County in the interest of New York, met at Westminster Sept. 2nd, 1777. The following protest made by a member of that Committee showed the feeling and sentiment of the people in Eastern Vermont: viz., "Whereas I, the subscriber, a member of the County Committee of Cumberland to represent the town of Windsor in Convention this third day of instant June, do now in behalf of said town enter my protest against any proceeding under the State of New York, either directly or indirectly, as to any jurisdiction over said town.

EBENEZER HOISINGTON."

In June, 1777, an inquiry was made as to the temper of the people in eastern Vermont, and the reply from Cumberland County was, that the New Hampshire Grants had declared themselves independent and would not let the County Committees sit, nor permit anything to be transacted under the jurisdiction of New York." The adherents of New York held meetings in good many of the towns in the interest of that State, but as time went on, those adherents became less, and the opponents of Vermont fewer. On June 15, 1777,

Gen. Jacob Bagley, who had been a member from Gloucester County to the New York Congress, wrote and declared that the people of that County were almost to a man violent for a separation from New York.

The New Hampshire Grants had endeavored through their delegates to get Congress to recognize them as independent of New York and as a member of the Union, but Congress was slow to act to settle the dispute between the Grants and New York, or to recognize them as an independent State. On the 30th of June, 1777, Congress passed a resolve, "That the independent government attempted to be established by the people, styling themselves inhabitants of the New Hampshire grants, can derive no countenance or justification from the act of Congress, declaring the United Colonies to be independent of the Crown of Great Britain, nor from any other act or resolution of Congress."

This looked like turning the cold shoulder to the brave Green Mountain Boys. The Committee of the House of the State of New Hampshire, on the 2nd of April, 1779, reported to the House of that State, that that State "should lay claim to the jurisdiction of the whole of the New Hampshire grants, so-called, lying to the westward of Connecticut River." This looked like annihilation. But the same report conceded, that, if the Continental Congress allowed the Grants westerly of Connecticut River to be a separate State by the name of Vermont, the state of New Hampshire would acquiesce therein. This report was ordered to lie, but it was taken up at the session of the House, on June 24, 1779, and passed. This concession seemed to open a door whereby Congress might settle the whole controversy by admitting all the Grants westerly of the west bank of Connecticut River, as a separate State.

Ira Allen through the appointment by the Leglature of Vermont and the instruction from the Governor and Council, waited upon the General Court of New Hampshire to settle the controversy of the two jurisdictions. Allen's position was, that New Hampshire had no just claim to the Grants. And after admitting that there was a small minority of the people in favor of uniting with New Hampshire, stated that Vermont had been to great expense in sending agents to Great Britain to present their claims to the King and his Council, to be separate from New York, at a time when New Hampshire refused to exert herself to recover her jurisdiction over the Grants, and substantially surrendered her claims to New York; that New Hampshire having left the Grants to contend alone against New York, she should not now claim her territory; that in fact the Green Mountain Boys had been deserted by New Hampshire, and had to contend against the New York Land jobbers without her aid; that this was a time when the Green Mountain Boys were few in number, generally poor, and had but little more than Heaven to protect them and their families, and in this situation, stimulated by a patriotic spirit of freedom, baffled all their adversaries for more than seven years. And when New Hampshire was appealed to to exert herself to obtain jurisdiction of the Grants again, when the Green Mountain Boys were hard pressed by both Great Britain and New York, she said, "the King gave and the King hath taken away, and blessed be the name of the King," and made no exertions to obtain the land for herself, or to aid the Grants. Consequently her jurisdiction was curtailed to the west bank of Connecticut River. Allen claimed it was conceded by the United States that Vermont had borne her equal share of the burdens of the Revolutionary war, and consequently was entitled to equal privileges with the rest of their brethren of America.

On the 3d day of June, 1779, Thomas Chittenden, Governor and Commander-in-Chief in and over the State of Vermont, issued his proclamation of full and free pardon of all public offences, except treason and misprison of treason and capital offences committed since January 15th, 1777. On the 23d day of February, 1778, Gov. George Clinton of New York, for the purpose of inducing the people of Vermont to submit to the authority of New York, issued his proclamation, among other things setting forth, "that all persons actually possessing and improving lands, by title under grant from New Hampshire or Massachusetts Bay, shall be confirmed in their respective possessions."

Ethan Allen made a reply to this proclamation, and while admitting there were disaffected persons within the boundaries of the territory of the New Hampshire Grants, asserted that almost the whole of the inhabitants of the State were disaffected with the government of New York, and it was not a fact that the ancient, original and true bounds of New York included the lands within the territory then called Vermont, and that the first claim of that kind was asserted in the proclamation of Gov. Tyron, dated the 11th of December, 1771, where he claimed that New York extended to Connecticut River. Allen did not recognize the act of the English King in 1764, attempting to change and curtail the territory of New Hampshire, and extend the Eastern boundary of New York to Connecticut River, and had no doubt but Congress would curtail the claims of New York. And as to the overtures made by the Governor of New York to undo the grants made by New York of the lands in Vermont, and confirm the New Hampshire Grants, so-called, in their titles, Allen stated with great force that the Legislature of New York had no such right or legal power. As to the lands that had been granted by New York, that State could not nullify or defeat their own grants. He said, "It is contrary to common sense to suppose that the property of the subject is at the arbitrary disposal of the Legislature; if it was, they might give a grant to-day and vacate it to-morrow, and so on *ad infinitum*. But the truth of the matter is, the first conveyance will and ought to hold good; and this defeats all subsequent conveyances."

Allen claimed that the overtures, made in the proclamation of Gov. Clinton, were calculated to deceive *woods* people, who, in general, may not be supposed to understand law or the power of a legislative authority. But very few of the people of Vermont accepted of the overtures. Allen claimed that the best way of vacating those New York interfering grants was to maintain inviolable the supremacy of the legislative authority of the independent State of Vermont. That would overturn every New York scheme for their ruin, and made the Green Mountain Boys free men, and confirmed the title to their property, and put them into the enjoyment of the great blessings of a free, incorrupted and virtuous civil government.

Another reason that Allen gave in his reply, why Vermont should not be under the jurisdiction of New York, was because the local distance of Vermont from the seat of government in the State of New York was 450 miles, which would make it inconvenient and would constitute a sufficient reason for the independence of Vermont, and said, "if the inhabitants were obliged to submit to the government of New York they would wish to have the distance ten times greater."

He also asserted that the people of Vermont considered themselves as being in union with the United States from the time they took possession of Lake Champlain and the garrison depending thereon in behalf of the United States, in May, 1775; and had pursued the same object, viz., liberty; and had participated in all their troubles, and had hazarded all that was worth living or dying for, and that it only needed a formal declaration to constitute them a member of the Union. And, lastly, he said that a confederation of the

State of Vermont with the other free and independent States could not fail of being attended with salutary consequences to the Confederacy for ages to come; that her people were stimulated with a spirit of liberty, having a perfect detestation of arbitrary power, and would instil the principles of liberty and social virtue into their children, which will be perpetuated to future generations; that the State being removed from the sea coast, her people will be in a great measure exempted from luxury and effeminacy, and be a valuable support to the rising empire of the new world.

CHAPTER IV.

THE EARLY HISTORY OF VERMONT CONTINUED.

Notwithstanding the great efforts that the people of Vermont made for a separate existence as a State and the earnest pleading to be recognized as a member of the Confederacy, on equal terms with the other thirteen jurisdictions, they received no favorable consideration from the action of Congress, although they had the sympathy of some of its members. New York continued to treat the Green Mountain Boys as rebels, outlaws and felons, and passed laws to which was attached the death penalty for their violation, all of which was designed to crush out the spirit of liberty and the purpose to form an independent State. It only served to nerve the Green Mountain Boys to a more determined resistance to arbitrary power.

The Green Mountain Boys issued their manifesto in respect to those laws and as to their enforcement, signed by Ethan Allen, Seth Warner, Remember Baker and others, declaring, among other things, that if the officers acting under New York government should attempt to enforce those unjust laws, and arrest any of their number, "that they were resolved to inflict *immediate death* on whomsoever may attempt the same. And provided that if any of us or our party shall be taken

and we have not notice sufficient to relieve them,
or whether we relieve them or not, we are resolved
to surround (their captor or captors) whether at
his or their own house or houses, or anywhere
that we can find him or them, *and shoot such person or persons dead.* And we will kill and destroy
any person or persons whomsoever that shall presume to be accessory, aiding or assisting in taking
any of us." The Green Mountain Boys could not
be protected in life and property under the laws of
New York unless they gave up the latter to secure
the former, and, therefore, resolved to maintain
both, or to hazard or lose both.

In June, 1779, the Legislature passed an act to
prevent persons from exercising authority unless
lawfully authorized by the State of Vermont; that
statue was aimed against all persons who should
attempt to act in the name and by the authority
of the State of New York. The penalty for the first
offense under the act was a fine; for the second,
not exceeding forty stripes on the naked body;
and for the the third, the right ear was to be
nailed to a post and cut off, and the forehead was
to be branded with the letter "C" [contumacious]
with a hot iron.

Gov. Chittenden referring to this matter in his
message to the Legislature, October 14th, 1779,
said, "I am unhappy to inform you that the disaffected inhabitants in the lower part of Cumberland
County continue in their unjustifiable obstinacy
against the authority of the State;" but he recommended the suspension of the laws intended to
have been executed against those offenders, in con-

sequence of a letter received from John Jay, President of Congress, inclosing acts passed by that body relating to a final settlement of the differences subsisting between Vermont and the adjacent States.

By November 1st, 1779, the lawful money of the State, or bills of credit, had become very much depreciated, as $16 in lawfnl money was equal to but one silver dollar, so that the Governor's yearly salary, which at this time was one thousand pounds, was not actually a large sum.

At an early day the Legislature passed acts ensuring the people of the State the freedom of conscience in religious matters, as appears by an Act passed in 1780, viz.: "An Act for the purpose of empowering the inhabitants of the respective towns of this State to tax themselves for certain occasions." The act provided that no person should be compelled by the major vote of the town to build or repair a meeting house; or support a worship, or minister of the Gospel, contrary to the dictates of his conscience, provided said person or persons shall support some sort of religious worship as to him may seem most agreeable to the Word of God.

The settlers in Vermont, in an early period in her history, were annoyed by the hostile disposition of Indians. On the 9th of August, 1780, a party of twenty-one Indians visited Barnard and captured Thomas M. Wright, Prince Haskill and John Newton, and carried them to Canada. Newton and Wright escaped in the spring of 1781, and Haskill was exchanged in the autumn of that year.

They suffered many hardships while remaining prisoners, but on returning, resumed their farms and lived on them many years. A small band of Indians captured two young sons of one Brown, in the town of Jericho, and carried them to Canada, but after several years and the close of the Revolution they were permitted to return to their home.

On the 18th of August, 1780, the Governor and Council ratified an agreement that Stephen R. Bradley made with a Mr. Green of New London, Conn., to remove his printing apparatus from thence to the State, for the purpose of printing agreeable to the agreement.

On the 25th of July, 1780, Gov. Thomas Chittenden issued his proclamation giving the Tories a limited time to leave the State and join the enemy, their room being better than their company. There were but nine persons, so far as known, who availed themselves of the proclamation.

The Governor and Council and the Legislature, from time to time sought the favorable action of Congress to admit the State into the Confederation as a State. And on the 18th day of August, 1780, the Governor and Council, resolved that Stephen R. Bradley, Esq., be and he is hereby requested as agent in this State, to repair to Philadelphia, in company with Col. Ira Allen, to transact the political affairs of this State and report to this Council."

At the session of the Assembly October 13th, 1780, Gov. Chittenden requested the House verbally to accept his resignation of the office of Governor, but on repeated requests he withdrew his request and took the oath of office.

A question arose in the State regarding the re-granting of land that had before been granted by New York, and as to the validity of such grants. The Committee who had that matter in charge were of the opinion that the prior grants made by the authority of New York, since the King's prohibition, ought not to be considered as a sufficient bar against granting the same to other respectable, worthy petitioners, and asked the sense of the Assembly on the subject. And thereupon the Assembly resolved unanimously that the said previous grants, made by virtue of the authority of New York, were not a bar against granting the same to respectable and worthy petitioners. In February, 1781, the Assembly passed an Act for quieting disputes concerning landed property. The act constituted the Governor, Council and House of Representatives a court for the trial of cases, where two or more charters had been made of the same tract of land, to different proprietors.

In the Center village of the historical town of Bennington stood "Catamount Tavern" House which had been a notable place of early times and until it was burnt to the ground the 30th of March, 1871. It was erected by Captain Stephen Fay, about 1768. It was two stories high and and about 44 feet by 34, with high fireplaces in each story. On the top of the high sign post was placed the stuffed skin of a catamount, from which came the name of the house. It was widely known as the Headquarters of the settlers in their contest with the New York land claimants. It was the home of Ethan Allen when he first came to the New Hampshire Grants. One Doctor Samuel Adams of Arlington became an advocate of the New York titles, and advised his neighbors to purchase their land from New York. He was warned to desist from such a course, but he persisted therein and threatened death to anyone who should molest him. He was taken to the tavern, tried and ordered to be tied in an arm chair and hoisted up to the sign, where he was required to remain two hours. This had a salutary effect, but he afterwards at the time of Burgoyne's invasion, became a violent Tory, and fled to Canada. From the Council room of this tavern Ethan Allen issued his order for mustering the Green Mountain Boys for the capture of Ticonderoga—which capture was effected seven days after. In this house sat the Vermont Council of Safety during the trying campaign of 1777; here Gen. Stark and Warner, with the aid of the Council, planned the famous attack on Banm's entrenchments, where was won the brilliant victory, which turned the current of success from the British to the American arms. Here it was that David Redding, a traitor and spy, was tried, condemned and hung.

From what has already been said respecting Massachusetts Bay, New Hampshire and New York, it appears that each party asserted that their respective claims to Vermont territory were sound and right. It was stated in the introduction to Vermont's appeal to the candid and impartial world: that, "'tis very curious to see how many shapes Massachusetts Bay, New Hampshire and New York, are able to make His most Sacred Majesty appear in; he certainly according to the vulgar notions, much exceeds the devil; while his adjudications were in their favor he had the immutability of a God, but when against them the design of a villain."

The Governor and Council on the 10th day of December, 1779, published to the world what is called Vermont's Appeal to the candid and impartial World, containing a fair statement of the claims of Massachusetts Bay, New Hampshire and New York, and the right that the State of Vermont had to independence, with an address to Congress and the inhabitants of the 13 original United States. It is a document clear in statement, grand and eloquent, and as able a paper as any statesman has ever written. We take the following extract from it, viz.:—

"COUNTRYMEN, FELLOW CITIZENS AND BRETHREN: Under the strongest ties of friendship, as men who have equally suffered together, from the iron rod of tyranny in the late cruel measures of Great Britain, and who have gone hand in hand, and stood by each other, in times when threatened with ruin, tyranny and death; we beg your most serious attention by our address to this very important subject. * * * It gives us pain and grief to mention the intrigues and artifices, used by wicked and designing men, to destroy the inestimable liberties and privileges of the State of Vermont; and that too, by those ungrateful ones, who have been preserved from Indian cruelty by our brave and strenuous exertions during the present war. * * * We beg leave to recall your attention to the present most critical situation of the inhabitants of the State of Vermont; many of us were soldiers in the Provincial army during the last war between France and Great Britain and suffered inconceivable hardships, in successive campaigns, in striving to support the honor of the British nation, and to conquer and defend this territory of land from Indians, Canadians, and French, at which time 'twas that we discovered the excellency of the country, and determined, if ever circumstances would permit, to settle the same."

And then after fully stating the contest of the Grants with New York, the appeal continues as follows: "We have now existed as a free, independent State almost four years, have fought Britains, Canadians, Hessians, Waldeckers, Douchmen, Indians, Tories and all, and have waded in blood to maintain and support our independence. We beg leave to appeal to your own memories, with what resolution we have fought by your sides, and what wounds we have received fighting in the grand American cause; and let your own recollection tell what Vermont has done and suffered in the cause of civil liberty and the rights of mankind. And must we now tamely give up all worth fighting for? No, Sirs, while we wear the name of Americans, we never will surrender those glorious privileges for which so many have fought, bled and died; we appeal to your own feelings as men of like sufferings, whether you would submit your freedom and independence, to the arbitrament of any court or referees under heaven? If you would after wasting so much blood and treasure, you are unworthy the name of Americans; if you would not, condemn not others in what you allow yourselves. To you we appeal as the *dernier resort* under God; your approbation or disapprobation, must determine the fate of thousands. * * * We have coveted no man's estate, we have at all times been ready to submit all differences relative to the fee of lands in dispute to impartial judges, and now solemnly declare to all the world that we are contending for liberty, the gift of the Creator to all his subjects, the right of making our own laws, and choosing our own form of government; and will God be pleased to dispose the hearts of our countrymen to save the inhabitants of the State of Vermont from tyranny and oppression, to grant them their liberties in peace, and to see the things which belong to their political salvation before they are hidden from their eyes."

Ira Allen, by the order of the General Assembly of Vermont expressed in a resolution passed Oct. 21st, 1779, was sent to the General Assemblies of the States of New Jersey, Pennsylvania, Virginia, Maryland, and some other places in the interest of Vermont, and to vindicate their position, and the opposition of Vermont to the Government of New York. Mr. Allen attended those Legislatures. He addressed a letter to the Council of Pennsylvania, setting forth the unjust claims of New York and the right of Vermont to take her place as one of the States of the Union. He said the citizens of Vermont have viewed themselves in the Union with the other free States of America ever since they took Ticonderoga, Crown Point, etc., in favor of the United States, and were willing to furnish their quota of men for the common defence, and pay their proportion of the expense of the war when admitted a seat in Congress.

By the resolution of Congress of Sept. 24th, 1779, the first day of February, 1780, was assigned for action on the claims of New York, New Hampshire and Massachusetts to the jurisdiction of Vermont, but action was postponed. As Vermont had no representation in Congress any hearing there had must be *ex parte*. But the agents of Vermont, Jonas Fay, Moses Robinson, and Stephen R. Bradley, transmitted to that body information that they were in town (Philadelphia), ready with full powers to close an equitable union with the other independent States of America. Peter Olcott and Bezaleel Woodward were appointed agents for towns in the northern district of New Hampshire Grants on both sides of Connecticut River, who represented to Congress that it was the wish of the people in that district between the heights of land on both sides of the river that they should be included in one State, if a new State should be formed. The matter was postponed in Congress from time to time till June 2nd, 1780, when Congress resolved that the Grants, "and they be and hereby are strictly required to forebear and abstain from all acts of authority, civil or military, over the inhabitants of any town or district who hold themselves to be subjects of and owe allegiance to any of the States claiming jurisdiction of the said territory (Vermont), in whole or in part, until the decisions and determinations in the resolutions aforementioned shall be made."

CHAPTER V.

THE EARLY HISTORY OF VERMONT CONTINUED.

The Vermonters continued to act and conduct their affairs as an independent State without much regard to the resolution of Congress. Indeed, Gov. Thomas Chittenden, in a reply addressed to the President of Congress, to the resolutions, denied that Congress had the right or power to prevent Vermont being a free and independent State. And in that address said, "If Vermont does not belong to some one of the United States, Congress could have no such power (to judge of the jurisdiction of Vermont) without their consent; so that, consequently, determining they have such power, has determined that Vermont has no right to independence; for it is utterly incompatible with the rights and prerogatives of an independent State, to be under the control or arbitrament of any other power. Vermont has, therefore, no alternative; they must submit to the unwarrantable decree of Congress, or continue their appeal to heaven and to arms."

* * *

"The cloud that has hovered over Vermont, since the ungenerous claims of New Hampshire and Massachusetts Bay, has been seen, and its motions carefully observed by this government;

who expected that Congress would have averted the storm: but, disappointed in this, and unjustly treated as the people, over whom I preside, on the most serious and candid deliberation, conceive themselves to be, in this affair, yet blessed by heaven, with constancy of mind, and connections abroad, as an honest, valiant and brave people, are necessitated to declare to your Excellency, to Congress and to the world, that, as life, liberty and the rights of the people, intrusted them by God, are inseparable, so they do not expect to be justified in the eye of heaven, or that posterity would call them blessed, if they should, tamely surrender any part." * * * And closed his reply as follows: "Notwithstanding the usurpation and injustice of neighboring governments towards Vermont, and the late resolutions of Congress, this government from a principle of virtue and close attachment to the cause of liberty, as well as a thorough examination of their own policy, are induced, once more, to offer union with the United States of America, of which Congress is the legal representative body. Should that be denied, this State will propose the same to the Legislatures of the United States, separately, and take such other measures as self-preservation may justify."

While the matter, concerning the jurisdiction of Vermont, was before Congress, there was an effort made by Ira Allen, Luke Knowlton and others, to unite thirty-five towns east of Connecticut River and that part of New York east of Hudson River (extending from North Latitude 45° to the north line of Massachusetts) with Vermont under the same jurisdiction, but this scheme was finally abandoned.

Vermont not having been made a party to the deliberations in Congress as to the settlement of the claims to the Vermont lands and her jurisdiction, Ira Allen and Stephen R. Bradley, the Vermont agents, remonstrated against the proceedings of Congress althongh they were invited to attend the deliberations and declined because they were not treated by Congress as the agents or representatives of any State or people invested with legislative authority. On the 22nd day of Sept. 1780, the Vermont agents sent in to Congress their formal remonstrance against their proceedings, which closed with the following warning, "It gives us pungent grief that such an important cause, at this juncture of affairs, on which our all depends, should be forced on by any gentlemen professing themselves friends to the cause of America with such vehemence and spirit as appears on the part of the State of New York; and shall only add, that if the matter be thus pursued, we stand ready to appeal to God and the world, who must be accountable for the awful consequences that may ensue." Congress having heard the evidence produced by New York and New Hampshire, on the 27th day of Sept., 1780, resolved that the further consideration of the subject should be postponed. On the 22nd day of November, 1780, Gov. Chittenden made demand on the Legislature of New York, by letter to Gov. Clinton, to give up and fully relinquish their claims to jurisdiction over Vermont. Governor Clinton on Feb. 5th,

1781, transmitted the letter with his message to the New York Assembly, in which he said, "Nothing but the desire of giving you the fullest information of every matter of public concern, could induce me to lay before you a demand, not only so insolent in its nature and derogatory to the honor of the State and the true interests of your constituents, but tending to subvert the authority of Congress." This message and letter was referred to the New York Senate to a committee of the whole, and in the House to a committee of nine. On the 21st of February, 1781, the Senate considered the subject, and a resolution was reported, "declaring it inexpedient for the State to insist further on its right to jurisdiction over Vermont," and provided for commissioners to meet commissioners of Vermont to settle the terms for a cessation of jurisdiction by New York. On the same day the Senate adopted the resolutions with only one dissenting voice, and sent them to the House for concurrence, where they were made the order of the day for Feb. 27th, 1781.

Before a vote was taken in the House on the resolutions, Gov. Clinton sent in his message, declaring that, "if the House should agree to carry those resolutions into effect, the duties of his office would oblige him to exercise the authority vested in him by the constitution, and prorogue them." This threat prevented the adoption of the resolutions. The Vermont Assembly, by an act of Feb. 14th, 1781, endeavored to promote the project of consumating the east and west union which was to include towns east of Connecticut River as far as the Mason line, and on the west to Hudson river, but the defeat of the resolutions in the New York House by the threat of Gov. Clinton, suspended the movement.

Gov. Chittenden had also made demands to the Governors of Massachusetts and New Hampshire, for their respective States to relinquish their claim over the jurisdiction of Vermont. Massachusetts responded favorably. New Hampshire would acquiesce in such determination as Congress should make. Connecticut and Rhode Island seemed to be favorably disposed towards Vermont, and appointed commissioners to take into consideration the subject matter of the policy and justice of admittiug into the Union the people calling themselves the State of Vermont, to meet commissioners from the other New England States and the State of New York, in convention, to be holden in Providence on the 12th of April, 1781, to confer on that subject, and for conferring on the matter of their common defence against the British.

On Jan. 16th, 1781, delegates from forty-three towns in New Hampshire met in convention at Charleston, a town on the east side of Connecticut River, to deliberate on the subject of forming a State of towns situated on both sides of Connecticut River, and a resolution was adopted by the convention favoring that object. Twelve delegates of the convention remonstrated against such action. The convention adjourned to meet at Cornish in February, three miles from Windsor, Vt., where the Vermont Assembly would then be in session. On the 12th of Feb., 1781, the Governor, Council and House at Windsor took up the matter, and appointed a committee of seven, who reported back to the Vermont Assembly. The report, after giving a history of the attempts to unite the towns east of Connecticut River with Vermont, and the attempt of New York to extend jurisdiction over all of Vermont, recommended that the Legislature lay a jurisdictional claim to all lands east of Connecticut River to the Mason line, north of Massachusetts, and south of latitude 45°, and west to the center of the deepest channel of Hudson River, but not to exercise jurisdiction for the time being; which report was accepted. Articles were drawn up and approved, and on April 6th, 1781, representatives from the towns east of the river took their seats in the Vermont Assembly.

Lieut. John Patterson and 37 other citizens of Camden, and John Austin and 79 others of Cambridge (towns within the jurisdiction of New York) petitioned to have Vermont extend their jurisdiction to the west so as to include their towns, and this was agreed to by the Vermont Assembly. On June 15th, 1781, the representatives of the western district, informed the House, then setting at Bennington, that they were ready to take their seats according to the Articles of Union, and the several representatives were duly received by the Assembly.

An act was passed by the Legislature directing that all the territory, as far west as the deepest channel of the waters of Hudson River, be divided into townships and annexed to Bennington and

Rutland Counties. And Gov. Chittenden issued his proclamation, for all to take due notice of the laws and orders of the State.

The intercepted correspondence between the Vermont authorities and the British in Canada, carried on for some purpose, seemed to open the eyes of some in Congress and out, and brought some of them who had been lukewarm toward Vermont, or actually hostile to her, to look more favorable to her independence.

James Madison wrote to Edmund Pendleton, August 14, 1781, that "the controversy relating to the district called Vermont, the inhabitants of which have for several years claimed and exercised the jurisdiction of an independent State, is at length put into a train of speedy decision. Notwithstanding there is an objection to such an event, there is no question but they will soon be established into a separate and Federal State. A relinquishment made by Massachusetts of her claims; a despair of finally obtaining theirs on the part of New York and New Hampshire, the other claimants on whom these enterprising adventurers were making fresh encroachments; the latent support afforded them by the leading people of the New England States in general from which they emigrated; the just ground of apprehension that their rulers were engaging in clandestine negotiations with the enemy; and lastly perhaps, the jealous policy of some of the little States, which hope that such a precedent may engender a division of some of the large ones, are the circumstances which will determine the concurrence of Congress in this affair."

The information given by the intercepted correspondence with the enemy, Ira Allen said, had greater influence on the wisdom and virtue of Congress than all the exertions of Vermont in taking Ticonderoga, Crown Point, and the two divisions of General Burgoyne's army or their petition to be admitted as a State." Undoubtedly the fear that the New Yorkers had that the Grants might cast in their fortunes with the British and thereby leave their people exposed to fresh ravages from the enemy, and perhaps endanger the revolutionary cause, served to modify their attitude towards Vermont and make them less hostile to the independence of Vermont. It was the purpose of Vermont in the negotiations with Canada to secure Vermont from British invasion, but rather than submit to the jurisdiction of New York they would oppose such a union with force of arms, and would join the British in Canada.

On the 18th of August, 1781, the committee of Congress and the agents for Vermont, had an interview. The committee from Vermont proposed that Vermont be recognized as an independent State, and to fix the western boundary, about where it was finally determined upon when the State was admitted; and that Vermont have the same right as any other State, and matters of dispute be settled by Congress on hearing.

Congress on August 20th, 1781 passed a resolution, "that it be an indispensable preliminary to the recognition of the independence of the people inhabiting the territory called Vermont, and their admission into the Federal union, that she explicitly relinquish all demands of lands or jurisdiction, on the east side of the west bank of Connecticut River." New Hampshire became friendly to the independence of Vermont on condition of the relinquishment of the unions, but New York commenced active measures against Vermont and committed some depredations on the people in the west union. The New York forces took some of the Vermont militia prisoners. Gov. Clinton claimed that the Vermont militia taken prisoners were for the service of the enemy, the British. In this Gov. Clinton was mistaken. Gov. Chittenden demanded the release of the prisoners and declared that unless they were given up Vermont would render no assistance to New York against the common enemy. Gen. Gausevoort said he was much opposed to civil war, but it was the duty of New York to protect those who owed and professed allegience to Vermont. Ira Allen replied that Vermont had an equal right to protect those who acknowledged her jurisdiction; but it was advisable to use lenient measures on both sides, till Congress should have settled the boundary between the States—thus preventing the horrors of civil war when the common cause required all to be united against Great Britain. There was at this time considerable friction created, and sharp sparring between Col. John Abbott, Col. E. Walbridge and Gov. Chittenden on behalf of Vermont and Col. H. VanRensselar, Gen. Gausevoort and Gov. Clinton on behalf of New York growing out of the occupancy of the lands in the western union, but no actual clash of arms took place. Gen. Gausevoort retired from the district and left the same in possession of the Vermonters and those claiming that a union had been effected between that district and Vermont. In the eastern union New Hampshire authorities were active in exercising their authority as a State over the country lying between the Mason line and Connecticut River after the union had taken place as stated in this chapter. And Vermont was equally determined to maintain their authority over the district, and the civil officers of each state were in conflict, and the contest hot, and civil war seemed inevitable for a time. The New Hampshire House on January 8th, 1782, resolved to raise one thousand men to enable the civil officers to exercise their authority in that quarter. Col. Hale gave Gov. Weare a humurous account of his own arrest, which I insert here as he expressed it in writing, including spelling and grammar. He said, "the Vermont party had a force of forty men, and for a frunt gard they Raised some of their most ablest women and sent forward with some men dressed in Women's apparil which had the good luck to Take me Prisoner Put me aboard one of their slays and filled the same with some of the Principal women and drove off Nine miles to Wellan Tarvern in Warpole. the main body following after with aclimation of Joy, where they Regailed themselves and then set me at liberty, Nothing Doubting but they had entirely subdued New Hampshire."

President Weare issued a proclamation giving Vermonters forty days to leave the last union, or subscribe an oath acknowledging that New Hampshire had jurisdiction to Connecticut River. On February 22nd, 1782, forty days from the date of the proclamation, the General Assembly of Vermont resolved to dissolve both the Eastern and Western Unions; this action was largely due to the intervention of Gen. Washington, whose letter, and the resolutions of Congress of August, 1781, were accepted as pledges that on the withdrawal of Vermont to its former boundaries, the State would be admitted into the Union. This assurance was not fully made good, for when the question of the admission of Vermont into the Union next came up in Congress a majority decided against it. The first union of towns in New Hampshire with Vermont was dissolved at the request of New Hampshire on the 12th day of February, 1779, by the Legislature of Vermont, and she relinquished all her claims to the New Hampshire Grants to the eastward of Connecticut River. In March, 1779, the Legislature of New Hampshire proposed the laying of their jurisdictional union to the whole of New Hampshire Grants, which included the State of Vermont, against which Vermont strenuously remonstrated at the General Court of New Hampshire, but to no purpose. New Hampshire thereby violated their settlement of the boundary line; consequently on the 4th day of February 1781, the Legislature of Vermont laid a jurisdictional claim to both the New Hampshire Grants east of Connecticut River and the New York territory, believing and claiming that the inhabitants of both of those districts were, by natural situation to the waters of the Northern lakes and exposure of the inhabitants of the old territory of Vermont to the incursions of the enemy from Canada in times of war, would render it expedient that they should belong to this State, and that self-preservation and mutual defence rendered it indispensably necessary that the inhabitants of those districts, with those of the old territory, should unite in one entire State. The purpose of Vermont, the second time, to extend their claim of jurisdiction to the Mason line on the east, and to the Hudson River on the west, was to counteract the efforts of those two adjoining States in assuming jurisdiction over the old territory of Vermont, and to quiet some of her own internal dissensions occasioned by those two governments, and to make them experience the evils of intestine broils, and strengthen Vermont against insult. The condition upon which Vermont admitted the East and West Unions was, that in case Vermont should be admitted into the Federal Union with the United States, Congress should determine boundaries.

Queries may arise as to whether it was good policy, or honest, for Vermont to extend her jurisdiction into the States of New Hampshire and New York. It will be borne in mind that Vermont had urged Congress to admit her as a State and was willing to let Congress determine her boundaries, but this action was strenuously opposed by both New Hampshire and New York, as well as the offer to those States to refer the disputes respecting boundary lines to the final arbitrament and decision of indifferent men. Both States laid their respective claims to Vermont; and both refused to make an alliance with Vermont against the common enemy, and would not confer on the subject. This silence on that matter, and their entire conduct indicated that they intended to let Vermont struggle, as they thought, in their impracticable notions of independence—they said, "it was a forlorn hope;" they said, "the Vermonters are nicely situated to Canada, and when the war is terminated, if any of them remain alive, we, old Confederate States, can easily subject them; we have a right to call upon the whole Confederacy to crush them; they will go through the hazards and fatigues of that exposed part of our frontiers better than as though they had, sometime past, been subjugated; we know the length of their tether, and can shorten it when we please, and have sometime since divided their territory between us; we have them snug enough, and scorn to answer any of their proposals." The Vermonters claimed it was as honest in them to lay jurisdictional claim to the Grants east of Connecticut River, as it was for New Hampshire, previously to break over the mutual settlement of their boundary line with Vermont on Connecticut River and lay claim to the whole territory of Vermont. It was rumored that the whole Confederacy of the United States would join to extirpate Vermont. But the Vermonters had too much confidence in the representatives of the people of the United States to believe they would be engaged in such a work of destruction. They said it was not supposable that the eleven States will be duped to espouse the cause of the two claiming States, the reward of which would be nothing but infamy and disgrace.

They said, "How inglorious would be the victorious Continental troops, just returned from the capture of a proud and haughty army, with a Cornwallis, the pride of England, at their head, appear in arms puissantly tramping on the rights of a brave and meritorious people, and sacrificing their liberties which they have been valiantly supporting. Did not Vermont strike a respectable part of the martial blow towards capturing General Burgoyne, which brought the alliance with France, and, in the chain of causes, brought the French fleet to Chesapeake, and brought about a second memorable era in America?" Continuous efforts were put forth, by New York and New Hampshire, to prevent Vermont's admission into the American Union, while on the other hand Vermont was pressing her claims for admission, but Congress took no decisive steps on the subject. A committee of the Vermont Assembly regarded the resolution of Congress of the 7th and 21st of August, 1781, guaranteeing to the respective States of New York and New Hampshire, all the territory without certain limits, therein expressed, as having determined the boundaries of Vermont, and the Assembly resolved, accordingly, on Feb. 20, 1782.

And on Feb. 26th, 1782, the House chose three persons to represent the State in Congress, and commissioned and gave private instructions to two of them, Moses Robinson and Paul Spooner,

Esquire., to repair to Philadelphia and consider themselves invested with full power to agree on terms upon which the State should come into an union with the United States, and to sign and ratify articles of Federal union with the Confederated States of America, and take seats in Congress if the union was effected.

On March 16, 1782, Gov. Chittenden addressed a letter to General Washington, in which he said, "as the dispute of boundary is the only one that hath prevented our union with the Confederacy, I am very happy in being able to acquaint your Excellency, that that is now removed on our part, by our withdrawing our claims upon New Hampshire and New York. * * * Since, therefore, we have withdrawn our jurisdiction to the confines of our old limits, we entertain the highest expectations that we shall soon obtain what we have so long been seeking after, an acknowledgement of independence and sovereignty. For this we have appointed commissioners, with plenary powers, to negotiate an alliance with the Confederated States, and, if they succeed, to take seats in Congress, and should Heaven prosper the designs of their negotiations, we please ourselves much, that we who are of one sentiment in the common cause, and who have but one common interest, shall yet become one nation, and yet, be great and happy. The glory of America is our glory and with our country we mean to live or die as her fate shall be."

At this juncture of affairs, the independence of Vermont, and its admission into the Confederacy, was favored by the Eastern States, except New Hampshire and New York; the cause and interest of these two States to oppose Vermont was obvious from what has been said as to their position and action, but when New Hampshire gained her object and Vermont limited her claim to the west bank of Connecticut River, she became indifferent to Vermont's independence, though it became probable that her action, in the near future, would harmonize with the other Eastern States in favor of Vermont.

The Middle States, save New York, were inclined to favor Vermont's claims for admission, as Vermont would act with them in opposing the claim of Virginia and other large States to Western territory; and the smaller States would favor Vermont, as it would strengthen the interest and influence of the little States. Virginia, North Carolina, South Carolina and Georgia opposed her independence and admission as a separate State out of jealousy of a predominance of Eastern influence, and because it would give another small State an equal vote in the Senate, in deciding on all of the grand interests of the Union, and be an example for the dismemberment of the other States. These conflicting interests engendered and kept up the controversy and served to delay Vermont's admission.

At this point we will suspend the consideration, for the present of the controversy both in and out of Congress, respecting the admission of Vermont as an independent State of the Union, and take the reader to the consideration of the internal affairs of the State, and to the nature and extent of the doings and legislation of the Vermont Assembly, and the Governor and Council.

CHAPTER VI.

LEGISLATION AND INTERNAL AFFAIRS OF EARLY VERMONT.

In 1782, a second and successful attempt was made to establish a printing press in Vermont, at which the State printing might be done. A committee of three was chosen by the House, to agree with persons to set up and continue the printing business in some convenient place in the State for the term of five years, and that a public newspaper be printed and published weekly at said printing office, and in consideration thereof such persons should receive the sum of three hundred pounds lawful money out of the public treasury of the State, and have the privilege of doing all of the State printing at a reasonable price.

Hough and Spooner of the Journal at Windsor, and Haswell and Russell publishers of the Vermont Gazette at Bennington, were the only printers in the State until Matthew Lyon started the Farmer's Library at Fair Haven in 1793.

On Oct. 21, 1782, a permit was granted by the Governor and Council to Lieutenant William Blanchard and John Blanchard to pass the present lines to the Northern part of the State, for the purpose of hunting. On Feb. 14, 1783, a petition was presented to the Council, requesting that Ebenezer Willoughby, late of Shaftsbury, who had been some time absent from the State, be permitted to return thereto and enjoy the privileges of a freeman thereof, which request was granted for him and his family and effects, to return to the State "by his dispensing with such of his interest as has been disposed of by this State for its use, to atone for his past offences committed against this State." Willoughby had previously joined the enemy, but was captured and his property confiscated.

Certain persons had been convicted by the Supreme Court of conspiring and attempting an invasion and rebellion against the State and were banished from the State. The Assembly passed an act giving His Excellency the Governor, and the Honorable Council, power to pardon such as had become penitent, the Assembly setting forth that, "this Assembly being desirous at all times of showing mercy when it can be done consistent with the public safety."

Postal arrangements in that early day in Vermont were meager and primitive. At a special session of the Council held at Bennington Nov. 26, 1783, it was resolved that Samuel Sherman be paid nine shillings per week out of the public treasury, for riding post, carrying and bringing the public intelligence to and from Albany, until the setting of the General Assembly in February next, and "he to be accountable for all the money he shall receive as postage on letters, which is to be deducted from the nine shillings per week." It was provided that postage would be under the same regulations as in the United States.

At a session of the Assembly and Council held at Bennington in February and March 1784, a bill was passed prescribing the mode in which the House and Governor and Council should enact laws for the State. One object of which was to make the two Houses coördinate in their powers of legislation as far as the Constitution would then permit.

The General Assembly, from time to time, by resolution, impeached justices of the peace and other State officers for wrong doing and mal-administration in office, and on trial before the Governor and Council convicted them, and suspended or removed them from office. On Feb. 24, 1784, the Council appointed a committee of two to join a committee from the General Assembly to consider and report upon the most effectual measures for the securing and settling of all the small islands in Lake Champlain east of the deepest channel.

On Oct. 15, 1784, after His Excellency Thomas Chittenden and other State officers and members of the Council had been declared elected for another term, Joseph Fay, the retiring secretary of the Council, caused to be published the following viz.:—

"To the Printers of the 'Vermont Gazette:'

Gentlemen: By inserting the following extract of an official letter received last evening, you will not only gratify the public by giving early knowledge of the choice of their rulers for the year ensuing, but sting the ears of our enemies with the unwelcome news of the uniformity of the people by continuing in office those gentlemen who have been the guardians and faithful servants of the public during a bloody war with Great Britain and the contest with the several neighboring States for eight years past. Such a steady firmness does honor to the people, and by a continuance, with due observance of good and wholesome laws, cannot fail to render this little republic happy, important, and the dread of her enemies."

The great results the Green Mountain Boys had accomplished in behalf of the New Hampshire Grants and the State of Vermont against obstacles seemingly overwhelming, shows what a few, but brave, persevering and determined people, adhering to principle and aiming at liberty and independence, may accomplish.

The General Assembly, on October 29th, 1784, resolved that, "the treasurer be and is hereby directed to pay His Excellency, Thomas Chittenden, Esq., thirty-six shillings, L. Money, on the two penny tax for cash expended by him for distilled spirits for the use of the Militia on the day of general election." And at the same date three agents, Hon. Ira Allen, Major Joseph Fay and Hon. Jonas Fay were appointed agents or commissioners to transact the necessary business of opening a free trade to foreign powers through the Province of Quebec.

On June 7th, 1785, it was represented to the Council that Abijah Prince and his wife Lucy and family were greatly oppressed and injured by John and Ormas Noyce in the possession and enjoyment of a certain farm. The Council having taken the matter into consideration and made due inquiry, were of the opinion that they were much injured, and unless some method was taken to protect them, they must fall upon the charity of the town, and resolved, that His Excellency be requested to write to the selectmen of the town of Guilford recommending to them to take some effectual measures to protect said Abijah, Lucy and family in the possession of said lands, till the dispute can be equitably settled.

The Council from time to time remitted fines that had been imposed by the courts. The Assembly passed acts, concurred in by the Council, to confirm persons in the quiet and peaceable possession of their farms, and render all judgements respecting the same, entered by any Court of law, null and void. On election day it was the custom to have an election sermon preached in the House of Representatives.

The General Assembly and Governor and Council, from time to time, on petition, granted farms, lying in Gores between chartered towns, to persons, and appointed committees to dispose of lands in such Gores to the inhabitants living therein, and to others under proper regulations and restrictions; the committees to be accountable for the avails.

As late as 1785, Addison County embraced all territory north of Rutland County, west of the mountain to the northern boundary of the State; and Orange County all territory north of the County of Windsor, east of the mountain, to the northern boundary of the State.

On October 27, 1785, the Assembly concurred in an act directing what coin and money should be legal currency in the State, and on Feb. 20, 1787, an act was read and approved to ascertain the value of contracts made for Continental money or bills of credit of the United States. Lawful money or bills of credit, down to Sept. 1, 1777, were of the value of gold and silver, and said bills of credit had so far depreciated by Sept. 1, 1780, as fixed by said act, that seventy-two of them were worth but one dollar in gold or silver coin.

During the trying times through which Vermont passed, Isaac Tichenor was a prominent figure. He was born in Newark, N. J., and came to Bennington June 14, 1777, and was representative of that town in the Vermont Assembly from Oct. 1781, to Oct. 1785, and speaker in 1783; member of the Council from Oct. 1786, to Oct. 1792; judge of the Supreme Court five years from 1791, and chief justice two years; and a member of the Council of Censors in 1792; and United States Senator in 1796-7, when he resigned to take the office of Governor; and again U. S. Senator from 1815 to 1821, in all seven years. He was Governor from 1797 to 1807, and 1808-9, in all eleven years. He was elected agent and delegate to the Continental Congress in 1782 and 1783, 1787, 1788 and 1789; and in 1790, he was one of the commissioners of Vermont who settled the protracted controversy with New York. He was a man of good private character and talents, accomplished manners and insinuating address. It is said that his fascinating qualities acquired for him at an early day the soubriquet of the "Jersey Slick." He died Dec. 11, 1838, in his 85th year, and left no descendants.

Governor Chittenden had his attention called to an address of President Wheelock of Dartmouth College which address suggested to the State to squester to the use of the College, "a part of the public lands in the State, those only which were left to a society for the propagation of knowledge in foreign parts," in return for which the College promised to educate Vermonters free of tuition. The proposition was criticised as an attempt both to divert the glebe rights improperly, and to prevent the establishment of colleges in Vermont. On March 3d, 1787, the Assembly "resolved that the proposals of President Wheelock, made to this House in behalf of the trustees of Dartmouth College, are such that they cannot be accepted." A proposition for a college at Williamstown had been made by Hon. Elijah Paine and Cornelius Lynde; and subsequently another by Ira Allen, Governor Chittenden and others for a college at Burlington, which was accepted, and a charter was granted Nov. 3, 1791.

By an act passed Oct. 31, 1786, neat cattle, wheat, rye and Indian corn, (beef, pork and sheep were afterwards added,) were made lawful tender on an execution by the debtor; that when property was taken on an execution that had been issued for more than one pound, after four days had elapsed, it was to be appraised off to the creditor at the sign post in the town where taken.

On Feb. 17, 1787, the petition of Lieut.-Col.

Benjamin Randall and fifty-five others, inhabitants of Little Hoosack, in the State of New York, was presented, praying for compensation for the damages they sustained for their influence and zeal in adding the Western Union to this State. And thereupon the Assembly decided to grant to them a township six miles square as soon as vacant land could be found.

Drunkenness, even in the early history of Vermont, was not regarded as altogether commendable, for on Feb. 19, 1787, it was enacted by the General Assembly, that, "any person found so drunk as to be deprived of the use of reason and understanding, or the use of their limbs, was subject to a fine of six shillings for every offence, for the use of the poor; and for non-payment of fine and costs, the offender was to be set in the stocks not exceeding three hours." And it was provided by another act, that each town was to provide a good pair of stocks with lock and key, and the stocks should be erected in the most public place in town.

It was enacted that the penalty for a person convicted of adultery was that, "He, she, or they shall be set upon the gallows, for the space of an hour, with a rope or ropes about his, her, or their neck or necks, and the other end cast over the gallows; and also shall be severely whipped on the naked body, not exceeding thirty-nine stripes, and shall from the expiration of twenty-four hours after such conviction, during their abode in this State, wear a capital A of two inches long, and proportionable bigness, cut out in cloth of a contrary color to their clothes, and sewed upon their upper garment, on the outside of their arm, or on their back in open view." And the same penalty was prescribed for polygamy. The penalty for treason against the State was death. Cropping, or cutting off an ear and branding on a hot iron with the letter C was one of the penalties for counterfeiting.

On March 2, 1787, an act was passed giving subjects of the United States the same privileges as citizens of Vermont.

The first constitution had been established by legislative statutes in 1779, and 1782, so it was deemed prudent to establish the amended constitution in the same way, and it was read and concurred in on March 2, 1787. The opinion prevailed, at that time, that the Legislature was sovereign, and no idea was entertained, said Daniel Chipman, "that an act of the Legislature however repugnant to the Constitution, could be adjudged void or set aside by the judiciary." The original and amended Constitution were both adopted by the representatives of the several towns in conventions, and confirmed by the representatives of the same towns in the General Assembly.

On March 3d, 1787, an act was concurred in adopting so much of the common law of England, and also so much of the statutes of Great Britain, enacted previous to October 1, 1760, in explanation of the common law, as was not repugnant to the Constitution, or any statute of the State. On March 8, 1787, an act was concurred in directing what money or currency should be legal tender, and what should be its fineness ; and also an act establishing post offices in the State, at Bennington, Rutland, Brattleboro, Windsor and Newbury. An act was passed empowering the County Courts to license Innkeepers, and it provided that, "Any person who sold less than one quart of intoxicating liquor without a license was subject to a penalty of three pounds for the first offence, six pounds for the second, and so on doubling the penalty for each repetition."

At the October session of the Assembly, 1787, Addison County was divided, and Chittenden County was formed out of her territory and organized by an act of the Assembly. An act also was passed at that session establishing a County grammar school at Castleton, in the County of Rutland.

Acts were frequently passed giving liberty for persons to raise money to establish and carry on various enterprises. On March 7, 1789, the Governor and Council, on account of the distressed situation of the inhabitants in the Northern part of the State for the want of grain, occasioned by the failure of crops, issued an ordinance that from the 20th day of March until the 18th day of April next ensuing, no one should export out of the State (being the products of the State) any wheat, rye, Indian corn, barley, or the meal or flour of any of said articles, and making it lawful for any sheriff, constable, grand juror, or selectman, to stop and examine any and every sleigh, cart, wagon or carriage or other conveyance which they apprehended was loaded with any of said articles for transporting out of the State contrary to the true intent and meaning of the ordinance.

In the year 1789, the freemen of Vermont made no choice of Governor, and on the 9th day of October, 1789, the Council and the Assembly met in Grand Committee at Westminster and chose Moses Robinson of Bennington Governor for the ensuing year. The retiring Governor, on the announcement of the election of his successor, addressed the Council and the gentlemen of the House, and said, in part, "Since I find that the election has not gone in my favor by the freemen, and that you gentlemen, would prefer some other person to fill the chair, I can cheerfully resign to him the honors of the office I have long since sustained, and sincerely wish him a happy administration, for the advancement of which my utmost influence shall be exerted."

The House, through their speaker, addressed the retiring Governor, who said in part, "The Representatives of the people of Vermont upon this occasion request Your Honor to accept for your past services all that a noble and generous mind can give, or wish to receive, *their gratitude and warmest thanks.*"

Moses Robinson was the second Governor of Vermont, and assumed the duties of his office Oct. 13, 1789. He was Governor one year and was succeeded by his predecessor, Thomas Chittenden. It was said at the time that Gov. Robinson bore the loss of his chief magistracy with a fortitude which becomes the character of a philosopher and a Christian.

The population of the State in 1791, was 85,533. On January 22, 1791, an act was passed by the Assembly and concurred in directing the width of sleds to be used in the Counties of Orange and Windsor.

There were many changes of the names of towns in the early history of Vermont. The town of Alburgh had had six different names before it received its present name in 1791; the town of Wilmington was changed to Draper in 1763, and subsequently it was changed back to Wilmington; the town of Bradford was called Moretown; Brandon was formerly called Neshbe; Lowell was called St. George; Johnson was called Browningtston; Newport was called Duncanburgh; Sutton was called Billymead; Fairfield or a part of that town was previously called Smithfield; Sheldon was called Hungerford; Jay was called Myllis; Craftsbury was called Mendon; Morgan was called Caldersburgh; Waterford was called Littleton; Barre was called Wildersburgh; Barton was called Providence; Albany was called Lutterloh; Hartland was called Waterford.

Early in Vermont history there were towns in Bennington County called Somerset and Bromley; in Windham County, Hindale and Fulham; in Windsor County, Saltasth; in Rutland County, Harwitch; in Addison County, Kingston; in Caledonia County, Deweysburgh, Hopkinsville, and St. Andrews; in Essex County, Ferdinand, Minehead, Lewis and Norfork; in Franklin County, Huntsburgh; in Orleans County, Kelleyvale.

The Counties of Washington and Lamoille were made up from towns in adjoining Counties. The old maps show that Chittenden County included Middlesex, Worcester, Stowe, Waterbury, Waitsfield, Moretown, Duxbury, Fayston and Starksboro. Orleans County included Morristown, Elmore, Hyde Park and Wolcott. Franklin County included Sterling, Johnson, Cambridge, Coits Gore (now Waterville), and Belvidere.

Previous to the Declaration of Independence of Vermont in 1777, the State was included within the limits of four Counties. The County of Cumberland, embracing that portion of the State lying east of the Green Mountains and extending as far north as the south line of Orange County, was established by the Colonial Legislature of New York in 1766. This act was annulled by virtue of a Royal decree in 1767, but was renewed in 1768, and the County was incorporated in March of the same year. The first Shire town was Chester, but the County seat was removed to Westminster in 1772.

The County of Gloucester, embracing all of the State lying east of the Green Mountains and north of Cumberland County, was established in 1770. The Shire town was Newbury.

The County of Charlotte, embracing a portion of the State of New York and that portion of Vermont lying west of the Green Mountains and north of the towns of Arlington and Sunderland, was constituted in 1772, with its Shire located at Skeensborough (now Whitehall), N. Y.

The remainder of the State, lying west of the Green Mountains and south of the County of Charlotte, was embraced in the County of Albany in the State of New York.

CHAPTER VII.

THE STRUGGLE OF VERMONT FOR ADMISSION INTO THE UNION.

In this chapter we resume the consideration of the controversy respecting the admission of Vermont as one of the United States of America from where we left the subject at the close of Chapter III. At that period of the controversy there was a sentiment in the Eastern States and in most of the Middle States favorable to the admission of Vermont, but when Congress took up the question again on Nov. 5, 1782, a material change in that body became manifest, which was due to the new friends that New York had gained through the acceptance by Congress, in October previous, of her cession of Western territory, and by Vermont's rigid enforcement of her authority in September against the insurrection that had been stirred up by the adherents to New York in Windham County. In April, 1782, the Legislature of New York passed two acts, for pardoning certain offences, and quieting the minds of the inhabitants of Vermont. The New York sympathizers in Windham County got up and circulated a remonstrance against the action of the authorities in Vermont, asserting therein, that the principal men of Vermont were engaged in a treasonable correspondence with the British Commander and Governor of Canada, and had made an agreement to raise a force to be employed under British pay for the destruction of the liege subjects of the United States, and asked New York to raise one regiment or more in the County of Cumberland, to be paid by New York, for the protection of the people. This document was sent to Gov. Clinton, who replied to the committee remonstrants in Cumberland County, promising to use his best endeavors to render them aid, and requested them to "diffusively and expeditiously disperse" among the people copies of those New York quieting acts, and to soothe and quiet the Vermonters, and said that "we never had it in contemplation to deprive individuals of their property." And said in the same reply, that the State of New York is determined not to relinquish its right of jurisdiction to the country distinguished by the name of New Hampshire Grants, unless Congress should agreeable to our act of submission, judicially determine it not to be comprehended within our boundaries. This expression that, "we never had it in contemplation to deprive individuals of their property," was not consistent with the acts of the New York authorities in attempting to oust the Grants from their land by writs of ejectment, writs of possession, and by force. Governor Clinton in said reply, said, "that there is the fullest evidence of a criminal and dangerous intercourse between some of the leaders in the assumed government and the common enemy, and this, I trust, will be an additional inducement with such who profess to be friends to the cause of America, to interest themselves in prevailing with their fellow citizens to return to their allegiance, and by that means disappoint the views of a combination who from motives of self interest and ambition would enter into a league with the enemy and sacrifice the liberties of their country." The adherents of New York in Guilford immediately called a meeting in which the instructions of Governor Clinton, in his reply, were adopted, and voted, "to stand against the pretended State of Vermont until the decision of Congress be known, with lives and fortunes."

Numerous justices of the peace were appointed by New York for Cumberland County, and charged among other things, to take notice of all attempts to set aside the laws and ordinances of that State, and at the same time officers for a battalion of six military companies, in the towns of Brattleborough, Guilford and Halifax, were commissioned; which action of the New York authorities looked like a determined effort to enforce New York law in Vermont, and suppress all Vermont authority by military force.

On June 19, 1782, the General Assembly of Vermont passed an act for the punishment of conspiracies against the peace, liberty and independence of the State, which was aimed at the New York adherents at Guilford and vicinity. Governor Tichenor was appointed to go to the three above named towns and endeavor, by persuasive means, to unite the people in favor of the government of Vermont and save the necessity of resorting to compulsory measures, but his eminent persuasive powers failed to accomplish the purpose. And on June 21, 1782, the Vermont Assembly passed an Act empowering the Governor to raise men to assist the sheriffs. Both sides were preparing for the conflict. On July 29, 1782, judgement had been rendered by John Bridgeman, a Vermont justice, against Col. Timothy Church, the commander of the New York battalion; an execution was issued on the judgement, and the sheriff attempted to arrest the Colonel thereon, but was prevented doing so by Church and his friends. The sheriff then applied to the Governor and Council for an armed *posse* to assist him in executing Vermont laws in Windham County; thereupon Governor Chittenden was authorized to raise two hundred and fifty men for that purpose. Ethan Allen was commissioned as commander of the military force, and by the 10th of September had executed his orders, so thoroughly, that the offenders and the opposers of Vermont law had been, by September 19, 1782, tried, convicted and sentenced—some to banishment and confiscation of their property, and others to pay fines. Charles Phelps of Marlborough and Joel Bigelow of Guilford, two of the offenders, escaped and left the State for the purpose of acquainting Governor Clinton of the proceedings. Bigelow soon returned with a letter from Governor Clinton recommending the adherents of New York to abstain from acts of violence until Congress should decide on the questions in dispute, but if the prisoners were not released he deemed it justifiable and advisable that an attempt be made for their release; and if that could not be effected, then an equal number of insurgents should be taken to some place in New York and held as hostages for the security and indemnity of the prisoners held under Vermont law.

Said Bigelow, in his affidavit sent to Governor Clinton, represented that Ethan Allen had declared that he would give no quarter to man, woman or child who should oppose him; and he would lay Guilford as desolate as Sodom and Gomorrah. Thereupon Governor Clinton addressed a letter to the New York delegates in Congress, in which he said, "I feel the honor of the State and myself hurt that my repeated applications to Congress for a decision of the controversy have not only been ineffectual, but even unnoticed. You are fully sensible of my situation, and of the condition of the State to assert its rights, and I flatter myself you feel for our unfortunate fellow citizens who are thus exposed to outrage and injury. I have, therefore, only to add an earnest request to use every means for inducing Congress to attend to this very important business."

Governor Clinton, on Sept. 27, 1782, addressed a letter to the New York adherents in Cumberland County, in which he said, "there was every reason to believe that Congress will immediately interpose and exert their authority for your relief and protection." He also wrote to Jonathan Hunt, the Vermont sheriff, warning him of the dangerous consequences of his action. Some of the adherents of New York who had been released from their Vermont imprisonment, presented their petition to Congress and asked for aid in their impoverished and distressed condition, and for a restoration of their property that had been confiscated, but Congress gave them no aid.

On Oct. 4, 1782, when Timothy Church, William Shattuck, Henry Evans and Timothy Phelps, four of the chief offenders against Vermont under sentence of banishment, were released from prison, they were taken across the line into New Hampshire by a deputy-sheriff, Samuel Avery, who warned them that they would incur the penalty of death if they ever returned to Vermont.

The General Assembly setting at Manchester, on Oct. 17, 1782, chose Moses Robinson, Paul Spooner, Ira Allen and Jonas Fay agents to Congress, any two of them to be vested with powers as plenipotentiaries to negotiate the admission of the State into the Federal Union, and to agree upon and ratify terms of confederation and perpetual union with them when opportunity should present; and were commissioned as such agents.

The Legislature of New Jersey instructed their delegates in Congress to use their influence against the admission of the State, and to subdue the inhabitants of Vermont to the obedience and subjection of the State or States that claim their allegiance. They disclaimed every idea of imbuing their hands in the blood of their fellow citizens, or entering into civil war among themselves, regarding such a step to be highly impolitic and dangerous.

The Vermont affairs from time to time were before Congress down to January, 1783; and the discussion in Congress and the action of that body, were on the whole, unfriendly to Vermont, but not decisive against her independence. The unfavorable resolutions and action of Congress towards Vermont encouraged the New York adherents in Windham County, but Gov. Chittenden showed a firm purpose to maintain the authority of Vermont against all opposition and against the threatened hostility of Congress, as well as the insurrectionists in Windham County.

On January 9th, 1783, Governor Chittenden, by letter to the President of Congress, remonstrated against the unfriendly action of Congress, founded partly on the mutual agreement between Congress on the one part, and the State of Vermont on the other, that the latter should have been taken into the Union previous to the late action of Congress; and partly on the impropriety of the claim of Congress to interfere in the internal government of the State. The agreement referred to, the reader will remember, was the encouragement that Congress gave Vermont, that if she complied with certain resolutions of that body and relinquished all claim to the so-called East and West Unions, she should be admitted as one of the States of the Union of the United States of America.

And after Governor Chittenden received the letter heretofore referred to, from His Excellency George Washington, assuring him that if Vermont withdrew her jurisdiction to the confines of her old limits, Congress would admit Vermont as a State of the Union, Governor Chittenden and the people of Vermont confided in the faith and honor of Congress, that those assurances would be made good. Governor Chittenden in the remonstrance said, "How inconsistent then is it in Congress to assume the same arbitrary stretch of prerogative over Vermont, for which they waged war against Great Britain? Is the liberty and natural rights of mankind a mere bubble, and the sport of State politicians? What avails it to America to establish one arbitrary power on the ruins of another? Congress set up as patriots for liberty, they did well; but pray extend the liberty, for which they are contending, to others."

The remonstrance, in referring to the criminals that had been banished or fined, for which Gov. Clinton, the New York committee and Congressmen were so solicitous for their relief, continued, "The notorious Samuel Ely, who was ring leader of the late seditions in the State of Massachusetts, a fugitive from justice, was one of the banished; he had left that State and was beginning insurrections in this, when he was detected, and carefully delivered to the sheriff of the County of Hampshire in the State of Massachusetts, who, as I have been since informed, has secured him in goal at Boston, to the great satisfaction and peace of that State. This Samuel Ely, Timothy Church and William Shattuck, who were three of the banished, had previously taken the oath of allegiance to the State of Vermont; and so had a greater part of those who were fined; and every one of the towns in which they resided, had for several sessions of the Assembly, previous to their insurrection, been represented in the Legislature of the State."

It will be seen from the foregoing that matters were approaching, very fast, to a disagreeable and alarming issue. General Washington saw the necessity of bringing the controversy to a peaceful settlement; and on Feb. 11, 1783, he wrote Joseph Jones, a member of Congress, a long letter in which he said, "That the delegates of the New England States in Congress, or a majority of them, are willing to admit these people into the Federal Union as an independent and sovereign State; * * * that they have a powerful interest in those States and have pursued very politic measures to strengthen and increase it long before I had any knowledge of the matter, and before the tendency was seen into or suspected, by granting, upon very advantageous terms, large tracts of land; in which, I am sorry to find, the army in some degree have participated. Let me next ask, by whom is this district of country principally settled? And of whom is your present army comprised? The answers are evident,—New England men. It had been the opinion of some that the appearance of force would awe these people into submission. If the General Assembly ratify and confirm what Mr. Chittenden and his Council have done, I shall be of a very different sentiment; and moreover, that it is not a trifling force that will subdue them, even supposing they derive no aid from the enemy in Canada; and that it would be a very arduous task indeed, if they should, to say nothing of a diversion which may and doubtless would be made in their favor from New York by Carleton, if the war with Great Britain should continue. The country is very mountainous, full of defiles, and extremely strong. The inhabitants, for the most part, are a hardy race, composed of that kind of people who are best calculated for soldiers; who in truth are soldiers; for many, many hundreds of them are deserters from this army, who, having acquired property there, would be desperate in the defence of it, well knowing that they were fighting with halters about their necks."

Joseph Jones, in his reply to General Washington, said that, "If Vermont confines herself to the limits assigned her, and ceases to encroach upon and disturb the quiet of the adjoining States, and at the same time avoiding combinations, or arts, hostile to the United States, she may be at rest within her limits, and by patient waiting the convenient time, may ere long be admitted to the privileges of the Union." Vermont was accused of a want of sincerity and candor in her negotiations with Congress. That body had trifled so long with Vermont, her government and her people had but little respect for the Continental Congress.

Unquestionably the letter of General Washington, though written in his private capacity to Mr. Jones, had much to do in bringing about a more favorable sentiment in the Confederacy for the admission of Vermont. On Feb. 25, 1783, in a committee of the whole of both Houses in Vermont, it was resolved that the citizens of the State had from the first attempt to form a State government uniformly shown their attachment to the common cause and a desire of being connected with the Federal Union, and that neither the Executive or Legislative authority of the State had ever entered into any negotiation, truce, or combination with the enemy of the United States, except for the exchange of prisoners, and expressed their good intentions towards the United States. But notwithstanding that, Vermont, at all times, was determined that her existence as a State should not be swallowed by interested adjoining States by any action of those States or by Congress.

And in an address to Congress, made by a committee of the Vermont Assembly appointed Feb. 26, 1783, in reply to the resolutions of Congress adopted Dec. 5, 1782, unfavorable to Vermont's separate existence, the committee said, "All and every act of Congress which interferes with the internal government of this State and tend to prevent a general exercise of our laws, are unjustifiable in their nature and repugnant to every idea of freedom; * * * we cannot express our surprise at the reception of the late resolutions of Congress of the 5th of Dec. 1782, obtained ex parte and at the special instance of an infamous person," referring to Charles Phelps of Marlborough, a persistent opponent of Vermont. Phelps had been some of the time in favor of Vermont and at other times in favor of New York. Governor Chittenden, for the purpose of showing to Congress what an unreliable and worthless character he was, sent to Congress the affidavit of Phineas Freeman and Jonathan Howard, taken on Jan. 15th, 1783, in which it was stated that Charles Phelps declared, "that he would as soon come under the Infernal Prince as under the State of New York."

CHAPTER VIII.

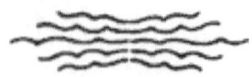

THE ACTION OF NEW HAMPSHIRE AND NEW YORK.

Let us refer to an attempt to divide Vermont between New Hampshire and New York after each of those States had failed in their efforts to absorb the whole. The proposition was for New Hampshire and New York to compromise the dispute and divide the State by the ridge of the Green Mountains, and New Hampshire take the Eastern and New York the Western part of Vermont. This scheme originated in 1779, and its proposal was made in Congress in March, 1782. Some of the towns on the east of the mountain favored such an object; and resolutions of a convention of committees of Newbury, Bradford, Norwich and Hartford favored it and inquired of the General Court of New Hampshire if they were desirous to thus extend their jurisdiction. On July 2, 1782, President Weare of New Hampshire wrote to Governor Clinton that, "It is represented that an agreement between the States of New York and New Hampshire, respecting the boundaries might probably tend to bring the matters to an issue, and the people, in general, between Connecticut River and the height of land, would be better satisfied to belong to New Hampshire than to Vermont, if Vermont could be made a separate State."

The House of Representatives of New Hampshire took into consideration the representation of the four towns expressing a desire to be under the jurisdiction of New Hampshire, and resolved, in substance, that New Hampshire had a just title to the whole of Vermont, but, for the sake of peace and good harmony with New York, and to accommodate the inhabitants east of the height of land, she was willing to extend their jurisdiction to that part of Vermont that lies east of said height of land, if the generality of the people desired it, and provided, New York would settle the boundary on the said heighth of land; and sent the resolutions to Governor Clinton.

Alexander Hamilton wrote to Governor Clinton from Philadelphia Jan. 1, 1783, that the New York Legislature "should take up the affair of Vermont on the idea of a compromise with Massachusetts and New Hampshire," and said, I have little hope that we shall ever be able to engage Congress to act with decision upon the matter, or, that our State will ever recover any part of the revolted territory but upon a plan that will interest those two States." Gouverneur Morris, a delegate from New York in Congress, wrote to John Jay, that "Vermont is yet Vermont, and I think no wise man will pretend to say when it will cease to be so." And after he left Congress he wrote Governor Clinton that, "I wish the business of Vermont were settled. I fear we are pursuing a shadow. * * * It is a mighty arduous business to compel the submission of men to a political or religious government. It appears to me very doubtful whether Vermont, if independent, would not be more useful to New York, than as the Eastern district. * * * If we have not the means of conquering these people we must let them quite alone. We must continue our impotent threats or we must make a treaty. If we let them alone, they become independent *de facto*, at least. Hundreds will resort to them for different reasons. They will receive lands from them, and cultivate them under the powers which are. When the dispute is again renewed these cultivators will, I believe, be better soldiers than logicians, and more inclined to defend their possessions, than examine their titles. If we continue our threats, they will either hate or despise us, and perhaps both."

During the winter of 1783-4, the civil powers of the State, aided by the military *posse*, were rigorously and successfully used. On Nov. 16, 1783, a party of Yorkers assaulted the house of Luke Knowlton of Newfane, forcibly entered, and captured and conveyed him into Massachusetts, and a Vermont military force were sent in pursuit. Knowlton was released and returned to the State. The civil power was at once brought to bear, and three of the offenders were quickly arrested, but the attempted arrest of the leader at Brattleboro, Dec. 1, was forcibly prevented by the adherents to New York, and on the same day another party of Yorkers, among whom was Charles Phelps of Marlborough, captured and carried away Benjamin Carpenter, formerly Lieut.-Governor of the State.

These acts aroused the Vermonters, and they

arrested William Shattuck and Charles Phelps, who were under the sentence of death for treason, and who had been permitted to be at large, and imprisoned them at Westminster. This so terrified the adherents of New York, they addressed a petition to Governor Chittenden asking that there might be some equitable and salutary measures taken to prevent all kinds of severity between the contending parties, and that Shattuck and Phelps might be released from their imprisonment. But Governor Chittenden left the civil and military authorities to deal with all offenders. Small detachments of militia were employed in searching and seizing the arms and persons of belligerent adherents of New York. Several leading New York adherents were arrested and imprisoned at Westminster.

These attacks and outrages on the part of New York sympathizers and Yorkers, and retaliatory measures on the part of the Vermonters, continued for some time. The New York adherents resisted the payment of taxes to the Vermont collector. And on the 16th of Dec. 1783, about twenty of them, armed, marched from Guilford to Brattleboro and surrounded the house of Landlord Arms where the constable and tax collector, Waters, was stopping, fired a number of balls into the house, wounded two men, burst into the house and took and carried away the constable with a design, it was supposed, to take from him a quantity of money that he had collected on taxes.

On Dec. 19th, 1784, it was learned there was a body of Yorkers, who were determined to oppose the collecting of taxes, were assembled at Guilford. Stephen R. Bradley with the sheriff immediately marched the *posse*, about 200 men, to Guilford, in order to reduce them to the obedience of law. When the troops appeared in sight, the whole body of Yorkers fled without firing a gun. Within two days some thirty of them came in and took the oath of allegiance and delivered up their arms. It was ascertained that there was another band of about forty Yorkers in Guilford near the Massachusetts line. Bradley and the sheriff took a detachment of 120 men and proceeded to disperse them. When the *posse* got within twenty rods of the Yorkers they fired one volley and retreated into Massachusetts. One man of the *posse* was badly wounded.

The abductors of Luke Knowlton and Cyril Carpenter, before referred to, were tried at Westminister before Chief Justice Moses Robinson and convicted, and sentenced. Many others of the New York adherents were convicted and fined or imprisoned for the offences charged against them. Charles Phelps was tried and was adjudged attainted of treason and sentenced to forty days' imprisonment and a forfeiture of all his property to the State.

On March 6th, 1784, an act was passed giving the Governor and Council the power to pardon any of the inhabitants of Windham County who have heretofore professed themselves subjects of the State of New York. On March 2, 1784, an act was passed to punish persons for the crime of high treason and misprision of treason against the

State. The penalty for the former was death, and the latter fine and imprisonment.

New York was powerless to effect anything by force. She could not reach the disturbed district without passing through Massachusetts, whose consent she probably could not obtain; or through Western Vermont, where they had met defeat before. Under these discouraging circumstances New York renewed the conflict in Congress. They set forth, anew, their complaints against Vermont, and said if Congress should delay the decision of the controversy, it ought to be considered a denial of justice. And on March 2, 1782, the New York House resolved "that until the affairs with Vermont were adjudicated by Congress, they would furnish no further aid to Congress."

New York asked for Federal troops to be used on the frontier. The frontier might mean Western frontier; but the design of New York was to use them against Vermont to protect the New York adherents in Eastern Vermont. Congress refused to permit her to control any troops. Congress was again urged by New York to decide her controversy with Vermont, but New York was only willing to have the dispute settled to their mind and not otherwise. In the instructions given to the delegates of New York in Congress, by their Legislature, after complaining of the procrastination of Congress in the settlement of their dispute with Vermont, it stated, "that if she (New York) must recur to force, for the preservation of her lawful authority, the impartial world will pronounce that none of the blood-shed, disorder or disunion which may ensue, can be imputable to this Legislature."

Governor Chittenden in his long letter to the President of Congress bearing date April 26, 1784, referring to the above threat, said, "As to this bloody proposition, the Council of this State have only to remark, that Vermont does not wish to enter into a war with the State of New York, but she will act on the defensive, and expect that Congress and the twelve States will observe a strict neutrality, and let the two contending States settle their own controversy. And as to the allegation of the State of New York against the conduct of this State in bringing a few malcontents to justice and obedience to government, whom they have inspired with sedition, I have only to observe, that this matter has been managed by the wisdom of the Legislature of this State, who consider themselves herein amenable to no earthly tribunal." These sentiments show that the Vermonters believed in the justice of their cause, and that they were able to cope with New York alone. In June, 1784, and again in April, 1785, Congress ordered a force of seven hundred men to be raised by all the posts in the United States, but they were not to be under the control of any State, thus defeating the ulterior purpose of New York to use the troops against Vermont. On May 29, 1784, the committee of Congress made their report to that body in favor of the admission of Vermont as a free, sovereign and independent State by the name of Vermont. No other direct action on the Vermont question was ever taken by the Continental Congress.

CHAPTER IX.

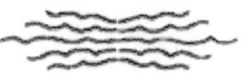

EARLY HISTORY AND ADMISSION OF VERMONT AS A STATE CONTINUED.

The people of New York sought opportunities to annoy Vermonters. On July 10, 1784, Hon. Micah Townshend, a citizen of Vermont, was arrested in the city of New York in an action of trespass at the suit of Seth Smith of the State of New York, for officiating in the line of his duty as the Clerk of the County Court of Windham County. Townshend petitioned the Legislature of Vermont that they would interfere in his behalf and indemnify him against loss and damage. Although the suit was aimed at Townshend, still it concerned the State at large and every officer and subject of the State.

A retaliatory act was passed by the Assembly appointing three commissioners to seize and sell so much of the lands in Vermont belonging to citizens of New York as would raise fifteen hundred pounds in specie, and directed them to pay to Townshend, as soon as the New York Court should render judgement against him, the amount of the judgement, cost and expenses of defending the suit, and a proper recompense for being unjustly sued. The suit however, was not pressed in the New York court, but discontinued.

Several acts were passed by the Vermont Assembly granting full pardon to many of the adherents of New York who were offenders against the laws of Vermont, and in many cases their confiscated property was restored. The Assembly in October, 1783, enacted a retaliatory statute declaring that, no person residing in New York shall commence any suit at law within the jurisdiction of the State against any inhabitant or resident thereof, for any civil matter or contract, until the Legislature of New York shall allow the inhabitants of this State full liberty to commence a like suit within their jurisdiction.

In 1784, the Revolutionary war had come to an end. The treaty of peace had been signed. The war with Great Britain had been greatly distressing to every part of the United States. The end of the war put an end to many embarrassments of Congress and to all fears of the people of Vermont. The people, weary of the long and distressing war, wished for repose and were heartily desirous of dropping all occasions of controversy and debate. The Confederacy was in an exhausted condition; their revenue was small and their currency had failed; their Continental money nearly valueless; their armies were dissatisfied and unpaid; and the public affairs of the Union were becoming more embarrassed with disorder, want of wisdom, credit and power.

Such being the case, an admission into the Union of the States, ceased to be an object of importance or desire. The evasive, irresolute, and what the Vermonters called contradictory acts of

Congress, had greatly destroyed the confidence that the people of Vermont had reposed in that body, and it was thought by many it would not be best to have any connection with them. Vermont as a separate jurisdiction stood in a better situation than the Confederation. Vermont was not subject to the calls of Congress for money; her Legislature had acquired wisdom and experience in governing the people; she had not contracted large debts, nor was it necessary to impose heavy taxes upon the people. The State had a large quantity of valuable lands to dispose of, and purchasers and settlers were constantly coming into it from all the New England States, so that the condition and prospect of the people became easy and more flattering than those of her neighbors.

At this time there was a general inclination not to be connected with the Union if they could fairly avoid it. This situation remained until the adoption of the Constitution of the United States. The adoption of the Constitution, and the wisdom and justice that soon marked the action of Congress, served to create a sentiment favorable to the Confederacy, but Vermont took no further pains to join it, further than to appoint delegates to Congress.

CHAPTER X.

LAND TITLES, BETTERMENT ACTS AND HARD TIMES.

It will be well here to consider the condition of the land titles in Vermont, and what is termed the Betterment Acts. It has been seen that when an independent Constitutional government was organized in Vermont in 1778, a large portion of its territory had been granted to citizens of the contending States. The same territory that had been granted by one of the contending States to proprietors was also granted by the other; hence arose conflicting titles and rights between the proprietors as well as between States; that in 1777, the Governor and Council entered upon the work of sequestering personal property of persons who had joined the enemy, and in 1778, the General Assembly established a board of confiscation with power to seize and sell the real estate, and at that time Vermont began to grant lands; and the grants from the State were greatly and speedily multiplied.

There had been no general systematic surveying, and the State had no map or plan of the surveys, and no public records within it of a large proportion of the grants; nor records of the deeds for many years. What actual surveys that had been made were the work of different persons. The proprietors of the territory covered by conflicting grants made sales as fast as purchasers could be found, and many of the latter occupied and improved their land, so purchased, relying upon the validity of their titles. This confused condition of things was a fruitful source of litigation in after years. The common law was adopted and courts were established in Vermont in 1778, by which titles could be ascertained, so far as practicable.

It was obvious that the results of common law trials would have been distressing to many persons who had in good faith purchased, occupied and improved their lands to which they had a faulty title. Measures of relief were resorted to. In the act of Feb. 1779, establishing the Superior Court, it was provided that that Court, "shall have no power to try any action or title of land, for the year ensuing," which left the disputes respecting lands to the Assembly and the Council. This act was continued in force till October, 1781, when a Betterment Act was enacted.

In June 1779, Ira Allen was appointed Surveyor General, for the purpose of procuring copies of all charters that ever were made of lands lying in the State, in order to make out one general plan, so as to know where the vacant lands were. In October of the same year a Board of Commissioners was constituted, for the better regulating the title of lands, whose duty it was to call for charters, patents, deeds and other papers respecting lands; and also having power given them to put claimants of lands upon their oath, and make reports of their doings and deposit them in the clerk's office of the town where the land was situated.

And the Board was, also, to report to the General Assembly at the opening of each session, and the reports when approved by that body were to be recorded in the town clerk's office.

The Betterment Acts were enacted to enable persons who had entered and made improvement on lands, under claim and color of title, who should be driven out of possession by a legal trial at law, to recover the value of the betterments or improvements that such persons had made, from the rightful owner of the land. And the Act provided that when any person or persons in actual possession of lands of which they had purchased a title, supposing such title to be good in fee, and should be prosecuted by action of ejectment, or writ of right, and final judgement should be rendered against them, such person should have a right of action to recover of him who had the legal title, so much money as should be adjudged *equitable* for the improvements; and the mode of proceeding was pointed out in the Act.

A new Betterment Act was passed in 1784, and another in 1785, which superceded the first act and a change was made as to the amount of the recovery and the mode of ascertaining the value of the betterments or improvements; but the main feature and purpose of the first act was retained. In the bill of 1784, the rule of recovery was, so much money as the true value of the estate exceeded its real value (after deducting the interest of such real value at six per cent per annum) at the time the settlement of the land began. By the act of June, 1785, the jury were to assess the value of the land as at the time of settlement by the possessor, and assess the value at the time of trial or assessment, as if the same was uncultivated, and allow the possessor one half of what the land had risen in value, and add thereto the value of the improvements; these two items was to be the amount of the recovery of the person who had been dispossessed of the land he had supposed he had purchased with a good title.

The Betterment Act met with considerable opposition. The opposers said, "the law makes every man a trespasser who enters upon the land of another without license and subjects him to damages; but by this Act you would compel the legal owner to pay him a bounty for his trespass." This law was clearly founded on the principles of natural justice and was in great favor with the people of Vermont. Daniel Chipman, commenting on the Act and on the uncertainty of the titles to land in New England, said, purchasers were not accustomed to receive the title deeds so as to have in their hands evidence of the title. Consequently a man so disposed could impose on one and sell him lands as well without the expense of a purchase as with. And swindlers took advantage of this state of things and made a business of selling lands without making a purchase.

Simeon Sears was one of these primitive swindlers, who had become notorious in that line of business, and the following anecdote was told. Some of the people of Bennington had been confined in the City Hall at Albany by the authorities of New York. The City Hall, of course, became a hated place, and an object of dread to the Green Mountain Boys and became a subject of conversation at all their meetings, and they began to consider ways and means to destroy it. And at one of the meetings a number of modes of effecting this were proposed, and among the rest, several modes of blowing it up. But Ethan Allen said, "No, the better way will be to employ Sim Sears to sell the d—d thing."

From 1784, to 1787, the times were hard and the people were becoming uneasy and discontented. They were burdened in their poverty-stricken condition at the close of the Revolutionary War, with the surveying and alloting the lands, the cutting of roads, subduing the wilderness, and erecting places of abode. Most of the people in all the new towns were burdened with debt, and dependent upon the productions of the soil to pay them; markets were distant, and the cost of transportation great. The capital of the richest men was mainly in land, and therefore but very few were able to loan money at any rate of interest, or on any security, however good; specie was rarely seen, and the paper currency was for the most part of little value. Many complained, but hardly knew where to fix the blame for the distress that was abroad. Some contemplated the same violent remedy that was attempted in other States, and that culminated in a neighboring State in Shay's Rebellion.

A disturbance of the proceedings of the courts in Rutland County in Nov. 1786, was threatened, and a mob that had gathered for the purpose of interfering with the business of the court and to prevent the session from being held, had to be dispersed by the militia. The leading rioters were arrested, tried, convicted and fined, and the rebellion quelled. A similar attempt had been made to interfere with the court and its proceedings at Windsor a few days before, with like result as in the Rutland County affair.

The General Assembly in session at Rutland in Oct. 1786, was active in passing laws for the relief and quieting the people. Jonathan Fassett, a leader in the Rebellion and a member of the Assembly, was impeached, and found guilty of riotous conduct. An Act for the prevention and punishment of riots, disorders and contempt of authorities, was passed by the Assembly, March 8, 1787. The leaders of the discontented aimed their shafts particularly at Gov. Chittenden and Ira Allen; the latter made an elaborate defence of himself, and Governor Chittenden appealed to the public in an address, in which he stated that the people of Vermont were in a much better condition than the people of the other States; that while the Revolution had left on the United States a debt of $42,000,375, exclusive of their own respective State debts, Vermont had but a trifle to pay. He said that, "In the time of the war we were obliged to follow the example of Joshua of old, who commanded the sun to stand still while he fought his battle; we commanded our creditors to stand still while we fought our enemies." And consequently, he said, the people were left in debt and behind hand, harrassed and destitute of provisions at the close of the war. He said one reason for their present distress was, that since the close of the war, "in lieu of exerting ourselves to the uttermost, to raise flax and wool and clothe ourselves, we have purchased on credit too many articles of the growth and manufactures of foreign countries, by which means we have drained the State of nearly all the cash we had, and a great part of our cattle, * * * and I know of no certain effectual method that can be taken to afford substantial relief, but by prudence, industry and economy, and these must be encouraged by government."

Shay's Rebellion broke out in the Commonwealth of Massachusetts in 1787, and the Governor of that State requested the assistance of Vermont in apprehending and returning certain of the rebels that had taken shelter in Vermont, to Massachusetts authorities. Governor Chittenden issued his proclamation enjoining upon all the citizens of the State not to harbor, entertain or conceal Daniel Shay, Luke Day, Adam Wheeler and Eli Parsons, leading rebels, and requiring all justices of the peace to issue their warrants when required, to apprehend them that they might be returned to the authorities of Massachusetts or delivered to some civil or military officer. And the citizens of this State were forbidden to take arms in support of the rebellion or contribute relief to its abettors and promoters.

On April 30, 1787, about one hundred of the rebels who had been driven from Massachusetts, met at Captain Galusha's in Shaftsbury to agree on measures to continue their opposition to their government, but the sheriff of the County, Jonas Galusha, commanded them to disperse, and they immediately left the State and met at White Creek in the State of New York. Several of the rebels were arrested in Vermont and returned to Massachusetts' authorities. Ethan Allen had been wrongfully accused with sympathizing with the rebellion, but he declared, "he had never had any communication with Shay or any of his adherents, directly or indirectly, but that he had heartily despised both of them and their cause."

CHAPTER XI.

VERMONT'S ACTS OF SOVEREIGNTY.

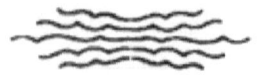

All the acts of Vermont, especially from 1778, to 1791, were really the acts of a sovereign State, and peculiarly so, as the internal police regulations were enforced against New York and the adherents of that State in Vermont, as well as against Congress. The act of issuing bills of credit and making them a legal tender for debts, coining money, regulating weights and measures, establishing post offices, naturalizing natives of other States and countries, corresponding with foreign governments in respect to commerce, which she exercised, were all acts of an independent and sovereign State.

It was enacted in 1781, that there be printed bills to the amount of twenty-five thousand one hundred and fifty-five pounds of lawful money for the payment of the debts of the State and other public purposes, and a committee were empowered to make a device and form for the bills. The bills were to be a lawful tender for payment on all contracts and executions, and should be redeemed by the treasurer of the State, by the time fixed in the act, in silver, at the rate of six shillings for one Spanish milled dollar, or gold equivalent. The penalty that a person was subject to, if found guilty of altering or counterfeiting the bills, or making instruments for that purpose, was death. The amount issued under this act was 24,750 pounds. By an act passed in Feb. 1782, the bills of credit were not to be legal tender after June 1, 1782, except in the treasury of the State.

On June 15, 1785, an act was passed granting Reuben Harmon, Jr., Esq., the right of coining copper, and by an act of Oct. 24, 1786, that right was extended for the term of eight years from July 1, 1786; the coins issued in 1785, and before Oct. 1786, had on the face of the coin the legend, "*Vermontensium. Res Publica.*"—meaning, The Republic of the Green Mountains, or Vermont; and the device was a rising sun, with mountains and trees in the foreground, and a plough in the field beneath—significant of a new and rising agricultural State. On the reverse, the device was an eye, radiating to thirteen stars, with "*Quarta. Demcima. Stella,*" for the legend—signifying that Vermont, as the fourteenth State, was looking for admission to the Union with the thirteen States.

By an act passed Oct. 24, 1786, both the legends and devices were changed—the device to a bust in a coat of mail, and the legend to *Vermon Auctori*—meaning by the authority of Vermont. On the reverse, was a female figure, seated with a shield at her side, and holding in her right hand an olive branch, in her left a rod. The legend was *Inde: et Lib*:—meaning independence and liberty. There were other devises and mottoes.

On Oct. 26, 1787, an act was passed, naturalizing Solomon Willard of New Hampshire, declaring him "to be entitled to all the privileges, benefits and immunities of a natural born subject and member of this Commonwealth, and shall forever hereafter have and enjoy the freedom of Vermont."

On March 10, 1787, an act was passed naturalizing Hon. St. John de Crevecoeur and his two children. The father was a citizen of France—was born in Normandy in 1731, educated in England and came to America in 1754, and settled on a farm near New York City, from which he was driven by the British during the Revolutionary war, and returned to England. Afterwards he became the author of several literary works.

An act establishing post offices in the State passed the General Assembly March 5, 1784, and Mr. Anthony Haswell of Bennington was appointed Post Master General within and for the State of Vermont. Five post offices were established within the State: viz., in Bennington, Rutland, Brattleboro, Windsor and Newbury, and the post riders from Bennington to Brattleboro were to be allowed three pence per mile for travel, and those on the other routes two pence per mile, and were to have the exclusive right of carriage, and enjoy the advantage of the fees arising from the carriage of letters and packets of every kind; and the rate of postage was to be the same as in the United States. The Governor had the right by the act to frank his letters or packets.

In these days of railroads run by steam or electricity, telegraphs, and telephones, we can hardly realize the meager facilities for communication and transportation during the early history of Vermont. It was a great event when in Nov. 1787, a stage wagon for the first time was erected to run, with four horses, between the city of New York and Stratford Ferry in Connecticut; which completed the stages from Portsmouth in the State of New Hampshire to Richmond in the State of Virginia, a distance of over 700 miles. January 21, 1788, Daniel Marsh advertised himself as post-rider from Clarendon to Onion River, Jericho being the end of his route; but there was no authority for establishing an office in Chittenden County, which then extended to Canada line, until June 1, 1792. At that time additional offices were opened in Manchester, Vergennes and Burlington, under authority of Congress.

On March 9, 1784, the Council resolved that the Governor be requested to take such measures as he should judge best for opening trade with the Province of Quebec, but the Assembly did not pass the act, and nothing definite was done on the subject till Oct. 29, 1784, when it was enacted that the Governor and Council be authorized and empowered to appoint not exceeding three persons as commissioners to confer and agree, with person or persons in Canada, having power to agree concerning trade and commerce, pertaining to "the opening a free trade into and through said Province of Quebec." Ira Allen, who was one of the commissioners, instituted negotiations with Great Britain through Lieutenant-Governor Hamilton in the city of Quebec.

By proclamation Lord Dorchester, Governor-in-Chief of the Province of Quebec, permitted the free importation and exportation of lumber, grains, produce, live stock and other things. 'It was supposed the intention was to make the privilege reciprocal, but neither the proclamation nor the ordinance limited the privileges to or with the State of Vermont, nor did it declare that they were granted in response to any application of Vermont; they applied to the United States as well as Vermont, but the advantages were enjoyed by the people of Vermont almost exclusively, on account of the proximity of the State to the Province. Lord Dorchester could not tolerate any separate intercourse with the people of Vermont without infringing upon the treaty of peace of 1783, with the United States—that treaty included Vermont within the boundaries of the United States. Pine timber and ashes constituted by far the largest part of the exports from Vermont for many years. Certain articles were prohibited from being exported or imported.

CHAPTER XII.

SETTLEMENT OF THE CONTROVERSY WITH NEW YORK AND ADMISSION OF VERMONT.

Certain gentlemen in New York, during the winter of 1784, presented a petition to the Assembly of that State, praying that they would pass a law to enable their delegates in Congress to apply for and consent to the sovereignty and independence of Vermont, and a bill was brought into the House to that effect; many were desirous to reach some kind of a compromise with the Vermont settlers in respect to the title of their lands that was in dispute. William Samuel Johnson, a delegate in Congress from New York, and who seemed inclined to favor an equitable settlement of the long-drawn-out controversy, thought it a favorable opportunity for the Vermonters, who had taken title to their lands under the New Hampshire grants and from the State of Vermont, to secure an indisputable title to their farms.

In the spring of 1787, Alexander Hamilton, a member for the City of New York introduced into the New York Assembly a bill entitled "An act to empower and direct the delegates, to acceed to, ratify and confirm the sovereignty and independence of Vermont, on conditions that Vermont should confine the limits of her territory between

Connecticut River and the line twenty miles east of Hudson River, and requiring Vermont to accede to the Union and preserving New York titles to land in Vermont.

Hamilton, in presenting the bill, said in part, "I believe there is not a member of this House but considers the independence of the district of territory in question, is a matter fixed and inevitable. All our efforts to a different point have hitherto proved fruitless, and long since we seem to have entirely given up the controversy. Vermont is, in fact, *independent*, but she is not confederated. And I am constrained to add that the means which they employ to secure that indpendence, are objects of the utmost alarm to the safety of this State, and to the confederation at large. * * * It is not natural to suppose, that a powerful people both by number and situation, unconnected as they now stand, and without any relative importance in the Union, irritated by neglect, or stimulated by revenge—I say, is it not probable, under such circumstances, they will provide for their own safety, by seeking connection elsewhere? And can he who hears me doubt but that connections have *already* been formed with the British in Canada? * * * Confederated with a foreign nation, we can be at no loss to anticipate the consequences of such a connection, nor the danger of having so powerful a body of people, increasing rapidly in numbers and strength, associated with a foreign power, and ready upon any rupture to throw their weight into an opposite scale. In their present situation, they bear no part of our public burdens; if they were a part of the Confederacy, they must of course participate in them; they are useless to us now, and if they continue as they are, they will be formidable to us hereafter."

The bill was taken up in the Assembly on March 28, 1787. Richard Harrison made a strong argument against the independence of Vermont, and said, among other things, in substance, that the adherents of New York, her citizens and those who had purchased lands in that territory by grants from New York, had the right to be protected in person and property; that the bill was unconstitutional, impolitic and destructive to the property and the rights of their citizens; that the constitution has declared the Counties of Cumberland, Gloucester and Charlotte shall be represented in the Senate and Assembly of New York. He treated the alleged connection between Vermont and the British Government a phantom, but if such a connection existed Vermont must be reduced to a sense of duty.

To this argument Hamilton made a candid and masterly reply, but it is too long to insert here the full text, and I shall be content to give only a few extracts. He asserted that the chief object of government to protect the rights of individuals by the united strength of the community, must be taken with this limitation:—The united strength of the community ought to be exerted for the protection of individuals so far as there is a rational prospect of success, and so far as is consistent with the safety and well being of the whole. * * * But is not bound to enter into and prosecute enterprises of manifest rashness and folly; or in the event of success, would be productive of more mischief than good. ° * * Are we now in a situation to undertake the reduction of Vermont, or are we likely to be in such a situation? Where are our resources? Where our public credit to enable us to carry on an offensive war? We ought to recollect that in war, to defend or attack, are two different things; to the first, the mountains, the wilderness, the militia, sometimes even the poverty of a country will suffice. The latter requires an *army* and a *treasury*. The population of Vermont will not be rated too high if stated at nearly one-half that of New York. * * * Can it be imagined that it would be able, finally to reduce such a people to its obedience? The supposition would be chimerical, and the attempt madness. Can we hope for a more favorable posture of affairs hereafter? Will not the population and strength of Vermont increase in ratio to our own? * * * The scheme of coercion would ill suit even the disposition of our own citizens. The habit of thinking to which the revolution has given birth, is not adapted to the idea of a contest for dominion over a people disinclined to live under our government. And, in reality, it is not the interest of the State ever to regain dominion over them by force."

On April 11, 1787, the bill passed the Assembly with a vote of 27 to 19, but the bill failed in the Senate. The vote in the Assembly and the discussion showed that New York was fast losing her grasp on Vermont. It would seem by a letter written by James Madison to George Washington March 18, 1787, that if Vermont now consented to become a State of the Union, it must be on two conditions: First, that neither the boundaries nor the rights of her citizens shall be impeached under the 9th article of Confederation; second, that no share of the public debt already contracted shall be allotted to her.

In 1788, no attempt was made to secure the assent of New York to the independence of Vermont, but during that year New Hampshire, Virginia and New York ratified the Constitution of the United States, and Kentucky, with the consent of Virginia made application for admission into the Union which the Southern States would favor, while the Northern States would favor the admission of Vermont as a counterpoise. Thus early a sectional feeling manifested itself. The most embarrassing question now was, how should the conflicting land titles be settled. Vermont was desirous to avoid having the titles to the lands left to the decision of the Supreme Court for fear that they would hold that the New York title would be held the better title. On July 15, 1788, Nathaniel Chipman wrote Hamilton, and asked him if it was not probable that the Federal Legislature, when formed, might on the concession to the Union, be induced on some terms, to make a compensation to the New York grantees out of their western lands, and said that if those difficulties could be removed, opposition of Vermont to becoming a member of the Union would be reconciled.

Hamilton in reply, on July 22, 1788, said that

"the accession of Vermont to the Confederacy is doubtless an object of great importance to the whole. * * * Upon the whole, therefore, I think it will be expedient for you as early as possible, to ratify the Constitution, upon condition that Congress shall provide for the extinguishment of all existing claims to lands under grants of the State of New York, which may interfere with claims under the State of Vermont."

In Grand Committee of both Houses, on Oct. 22, 1787, Moses Robinson, Ira Allen and Jonathan Arnold were elected agents to Congress; and on Oct. 25, 1787, the General Assembly resolved that it be the duty of the agents to Congress to use all due diligence to remove every obstacle to the accession of the State to the Federal government. John Jay and more than sixty others of New York presented their memorial to the New York Legislature suggesting it would be expedient to appoint commissioners with full powers to treat of and agree to, the independence of Vermont; and on Feb. 27, 1789, the New York Assembly again passed a bill on a vote of 40 to 11, declaring the consent of the Legislature of that State to erecting the district of Vermont into a new State by Congress.

This bill also was defeated in the Senate. But on July 6, 1789, the New York Assembly passed a bill, that became a law, appointing seven Commissioners to declare the consent of the Legislature to erect the Vermont territory into a new State on such terms and conditions and in such manner and form as they should judge necessary and proper, with the restriction that no person claiming lands in such district should have any right to any compensation whatsoever from New York.

On July 23, 1789, the Vermont Legislature appointed, also, seven Commissioners with like powers, purposes and restrictions. Upon this subject the following lines were published in the *Vermont Gazette* Jan. 25, 1790:—

> At Westminster, lately, the State of Vermont,
> After due consultation determined upon't,
> That *seven good men* were sufficient to join
> With New York to determine the government line,
> Remove all obstructions and point out the way
> For Vermont in the Union her stars to display;
> But alas! brother freeman, I fear it will prove
> We have raised *six or seven* new blocks to remove.

The Vermont Commissioners went to Albany to fulfil the duties of their appointment and to confer with the New York Commission; and a long correspondence took place between the two Boards of Commissioners. The New York Commissioners concluded the powers given them were not sufficiently broad to treat fully on all the subjects of the controversy. They, however, afterwards obtained ample power from their Legislature. The two Boards met at New York on Sept. 27, 1790, and after a long negotiation the two Boards of Commissioners agreed, and executed a formal instrument in writing as a basis of final adjustment of the whole controversy.

By this agreement New York was to give her consent that Vermont be admitted as one of the United States of America, and the boundary line between the two States, to be where it now is; and on the admission of Vermont, all claims of jurisdiction from the State of New York, within the State of Vermont, should cease; that if the Legislature of the State of Vermont should on or before Jan. 1, 1792, declare that the State of Vermont, should on or before June 1, 1794, pay the State of New York the sum of thirty thousand dollars, then all right and title of New York, to lands within the State of Vermont under grants from the government of the late Colony of New York, or from the State of New York, should cease. If Vermont should not elect to make such declaration, it was provided in the instrument how New York should be compensated in lieu of the thirty thousand dollars.

As Vermont made the required declaration and afterwards paid the thirty thousand dollars to New York, we omit the other provision. The Vermont Commissioners reported to the Legislature of Vermont that they closed the negotiations with New York on Oct. 7, 1790. And on Oct. 28, 1790, it was enacted by the Legislature of Vermont that the treasurer of the State pay to the State of New York the thirty thousand dollars on or before June 1, 1794, and that the boundary line, agreed upon, be made perpetual, and that all grants, charters, or patents made by or under the government of the late Colony of New York, in the Vermont district, except such as were made in confirmation of grants, charters or patents by or under the government of the late Province of New Hampshire, "are declared nul and void, and incapable of being given in evidence in any court of law within this State."

Alexander Hamilton exerted a greater influence in obtaining the consent of New York to the independence of Vermont and to her admission into the American Union, than any other citizen of New York. He was a man of great abilities and a statesman of whom Vermonters have ever had the highest regard, and her people regretted his untimely death.

An Act was passed by the Legislature of Vermont on Oct. 27, 1790, authorizing a convention to be called, to consist of one delegate from each town, to meet at Bennington Jan. 6, 1791, to deliberate upon and agree to the Constitution of the United States. The delegates were elected, and the Convention met as provided by the Act. The general question arose in the convention whether it would be expedient or inexpedient for Vermont to enter the Federal Union. Nathaniel Chipman, the delegate from Rutland and a lawyer of superior abilities, took a leading part in favor of the State entering the Federal Union and agreeing to the Constitution of the United States. His arguments were strong and convincing. He said in part, in substance, that the narrow limits of Vermont were wholly inadequate to support the dignity or to defend the rights of Sovereignty; the division of an extensive territory into small independent Sovereignties greatly retards civil improvements, but when small States are united under one general government, civilization has proceeded, more rapidly, and the kindly affections have much sooner gained an ascendent than when they remained under numerous neighboring governments; the weak are jealous of the strong and endeavor by art and cunning to supply their want of power; the strong are ever ready to decide every question by force according to their own interest, that creates a want of public faith, recrimination and animosities. In an extensive government, national prejudices are suppressed, hostilities are removed to a distance, and private injuries are redressed by a common judge; the people view all as members of one great family, connected by all the ties of interest, of country, of affinity and blood.

We are almost encircled by the United States that have become great and powerful, and our intercourse with them must be on very unequal terms. When our interests clash with those of the Union, it requires very little political sagacity to foretell that every sacrifice must be made on our part. In the event of war between Great Britain and the United States, Vermont would be in a situation much to be regretted. Our country, from its situation, would become a rendezvous and a thoroughfare to the spies of both nations. Confined to the narrow limits of Vermont, genius, for want of great occasions, and great objects, will languish, and the spirit of learning will be contracted and busy itself in small scenes, commensurate to the exigencies of the State, and the narrow limits of our government; but admitted into the Union, instead of being confined to the narrow limits of Vermont, we become members of an extensive empire, social feelings will expand, channels of information will be opened wide and the spirit of learning and laudable ambition will be called forth.

Daniel Buck, the delegate from Norwich, opposed the admission of Vermont. He said, in part, in substance, that Vermont, by her local situation, had a uniformity of interest; that there was no mercantile and landed interests found clashing here, and that of lord and tenant was not known; the laws, therefore, were simple and suited to the whole; the affairs of government were managed, as it were, under the eye of the people and the machine was so small that every one could look and see how the wheel moved, but if Vermont came into the Union the sacrifice she makes must be great—her interest must bend to the interest of the Union; that the people of the State must be much happier unconnected with any other power, than to be in the Union.

The Convention on Jan. 10, 1791, by a vote of 105 to 4, assented to and ratified the Constitution of the United States. The main act or resolution of the Convention was as follows: viz., "This Convention having impartially deliberated upon the Constitution of the United States of America as now established, submitted to us by an Act of the General Assembly of the State of Vermont passed Oct. 27, 1790, do in virtue of the power and authority to us given, for that purpose, fully and entirely approve of, assent to, and ratify the said Constitution; and declare that, immediately from, and after this State shall be admitted by the Congress into the Union, and to a full participation of the benefits of the government now enjoyed by the States in the Union, the same shall be binding on us and the people of the State of Vermont forever."

A duplicate of said Act and resolution was transmitted to the President of the United States. When the news of the result of the Convention was received at Albany, New York, Jan. 13, 1791, the independent company of artillery paraded in uniform, and fired a Federal salute of 14 guns, followed by three cheerful huzzas from the respectable citizens.

At Rutland, Vt., a celebration was held, and after a collation, fifteen toasts were drank, with the discharge of cannon. The following song composed for the occasion was sung: viz,—

> Come every Federal son,
> Let each Vermonter come,
> And take his glass
> Long live great Washington,
> Glory's immortal son ;
> Bright as the rolling sun,
> O'er us doth pass.
>
> Hail, Hail this happy day,
> When we allegiance pay,
> T' our Federal head,
> Bright in these western skies,
> Shall our new star arise,
> Strike our enemies
> With fear and dread.
>
> Come each Green Mountain Boy,
> Swell every breast with joy,
> Hail our good land,
> As our pines climb the air
> Firm as our mountains are,
> Federal beyond compare
> Proudly we stand.

Fill. Fill your bumpers high.
Let the notes rend the sky.
Free we'll remain,
By that immortal crown
Of Glory and renown,
Which our brave heroes won
On blood stained plain.

Then come join hand in hand
Like a firm Federal band.
Bound by our [one] law,
From our firm Union spring
Blessings unknown to kings.
Then each shout as he sings
Federal huzza.

On June 20, 1791, the General Assembly of Vermont passed an Act for the appointment of commissioners to look after the interest of the State in the matter of her admission into the Union; and Nathaniel Chipman and Lewis R. Morris were appointed such commissioners, and they repaired to Philadelphia in discharge of their duties. The Act for the admission of the State of Vermont into the Union was as follows; viz:—

"The State of Vermont having petitioned the Congress to be admitted a member of the United States—Be it enacted by the Senate and House of Representatives of the United States of America in Congress assembled, and it is hereby enacted and declared, that on the fourth day of March, 1791, the said State, by the name and style of, 'The State of Vermont,' shall be received and admitted into this Union, as a new and entire member of the United States of America."

This bill passed the House Feb. 14, 1791, and

it passed the Senate and was duly signed by John Adams, President of the Senate, and by George Washington, President of the United States, Feb. 18, 1791. And on Feb. 25, 1791, Congress enacted a law giving Vermont two Representatives in Congress, and on March 2, 1791, passed an Act giving effect to the laws of the United States within the State of Vermont, and constituting Vermont one judicial district, of which Nathaniel Chipman was appointed Judge by the President, with the advice and consent of the Senate.

We have now come down to a period in the history of Vermont when she first stood as one of the sovereign States of the United States of America. We have seen she has filled a unique place in history. She is the only State of the Union, save Texas, that for years held her place among the nations of the earth absolutely independent from all other nations, Kingdoms or States, rendering obedience to no other power. She established post offices and post routes within her borders, issued bills of credit, coined money, made treaties with foreign powers and agreed with them on the terms of exchange of prisoners in time of war, and other sovereign acts that the States of the Union could not exercise under the Constitution of the United States. She was not only the first State that was admitted into the Union after the original thirteen Colonies had become confederated, but was the first State that never had tolerated Slavery within her borders.

There has been a misunderstanding or dispute as to whether persons were ever held as slaves in

Vermont. The official printed reports of the census of the United States assigned sixteen slaves to Vermont in 1790, or 1791, all in the County of Bennington. The fact was discovered after the publication of the report, that the persons charged to Vermont in 1790, as slaves, were free blacks.

The most severe battle that was fought on the soil of Vermont while she was acting as an independent jurisdiction was near the present village of Bennington on August 16, 1777. The victory there won over the British forces was made possible by the heroism and the blood shed by the brave Green Mountain Boys. The defeat of the enemy on the field hastened the surrender of the British army under General Burgoyne at Saratoga, and the surrender of the Royal troops under General Lord Cornwallis, at Yorktown, and the close of the War of the Revolution.

It is but a few years since, that the spot where that battle was fought and victory won, was marked by the erection of a monument. The General Assembly of Vermont passed an act Nov. 28, 1876, incorporating the Bennington Battle Monument Association, for the purpose of erecting and maintaining a suitable monument commemorative of the achievements of General John Stark and the patriot soldiers of Vermont, New Hampshire and Massachusetts at the decisive battle of Bennington. The monument was erected, the shaft of which was 100 feet high, at the expense, with the grounds, of $90,000. The one hundredth anniversary of the Battle of Bennington was celebrated at Bennington on a grand scale, and with imposing ceremonies, on August 16th, 1877.

The Battle of Bennington was not commemorated by the erection of this monument on account of the large numbers engaged (for the numbers were small in comparison to the great battles of the world, like Waterloo and Gettysburgh), but it is remembered for the principle at stake, the heroism and self-sacrifice displayed. Judged by these standards, it will be reckoned among the memorable battles of the world.

At the time the chances seemed to be desperate. Burgoyne was making a successful march with a trained veteran army from Canada to the Hudson to connect with the British force under General Clinton. Ticonderoga had fallen, and the Vermonters had been defeated at Hubbardton, and it looked as though Burgoyne's march to Albany could not be prevented. The whole frontier of Vermont was exposed to the enemy composed of British troops and savages. The left flank of Burgoyne's army must be struck and vanquished, for it was nearing Bennington, where the supplies for the Vermont soldiers were stored. What was done must be done quickly. The situation was critical. Soldiers from Massachusetts, New Hampshire and the Green Mountain Boys from their farms were quickly gathered, and they under General John Stark, seconded by Warner, met the enemy on August 16, 1777, and won a victory that not only saved Vermont from the incursion of the British troops and savages, but the nation.

In that battle the Vermont farmers fought

with desperation; it was the last hope of the Hampshire Grants, who were fighting as Hon. E. J. Phelps said in his dedicatory address, "for all they had on earth, whether of possession or of rights. They could not go home defeated, for they would have had no homes to go to." Their victory sounded the first notes of the death knell of the power of Great Britain over the American Colonies. It revived the drooping spirits of the American Generals and of Congress.

Hon. John W. Stewart, Ex-Governor of Vermont, in an address delivered at the laying of the corner-stone of the monument the 16th day of August, 1887, said, that, "Our fathers did rally and stand here, like a wall of consuming fire, against the invading host, and their rally and battle and victory will forever stand in American history as one of the most dramatic and eventful episodes recorded on its pages. Probably few, if any, of those engaged in the battle began to measure the momentous consequences which hung upon its issue. It seemed to them simply a struggle for the capture or the retention of a quantity of supplies, and so far important; but the far-reaching consequences of the result could not then be foreseen. Our fathers builded better than they knew. We estimate the value of their services in the light of subsequent events. But their want of foreknowledge does not detract, in the slightest degree, from the moral quality of their action. That lies in their ready, unselfish loyalty to a perilous duty, and their prompt response to its call at the risk of life itself.

"No race of men ever trod this planet, who more than they revered and respected rightful authority, divine and human, and it was the rightness and righteous exercise of authority which commanded their respect and allegiance. Its abuse they knew was outside the functions of government and therefore intolerable. * * * On August 14 Baum had reached a point about six miles from Bennington and had captured a large quantity of wheat and flour at Sacoik mill. From here he wrote a dispatch to Burgoyne, that about 1800 militia were in his front, which would leave at his approach; of which another has wittily said, they did leave but took Baum's whole army along with them. On the night of the 14th Baum entrenched his army in a strong position. On the 15th it rained. On the 16th Stark attacked the entrenched and disciplined troops on all sides. They made a brave defense, but they were nearly all killed or taken prisoners. Immediately after the battle was over Col. Breyman, sent to reinforce Baum with five or six hundred men, was observed approaching, with whom a second battle was fought, continuing until sunset, when the enemy fled, leaving his artillery and escaping in the darkness. About 700 of the enemy were captured and 207 men killed. * * * Burgoyne in a private letter to the British minister, soon after the battle, said, the New Hampshire Grants, in particular, a country unpeopled in the last war, now abounds in the most active and most rebellious race of the continent and hangs like a gathering storm on my left."

CHAPTER XIII.

A RESUME AND EARLY HISTORY OF VERMONT CONCLUDED.

There has been presented in this and the previous chapters the main features of the struggle of the Green Mountain Boys for an independent existence from New Hampshire and New York. It is not possible to crowd into one volume of moderate size all the acts and a detailed history of the people of the territory named Vermont, and shall be content with a short resume.

Before the American Revolution the New Hampshire Grants were engaged in their conflict with New York. The Grants had taken and paid for their lands as a part of the Colony of New Hampshire, under grants from its governor as agent of the British Crown. New York, for more than a hundred years from the date of her own charter, attempted no jurisdiction over the Grants. But after the settlements began to be numerous and had grown to considerable importance, New York, greedy to enlarge her boundaries, arbitrarily began to claim that her eastern boundary extended to Connecticut River. The loosely drawn and even conflicting charters of New Hampshire and New York invited a controversy. The greater influence and power of New York obtained from the Crown an order establishing the Connecticut as the dividing line, and *then* claimed that all of the grants of land, that had been made by the Governor of New Hampshire, were void, and claimed the right to and did grant the same land to others, to some extent.

The Grants claimed that if the decree or order of the Crown had any effect it could not be retroactive; that it did not invalidate titles that had become vested in the possessor, whether acquired under the New Hampshire charters or grants or by adverse possession. The settlers resisted the claim of New York and their efforts to confiscate their land, and in 1767, succeeded in again bringing the subject before the King and Council, who reheard the matter and positively forbid New York making further grants of land that had been granted by New Hampshire prior to 1764, but New York, nevertheless, continued to make grants. The settlers were without money and had no means to resist the arbitrary course of New York. Justice was denied them in the Courts of New York. Then they set the authority of New York at defiance and resolved to protect themselves. How well the grants succeeded has been told in these pages. When the authority of Great Britain was thrown off, the organization of a separate government was a necessity unless they submitted to the arbitrary power of New York, as New Hampshire, after the Royal order of 1764, had withdrawn all claim to lands west of Connecticut River.

In 1777, a Constitution was drafted and ratified, and an election was held under it, and Thomas Chittenden was made Governor. Under this constitution Vermont was for thirteen years an independent community, when it was admitted as an independent State. Down to this time she had maintained herself against New York and against Congress. Hon. E. J. Phelps, said, in an oration delivered at the dedication of the Bennington Battle monument, that, "No oppression charged upon Great Britain by America, approached that sought to be visited by Congress and New York upon Vermont, while she was fighting side by side with them to her last man and last dollar, in the struggle for national independence."

The more closely we study the lives and achievements of early Vermont men, the greater is our admiration for their patriotism, their love of liberty, their character and capacity. It came to be seen by New York that the right of self-government ought not to be denied to Vermont, nor the lands of her people taken from them, and that such results could only be attained by a war of extermination. The demands of Vermont were finally conceded. So Vermont came more than a hundred years ago into the sisterhood of the States— the first accession to the thirteen original States. She came into the Union unconquerable in spirit, proud of her untarnished history, and reluctant to surrender the independence that had cost so much and been cherished so long. But she came to remain.

Mr. Phelps, in the oration referred to, referring to the monument, said, "Long before it shall cease to be reckoned as young, we and our children will have disappeared from the scene. It is our messenger to posterity. Here it shall wait for them, while the successive generations shall be born and die. Here it shall wait for them, through the evenings and the mornings that shall be all the days that are to come. Crowned with the snows of countless winters; beautiful in the sunlight and shadows of unnumbered summers; companions of the mountains which look down upon it, whose height it emulates, whose strength it typifies, whose history it declares. * * * It shall tell the story not only of Stark and Warner and Chittenden and Symonds, the Allens and the Fays and the Robinsons, and their compeers, but of that multitude of their humbler associates, less conspicuous, but just as devoted, whose names are only written in the memory of God."

I will close this history of the early days of Vermont and the acts of her sturdy and brave pioneers by quoting the eloquent words of Hon. L. E. Chittenden, taken from an oration delivered by him at Burlington, July 4, 1876. He said:—

"How was it possible that a few scattered settlers, deficient in resources and poor in purse, could accomplish the results which they did accomplish? In 1774, they numbered scarcely more than 1,500 families. They were dispersed from the Winooski and the Great Bend of the Connecticut to the Massachusetts line. They had no means of assessing taxes, no organization which was not purely voluntary. They had already maintained themselves against the power of New York through a struggle of nearly ten years. They sprang to arms at the summons of revolution. They captured Ticonderoga, raised a regiment which made the name of Green Mountain Boys historical, joined in the invasion of Canada, saved the remnants of Wooster's army, and barred their long frontier against invasion. Relieved for a space from arms, they came into convention, to form a constitution. The news of Burgoyne's invasion, and St. Clair's retreat, arrested their deliberations. Again they hurried to the frontier, fought the battle of Bennington, raised another regiment and paid its expenses out of Tory property. Again they kept an invading army idle for many months which almost outnumbered their population, and sent them back to the place from whence they came. Once more we find them in convention at Windsor, finishing that first Constitution, the most democratic, free and just ever yet adopted in any American State. They adopted it without even the form of a vote, and having launched the independent State of Vermont in defiance of New York, New Hampshire, King George, and I might say of all the evil powers of earth and air, they entered upon that singular struggle with Congress and the other States, which did not end until 1791, when all opposition worn out or overcome, Vermont took her seat at the national board in a Federal Union.

"Look now at the men whose characters our fathers could assimilate, whose diversities they could make an element of strength. Let us name a few of the leaders, who resembled each other in one respect only—they were all patriots.

"There was Ethan Allen, a man of giant frame

and iron muscle, in manner rough, but in soul as gentle as a woman, impatient of restraint, intolerant of opposition, his mind undisciplined and in constant revolt against all control, human or Divine.

"Ira Allen, his brother, a born diplomatist, smooth and polished in address, equally skilled in concealing his own thoughts and in discovering those of others.

"Seth Warner, the soldier, open and generous, into whose soul jealousy or vice of any kind could find no by-way to enter, the Bayard of Vermont, without fear and without reproach.

"Their First Governor, a plain, simple farmer, but shrewd and far-sighted, whom men could take into their confidence in spite of themselves, whose rule of life it was to make the best of everybody, because to use a rather Irish expression, which he applied daily, "he knew they always turned out better than he thought they would."

"The two Fays, Jonas and Joseph, masters of the caucus, so systematic that no convention could be held regular that had not a Fay for its secretary.

"The Robinsons, negotiators, pioneers in all missions to other States and powers: Nathaniel and Daniel Chipman educated trained lawyers, slightly aristocratic, faithful servants of the church by law established. Stephen R. Bradlay, a Democrat by nature, the best political writer of his time. Ebenezer Allen, who could not write a sentence correctly, but who could and did write the first American Emancipation proclamation. Remember Baker, who always doubted which he hated most, a Yorker, a Tory, or an Indian. Cochran, a hunter and guide, a philosopher and a patriot—and I might name a score of others, but these will serve to make leaders enough for all our political parties, for as many sects as ever opposed the Pope,—so unlike each other in all things that you would not suppose they could have sprung from the same race. Had they been like ourselves, they would have all been leaders, but each would have led a different party.

"We have to go deeper to find their points of unity. They all came from that iron-souled race of thinkers, who, early in the 17th century burst the letters of Church and State, and shook the centres of monarchy to their bases with the proposition, that the powers of government were derived from the people, should be employed for the benefit of the people, that any system or religion which taught the contrary was no true system or religion. For this faith they might be and were broken on the wheel, but from it they would not turn. They were Republicans in religion and in politics. Emigrating from Europe into the free air of this Western world these principles became a part of themselves, their descendants carried them into western Connecticut and Massachusetts, and from thence into this wilderness, where they confronted all the dangers and deprivations of a new settlement. They were patriots by birth, by growth and by education. However much they might differ in other affairs, they were all agreed that they would not tolerate any invasion of their rights of person or property. *That* was tyranny, and tyranny was to be resisted to the death. They were taught by their fathers—their lives were perpetual illustrations of the necessity of united action. In their case division was destruction,—*union, perfect union* of opinion, resources, characters, and powers alone could preserve them.

"I now ask your attention to some of the consequences to the person and the community of this common unity of action and opinion, among these men, who differed so widely among themselves. I need not remind you that in their time the telegraph, the railway and the steamboat had not been invented. There was scarcely a highway upon the Grants. Men went from place to place on foot or on horseback, following Indian trails or lines of marked trees. You will scarcely credit the assertion that under such circumstances the full effective strength of the new settlement could be mustered at any given point with nearly as much celerity as now. The statement is almost incredible, but you will hear my proofs before you reject it. I take them from history. It was on the 9th of May 1775, when Allen summoned his first man to march upon Ticonderoga. He lost a full day waiting for boats, on the shore of the lake, and even then captured the fort in the morning twilight of May 10th. There was then a block house near the north end of the bridge at Winooski. It was called Fort Frederic, garrisoned by men engaged in surveying or clearing the intervales above. They were under the command of Remember Baker. In some way, Allen's summons reached Baker in time to enable him to call in his men, equip them, embark them on a flat-boat, sail down the river to its mouth, row or sail up the lake, capture a boat filled with escaping British soldiers, on the way to Canada, and to reach Crown Point in time to take part in the capture of that fort, before noon of the 10th of May. Could you do much better now?

"I find the fact also recorded that in the winter of 1776, an express from Albany brought the news to Bennington that Sir John Johnson with five hundred Tories and a body of Indians was marching upon Tryon County, then at the eve of insurrection. The Yorkers—the people who had kidnapped Baker, and declared Allen an outlaw—implored the Green Mountain Boys to help them. Did they answer, You are the men who, with strong hand, without right, for more than ten years have been striving to rob us of our homes? No! no! Within *twelve hours after* the news reached the Grants, more than ninety Green Mountain Boys, armed, equipped and provisioned, were on the march, and every one of these Vermonters was furnished by a single town. They joined Schuyler, marched to Johnstown, and received the surrender of the invading force.

"David Wooster, a captain in the French war, had a New York grant of lands in the town of Addison. In 1761, the Vermonters who had expelled Col. Reid from the meadows of Otter Creek found Wooster serving writs on the settlers of the lands he claimed. They tied him and his sheriff to a tree, threatened them with the Beech seal, and released them only when they had withdrawn their writs, and promised to go and sin no more.

"We next hear of Wooster in midwinter of 1776. Montgomery has fallen. Wooster is in command of a defeated and dispirited army below Montreal, and the smallpox is epidemic among the frozen, starved and wounded patriots, who have traversed the wilds of Maine only to be defeated before Quebec. They are surrounded by an enemy twice their number. He is writing to Col. Warner. 'Our prospect is dubious,' he says, 'I have sent to General Schuyler, General Washington and to Congress. * * * but you know how long it will be before we can have relief from them.' 'You and the valiant Green Mountain Corps are in our neighborhood.' * * * 'You all have arms and ever stand ready to lend a helping hand to your brethren in distress.' Had I time I would read the whole of this touching letter. He implores Warner to send him help. 'Let the men set out at once * * * by tens, twenties, thirties or fifties.' 'It will have a good effect on the Canadians.' *'I am confident I shall see you here with your men in a very short time.'*

"This letter was written near Montreal on the 6th of January, and on the 22d, only 16 days later, Schuyler withdrew his request upon Washington for reinforcements, because, as he said, Warner had been so successful in sending men to Wooster's aid. Again the courage and celerity of the Vermonters saved the army. They formed Wooster's rear guard, standing like a wall between him and his pursuers, and fought all the way from the St. Lawrence to the islands of Lake Champlain. Nor did they relax their watchful care until June, when the last weary, wounded soldier of that army was safely sheltered within the walls of Ticonderoga.

"I could give many other illustrations of their promptness in marching to protect a friend or destroy an enemy. Let us now note their conduct in a difficult emergency.

"The embryo State never passed through a darker period than that between the advance of Burgoyne and the battle of Bennington. The retreat of St. Clair left the whole western frontier unprotected. Burgoyne scattered his proclamations, setting forth his own strength and offering protection to all who would abandon the patriot cause. All the provisions brought to his camp would be paid for in gold. The defection was frightful. Every wavering man accepted his offers. Even *one member of the Council*, to his eternal disgrace be it said, deserted. The people were poor. They had no money or credit. Alarm and confusion everywhere prevailed. A volunteer force must be raised, armed, fed and clothed, or the contest in this quarter was ended. How could it be done?

"But there was a little band of men known as the Council of Safety which was neither discouraged nor dismayed. They took account of their resources as cooly as a few weeks before they had discussed the provisions of the new Constitution. The prime necessity of the moment was to raise an adequate force of volunteers, and put a stop to these desertions. Both objects were accomplished by a single resolution, conceived, adopted, and its execution provided for, in a single session.

"Ira Allen, then a statesman 26 years old, was its author. It provided for a committee of sequestration, with power to confiscate the estates of the Tories and out of the proceeds raise and pay the volunteers. It stopped desertions instantly. Volunteers promptly came forward. This resolution was the first and a most fatal blow struck at the army of Burgoyne.

"Let me now call your attention to an illustration of the practical common sense which appears to have controlled the actions of our ancestors. I refer you to their first convention to frame a Constitution. It convened at Windsor in July, 1777. Half its members came direct from their regiments to the convention. Burgoyne was approaching with an army which twice outnumbered all the men on the Grants able to bear arms. Congress had just declared that the idea of forming a new State here was in substance derogatory to that body and a violation of the rights of New York.

"Cool and undismayed the delegates met in convention. Ira Allen has written that 'the business being new and of great consequence required serious deliberation.' No doubt of that. A draft of the Constitution was presented, by whom prepared we do not know. They examined it section by section. In the midst of the debate an express arrived with news of St. Clair's retreat before

Burgoyne. The families of the President and many of the members were exposed to the hireling and the savages in his train. Their first impulse was to adjourn and hasten to the defence of their homes. Just then a sudden July storm arose, which their venerable chaplain declared was an indication of the Almighty's will that the Constitution should be adopted then and there, and while awaiting its cessation, in the very conflict of the elements, the darkened hall illuminated by the flashes of the lightning, they formed a State. The Constitution was read through and virtually adopted. A vote appointing the Committee of Safety followed, an adjournment to December, the storm passed over, and within two hours of the arrival of the express the members were on their way to defend their families and their firesides.

"They came together again in December. Stirring events had happened meantime in which they had been actors. The battles of Bennington and Hubbardton had been fought; Burgoyne had surrendered, Ticonderoga had been retaken, the frontier had been cleared of the invader, and many of the volunteers had returned to their homes. The convention finished its work without delay. They adopted a preamble and ratified the Constitution. They decided that it was not expedient to submit their work to a popular vote. They named the 12th of March for their first election and sent Ira Allen to Connecticut to have the constitution printed."

CHAPTER XIV.

GENERAL ETHAN ALLEN.

Ethan Allen was a descendant of Samuel Allen, who came to New England in 1632. The most remarkable family that ever lived in Vermont, especially in the early history of the State, was that of the Allens. It was numerous and closely identified with the history of the controversy with New Hampshire and New York, resulting in the establishing a government under the name of Vermont. From Samuel Allen of Chelmsford (in 1632), and Windsor, Conn. (in 1636), descended the six sons and one daughter of Joseph Allen of Litchfield and Coventry, Connecticut: to wit, Gen. Ethan Allen, Captain Heman, Lydia, Maj. Heber, Lieut. Levi, Zimri, and Col. Ira Allen.

There were three Heman Allens in the Allen family: one was the son of said Heber, and one the son of Mathew the brother of Samuel Allen, and the other the son of Joseph Allen. From Mathew Allen descended Maj. Ebenezer Allen of Tinmouth and Heman Allen of Milton, Vt., and afterwards of Burlington. Joseph Allen married Mary Baker and they were the parents of Gen. Ethan Allen. Mary Baker was the sister of the father of Remember Baker, the brave associate of Ethan Allen. Remember Baker and the said six sons and daughters of Joseph Allen were cousins. The mother of Remember Baker was aunt to Seth Warner; and thus it is seen that the most distinguished of the early heroes and statesmen of Vermont were related by the ties both of blood and marriage.

Ethan Allen was born in Litchfield, Ct., January 10th, A. D. 1737. He was the eldest of his father's family and the one that his parents designed should receive a collegiate education, but the death of his father in straightened circumstances obliged Ethan to abandon, much to his bitter disappointment, the pursuit of a collegiate education in the 18th year of his age, while pursuing his preparatory studies. At an early age he was fond of political discussion and became interested in the affairs of the Colonies and in their contentions with Great Britain. He was a great reader and he said he had "acquainted himself with the history of mankind." We have but a meagre account of his early life, but it is said he followed the life of a hunter for several years. The first account we have of him in Vermont (New Hampshire Grants) was in the year 1766, and he immediately took a lively interest in behalf of the people inhabiting the Grants, who were suffering from the wrongs and oppressive measures of the authorities of New York.

Gov. Wentworth of New Hampshire had granted townships as far west as Bennington, and claimed the right under the Charter from the British Crown to do so. The settlers had paid for their lands in the several towns granted, and had taken possession of them, felled the forests, planted their crops and established their homes. The people in each town thus settled managed and controlled their own municipal affairs—each grant was sort of a primitive Republic. New York, another Province of Great Britain, denied the right of New Hampshire, and asserted a right in opposition. The settlers supposed that the conflict was simply a mere question of Colonial jurisdiction, and had no idea it was going to interfere with or disturb their title obtained under the grants from New Hampshire. But it was not long before they were undeceived, for soon the Colonial officials of New York ignored their rights and demanded pay for the lands again for the New York speculators who required the settlers to take the title of their lands under New York grants. The time had now come to oppose the claims of New York in their courts, or appeal to arms to maintain their rights. In such contests the Grants must have a leader who was bold, energetic and fearless, and who sympathized with them. They found such a leader and defender of their rights in Ethan Allen. He came to the front in their support. He at first put confidence in the courts of New York and when suits of ejectment were brought against those in possession of lands under the New Hampshire grants, by those who took their supposed title under grants from New York, Allen took his lawyer and went before the New York judges, and pleaded the Royal grant purchased and paid for with the money of the grantees, in full confidence that his claims would be respected by their courts, but he was mistaken. The courts there rejected the Royal grant and the titles obtained by the settlers under the grants from the Governor of New Hampshire, as so much waste paper, and judgement was pronounced in favor of the claimants under New York grants. The King's attorney told Allen he "better go home and advise his people to make the best terms they could with their landlords, for might often prevails against right." Allen answered, "The gods of the hills are not the gods of valleys." This the Yorkers found out later.

Allen saw that the magnitude of the work of defense of the settlers was great. He knew it demanded all his energies. He and the other Green Mountain Boys were a great power and held the Yorkers in wholesome dread. Allen was sleepless and untiring. He would be in Connecticut enlisting material aid for the defense of the Grants; next he would be holding meetings in the Vermont settlements, perfecting organizations for defence among the settlers; then would be employed in resisting the New York sheriff and his posse. One day he would be holding a court for the trial of a Tory justice, and the next would be executing the sentence with the twigs of the wilderness; and then he would appear where the enemy would least expect him. The enemy looked upon him with dread, and they denounced him as a rebel, the leader of the mob, a felon, and an outlaw. They were insane with rage, but he hurled back defiance. He told them, "if you come forth in arms against us, thousands of your injured neighbors in the several Provinces will join with us to cut off and extirpate such an execrable race from the face of the earth." Allen and the Green Mountain Boys had the British and the Indians as enemies to keep at bay, and treacherous Tories and spies in their midst to watch and subdue.

The first systematical and bloody attempt by the British at Lexington to enslave America electrified the mind of Allen and fully determined him to take part in the controversy against British aggression and in favor of the Colonies. And while he was wishing an opportunity would present itself that he might signalize himself in behalf of his country, directions came to him privately from the Colony of Connecticut, to raise men from among the Green Mountain Boys, and surprise and take the fortress of Ticonderoga. This enterprise he cheerfully undertook, cut off all intelligence between the garrison and the country, and made a forced march from Bennington and arrived at Lake Champlain opposite Ticonderoga on the evening of the 9th day of May, 1775, with 230 brave Green Mountain Boys. It was with great difficulty that he procured boats to cross the lake, but he succeeded in landing 83 men near the garrison and sent Col. Seth Warner back with the boats to bring up the remainder of the men. It began to grow daylight, and Allen felt himself under the necessity to attack the fort, before Warner could cross the lake with his command, though he viewed it hazardous. He addressed the 83 men as follows:—

"Friends and fellow soldiers, You have, for a number of years past been a scourge and terror to arbitrary power. Your valor has been famed abroad, and acknowledged, as appears by the advice and orders to me, from the General Assembly of Connecticut, to surprise and take the garrison now before us. I now propose to advance before you, and in person, conduct you through the wicket-gate; for we must this morning either quit our pretensions to valor, or possess ourselves of this fortress in a few minutes; and, inasmuch as it is a desperate attempt, which none but the bravest of men dare undertake, I do not urge it on any contrary to his will. You that will undertake voluntarily, poise your firelocks."

Every man poised his firelock. Allen at their head marched to the wicket-gate, where he found a sentry posted who snapped his fuse at Allen. On the approach of Allen the sentry retreated through the covered way into the fort and gave the alarm. Allen's party followed him into the fort. The garrison was taken by surprise and made but little resistance. One of the sentries who attempted to make some resistance was wounded by Allen and asked for quarter which was granted. Allen demanded that he show him the place of the commanding officer; this request was complied with and Allen quickly repaired to the place and ordered the commander, Captain De LaPlace, to come forth instantly, or he would sacrifice the whole garrison: at which the Captain came immediately to the door undressed, when Allen ordered the Captain to deliver him the fort instantly. He asked Allen by what authority he demanded it; Allen answered him in the ever memorable words, "In the name of the great Jehovah, and the Continental Congress." The Captain began to speak again when Allen interrupted him, and demanded, with his drawn sword over his head, an immediate surrender of the garrison, to which the Captain immediately complied. Fifty men and officers surrendered; there were taken about 100 pieces of cannon, one 13 inch mortar and a number of swivels.

This capture was carried into effect in the gray of the morning of May 10, 1775. Allen did not know the work that he and his men accomplished that morning, would be regarded by all future generations as one of the most wonderful exploits in American history, and his praises be told as long as Vermont shall continue a state and the United States exist as a nation. This brilliant exploit must have been a bright spot in the memories of the Green Mountain Boys during their whole lives. It gave great encouragement to the drooping spirits of the American Patriots. But little did Allen dream that in a few months the tables would be turned and he become a prisoner and compelled to drag out a miserable existence for two years and eight months in an English prison.

Col. Warner and his men soon after the capture of the fort joined Allen at the fort. Allen immediately sent Warner with 100 men to capture Crown Point which was garrisoned with a sergeant and 12 men, which was taken the same day with over 100 pieces of cannon.

The next thing that Allen sought to accomplish was to get possession of a British sloop of war which was laying at St. Johns. To accomplish this they proceeded to arm and man a schooner and sent Captain Arnold with it to accomplish the undertaking. Allen took command of a batteau. The schooner was the fastest sailing craft and Arnold arrived at St. Johns, possessed himself of the sloop, a Sergeant and 12 men before Allen could arrive, and sailed with the prize for Ticonderoga, when he met Allen, who went on board the sloops, where "several loyal Congress healths were drank." Now the Green Mountain Boys were masters of Lake Champlain and the garrison depending thereon.

The following is another account of this Canadian enterprise that has been furnished me, viz.:—

"After taking Ticonderoga, and in order to obtain complete control of Lake Champlain, Allen desired to get possession of a British armed sloop which was anchored in the Richelieu river at St. Johns. It was accordingly arranged between him and Benedict Arnold that the latter should start for St. Johns in a schooner which Capt. Herrick had taken at Skenesborough (now Whitehall), and that Allen should follow with three batteaux, which were at Crown Point. Arnold, on the 17th of May, got within thirty miles of St. Johns, when the wind failed him. He pushed forward in small boats, with thirty-five men; surprised the garrison at St. Johns and seized the sloop. Learning that a detachment of British troops, with artillery, was on its way to St. Johns from Montreal, Arnold did not await Allen's arrival at St. Johns, but started back, taking with him the sloop and twenty prisoners. Fifteen miles this side of St. Johns he met Allen with, as the accounts say, about one hundred men; but from Allen's letter it appears that he had a smaller number. Arnold informed Allen of the near approach of the British troops and advised him to turn back; but he refused to do so, saying that he would push on to St. Johns, and hold possession of the fort there. But the English troops were there before him, and when he appeared on the opposite side of the river, they opened fire on him with six field pieces and two hundred muskets. Allen returned the fire; but perceiving that he was heavily outnumbered, he abandoned the attempt, re-embarked hastily on his boats, leaving three men behind, and returned to Ticonderoga. He intended, as his letter shows, to return in stronger force and seize and fortify Isle aux Noix, but this purpose was not carried out at that time. We submit Allen's letter below:

COL. ETHAN ALLEN TO CAPT. NOAH LEE.

Sr.—This Hour Capt. Warner and myself Arrived at Ticonderoga with the soldiery, consisting of Seventy six men Including Officers. We met with Cannonading of Grape shot. The Musick was both Terrible and Delightful. We were across the water at the Distance of 80 or 100 rods. None of our party was killed, the regulars broke their ranks, but we know not as we killed any of them. The council of war agreed to immediately take Posession of the Isle of Noah, which is ten miles this side Saint Johns and fortify it and advance all the troops thither we can spare from every station on the lake. This is therefore (to) Desire and Earnestly request you to Lay this Letter before

Those of our friends that are at Your Station to repair here for the purpose above

Mentioned—I should think 5 or 6 men sufficient to occupy Your Station and forward Provisions Except Proper hands to manage the water Crafts for that purpose I Desire You would send all the Soldiers You Can and urge forward Provisions and Ammunition.

Fail Not. Given under my Hand, the 21st day of May 1775.

Ethan Allen Commander of the G. M. Boys.

N B.—this Express is by the Agreement of the Council of War.

To Capt. Noah Lee, Commandant at Skeensborough."

Early in September, 1775, the little army under the command of Generals Schuyler and Montgomery, was ordered to advance into Canada. Allen was at Ticonderoga at the time the orders were received. The Generals of the army requested Allen to attend them in the expedition; he complied with their request though he had no commission. He was told he should, as occasion required, command detachments of the army, and advanced with it to Isle-aux-Noix, containing about eighty-five acres, ten miles north of the boundary line of Vermont, where the British had a small garrison. From there he made two tours into Canada to observe the disposition, designs and movements of the inhabitants, and to let them know that the design of the army was only against the English garrisons, and would not interfere with their liberties or religion. While there he met Colonel

Brown, of the army under the command of General Montgomery, who desired that Allen should procure canoes, so as to cross the river St. Lawrence a little North of Montreal, and he, Brown, would cross it a little to the South of the town with near two hundred men, and capture the city. Allen's party consisted of 110 men, eighty of whom were Canadians. As agreed with Brown, Allen crossed the river in the night of the 24th of September.

The story of Allen's attempt to take Montreal and the result of his failure to do it I will give in his own words:—

"Soon after day-break, I set a guard between me and the town, with special orders to let no person whatever pass or repass them, another guard on the other end of the road, with like directions; in the meantime, I reconnoitered the best ground to make a defence, expecting Col. Brown's party was landed on the other side of the town, he having, the day before, agreed to give three loud huzzas with his men early in the morning, which signal I was to return, that we might each know that both parties were landed; but the sun, by this time, being nearly two hours high, and the sign failing, I began to conclude myself to be in premunire, and would have crossed the river back again, but I knew the enemy would have discovered such an attempt; and as there could not more than one-third part of my troops cross at one time, the other two-thirds would of course fall into their hands. This I could not reconcile to my own feelings as a man, much less as an officer: I therefore concluded to maintain the ground, if possible, and all to fare alike. In consequence of this resolution, I despatched two messengers, one to Laprairie, to Col. Brown, and the other to l'Assomption, a French settlement, to Mr. Walker, who was in our interest, requesting their speedy assistance, giving them, at the same time to understand my critical situation. In the mean time, sundry persons came to my guards, pretending to be friends, but were by them taken prisoners and brought to me. These I ordered to confinement, until their friendship could be further confirmed; for I was jealous they were spies, as they proved to be afterwards. One of the principal of them making his escape, exposed the weakness of my party, which was the final cause of my misfortune; for I have been since informed that Mr. Walker, agreeably to my desire, exerted himself, and had raised a considerable number of men for my assistance, which brought him into difficulty afterwards, but upon hearing of my misfortune, he disbanded them again.

The town of Montreal was in a great tumult. General Carleton and the royal party, made every preparation to go on board their vessel of force, as I was afterwards informed, but the spy escaped from my guard to the town, occasioned an alteration in their policy, and emboldened Gen. Carleton to send the force which he had there collected, out against me. I had previously chosen my ground, but when I saw the number of the enemy as they sallied out of the town, I perceived that it would be a day of trouble if not of rebuke; but I had no chance to flee, as Montreal was situated on an island, and the St. Lawrence cut off my communication to Gen. Montgomery's camp. I encouraged my soldiery to bravely defend themselves, that we should soon have help, and that we should be able to keep the ground, if no more. This, and much more I affirmed with the greatest seeming assurance, and which in reality I thought to be in some degree probable.

The enemy consisted of not more than forty regular troops, together with a mixed multitude, chiefly Canadians, with a number of English who lived in town, and some Indians; in all to the number of near five hundred.

The reader will notice that most of my party were Canadians; indeed it was a motley parcel which composed both parties. However, the enemy began the attack from wood-piles, ditches, buildings, and such like places, at a considerable distance, and I returned the fire from a situation more than equally advantageous. The attack began between two and three o'clock in the afternoon, just before which I ordered a volunteer by the name of Richard Young, with a detachment of nine men as a flank guard, which, under the cover of the bank of the river, could not only annoy the enemy, but at the same time, serve as a flank guard to the left of the main body.

The fire continued for some time on both sides; and I was confident that such a remote method of attack could not carry the ground, provided it should be continued till night; but near half the body of the enemy began to flank round to my right; upon which I ordered a volunteer by the name of John Dugan, who had lived many years in Canada, and understood the French language, to detach about fifty of the Canadians, and post himself at an advantageous ditch, which was on my right, to prevent my being surrounded. He advanced with the detachment, but instead of occupying the post, made his escape, as did likewise Mr. Young upon the left, with their detachments. I soon perceived that the enemy was in the possession of the ground, which Dugan should have occupied. At this time I had about forty-five men with me; some of whom were wounded; the enemy kept closing round me, nor was it in my power to prevent it; by which means, my situation, which was advantageous in the first part of the attack, ceased to be so in the last; and being almost entirely surrounded with such vast unequal numbers I ordered a retreat, but found that those of the enemy, who were of the country, and their Indians, could run as fast as my men, though the regulars could not. Thus I retreated near a mile, and some of the enemy, with the savages kept flanking me, and others crowded hard in the rear. In fine, I expected, in a very short time to try the world of spirits; for I was apprehensive that no quarter would be given me, and therefore had determined to sell my life as dear as I could. One of the enemy's officers, boldly pressing in the rear, discharged his fusee at me; the ball whistled near me, as did many others that day. I returned the salute, and missed him, as running had put us both out of breath: for I conclude we were not frightened: I then saluted him with my tongue in a harsh manner, and told him that, inasmuch as his numbers were far superior to mine, I would surrender, provided I could be treated with honor, and be assured of good quarters for myself and the men who were with me; and he answered I should; another officer, coming up directly after, confirmed the treaty; upon which I agreed to surrender with my party, which then consisted of thirty-one effective men, and seven wounded. I ordered them to ground their arms, which they did.

The officer I capitulated with, then directed me and my party to advance towards him, which was done; I handed him my sword, and in half a minute after, a savage, part of whose head was shaved, being almost naked and painted, with feathers intermixed with the hair of the other side of his head, came running to me with an incredible swiftness; he seemed to advance with more than mortal speed; as he approached near me, his hellish visage was beyond all description; snake's eyes appear innocent in comparison of his; his features distorted; malice, death, murder, and the wrath of devils and damned spirits are the emblems of his countenance; and in less than twelve feet of me, presenting his firelock; at the instant of his present, I twitched the officer, to whom I gave my sword, between me and the savage; but he flew round with great fury, trying to single me out to shoot me without killing the officer; but by this time I was nearly as nimble as he, keeping the officer in such a position that his danger was my defence; but in less than half a minute, I was attacked by just such another imp of hell: Then I made the officer fly around with incredible velocity, for a few seconds of time, when I perceived a Canadian, who had lost one eye, as appeared afterwards, taking my part against the savages; and in an instant an Irishman came to my assistance and drove away the fiends, swearing by Jasus he would kill them. This tragic scene composed my mind. The escaping from so awful a death, made even imprisonment happy; the more so as my conquerers on the field treated me with great civility and politeness.

The regular officers said that they were very happy to see Col. Allen: I answered them, that I should rather chose to have seen them at General Montgomery's camp. The gentlemen replied, that they gave full credit to what I said, and as I walked to the town, which was, as I should guess, more than two miles, a British officer walked at my right hand, and one of the French noblesse at my left the latter of which, in the action, had his eyebrow carried away by a glancing shot, but was nevertheless very merry and facetious, and no abuse was offered me till I came to the barrack yard at Montreal, where I met General Prescott, who asked my name, which I told him: He then asked me, whether I was that Col. Allen, who took Ticonderoga. I told him I was the very man: Then he shook his cane over my head, calling many hard names, among which he frequently used the word rebel, and put himself in a great rage. I told him he would do well not to cane me, for I was not accustomed to it, and shook my fist at him, telling him that was the beetle of mortality for him, if he offered to strike; upon which Capt. M' Cloud, of the British, pulled him by the skirt, and whispered to him, as he afterwards told me, to this import; that it was inconsistent with his honor to strike a prisoner. He then ordered a sergeant's command with fixed bayonets to come forward, and kill thirteen Canadians, which were included in the treaty aforesaid.

It cut me to the heart to see the Canadians in so hard a case, in consequence of their having been true to me; they were wringing their hands, saying their prayers, as I concluded, and expected immediate death. I therefore stepped between the executioners and the Canadians, opened my clothes, and told Gen. Prescott to thrust his baynets into my breast, for I was the sole cause of the Canadians taking up arms.

The guard, in the mean time, rolling their eyeballs from the General to me, as though impatiently waiting his dread commands to sheath their bayonets in my heart; I could, however, plainly discern, that he was in a suspense and quandary about the matter. This gave me additional hopes of succeeding; for my design was not to die, but to save the Canadians by a finesse. The general stood a minute, when he made me the following reply; "I will not execute you now; but you shall grace a halter at Tyburn, God damn you."

I remember I disdained his mentioning such a place; I was, notwithstanding, a little pleased with the expression, as it significantly conveyed to me the idea of postponing the present appearance of death; besides his sentence was by no means final, as to "gracing a halter," although I had anxiety about it, after I landed in England, as the reader will find in the course of this history. Gen. Prescott then ordered one of his officers to take me on board the Gaspee schooner of war, and confine me, hands and feet, in irons, which was done the same afternoon I was taken.

The action continued an hour and three-quarters, by the watch, and I know not to this day how many of my men were killed, though I am certain there were but few. If I remember right, 7 were wounded.

I now come to the description of the irons, which were put on me: The hand-cuff was of the common size and form, but my leg irons, I should imagine would weigh thirty pounds; the bar was eight feet long, and very substantial; the shackles, which encompassed my ancles, were very tight. I was told by the officer, who put them on, that it was the king's plate, and I heard other of their officers say, that it would weigh forty weight. The irons were so close upon my ancles, that I could not lay down in any other manner than on my back. I was put into the lowest and most wretched part of the vessel, where I got the favor of a chest to sit on; the same answered for my bed at night; and having procured some little blocks, of the guard who day and night with fixed bayonets, watched over me, to lie under each end of the large bar of my leg irons, to preserve my ancles from galling, while I sat on the chest, or lay back on the same, though most of the time, night and day, I sat on it; but at length, having a desire to lie down on my side, which the closeness of my irons forbid, I desired the captain to loosen them for that purpose; but was denied the favor. The Captain's name was Royal, who did not seem to be an ill-natured man; but oftentimes said, that his express orders were to treat me with such severity, which was disagreeable to his own feelings; nor did he ever insult me, though many others, who came on board did. One of the officers by the name of Bradley, was very generous to me; he would often send me victuals from his own table; nor did a day fail, but he sent me a good drink of grog.

The reader is now invited back to the time I was put in irons. I requested the privilege to write to General Prescott, which was granted. I reminded him of the kind and generous manner of my treatment of the prisoners I took at Ticonderoga; the injustice and ungentleman-like usage I had met with from him, and demanded better usage, but received no answer from him. I soon after wrote to Gen. Carleton, which met the same success. In the mean while, many of those who were permitted to see me, were very insulting.

I was confined in the manner I have related, on board the Gaspee schooner, about six weeks; during which time I was obliged to throw out plenty of extravagant language, which answered certain purposes, at that time, better than to grace a history."

On one occasion Allen on being insulted, in anger twisted off with his teeth a ten-penny nail that went through the bar of his hand cuff; one of the bystanders said, he could eat iron. Allen was put on to an armed vessel laying off against Quebec, the officers of which treated him kindly. One of the officers, Capt. Littlejohn said, "that a brave man should not be used as a rascal, on board his ship." While the ship was laying there Capt. Littlejohn was challenged on the plains of Abraham. The fight was to take place the next morning. The Captain acquainted Allen of the affair, whereupon, Allen told him he would be glad to testify his gratitude to him by acting the part of a faithful second; Littlejohn replied he wanted no better man, but said, I am a King's Officer and you a prisoner under my care, you must, therefore go with me, to the place appointed in disguise, and engage upon the honor of a gentleman, that whether I die or live, you will return to my Lieutenant on board this ship. To this Allen solemnly agreed. The controversy was settled without fighting.

On Nov. 11, 1775, Allen was put on the vessel called Adamant with other prisoners, under the power of an English merchant, Brook Watson, a man of cruel and malicious disposition. During the voyage Allen was insulted by every blackguard sailor, and Tory on board. Allen appealed to Watson's honor for better treatment. Watson told him it was impertinent for a capital offender to talk of honor or humanity; that anything short of a halter was too good for him and that would be his portion soon after he landed in England. A lieutenant among the Tories told him he ought to have been executed for rebellion against New York, and spat in his face, for which act Allen sprang at him and partly knocked him down, when the lieutenant fled to others for protection. Allen and the other prisoners were kept in a filthy dark room forty days without means of clensing their bodies, and covered with body lice, resulting in sickness.

Allen was landed at Falmouth, England, in the same suit of clothes in which he was taken prisoner, and there was exhibited to the citizens, of that place, who were excited by curiosity. In England Allen was anxious on the question as to what should be his fate. It was talked generally that he would be hanged. Parliament was divided on the question. But the Americans had the most prisoners in their power, and if the British resorted to hanging, it was a game that two could play at; Allen was well treated in the Castle where he was imprisoned. He requested the privilege of writing to Congress, and after a while got permission to do so. He wrote giving an account of his treatment, after having been taken prisoner, under the orders of General Carleton. He desired Congress to desist from matters of retaliation until they knew the course that the English would take respecting their treatment towards him, and that if retaliation should become necessary, it might be exercised, not according to the smallness of his character in America, but in proportion to the importance of the cause for which he suffered. The design of the letter was to save his neck from the halter. He managed to have the letter fall into the hands of Lord North before it was sent to Congress, although he did not tell the officers, to whom it was delivered, that that was his purpose. The next day after it had been delivered to the officer in charge, who had given Allen license to write, the officer said to him, "Do you think we are fools in England, and would send your letter to Congress with instructions to retaliate on our people. I have sent your letter to Lord North." Allen at the Castle behaved in a daring soldier-like manner, thinking that would tend to his preservation better than concession and timidy. But he had determined, that if cruel death was inevitable he would face it undaunted ; and when he arrived in the world of spirits, he said, he expected he "should be as well treated as other gentlemen of his merit." While imprisoned in the Castle people came for fifty miles distant to see, question, and make free with him in conservation. One asked him what had been his occupation in life, and Allen replied, he had studied divinity, but was a conjurer by profession, and had conjured them out of Ticonderoga. They would take him on the parade in the Castle where large numbers could see and hear him. He would harangue his audiences on the impracticability of conquering the American Colonies, and expatriated on American freedom.

Allen refused to take a bowl of punch that he had ordered from the hand of a servant. He used to argue, with learned gentlemen who came to see him, on moral philosophy and Christianity, and they seemed to be surprised at his power of argument. On his passage to England he was forbidden to walk on deck, but he disregarded the order and went on deck; this enraged the captain who said to him, "Did I not order you not to come on deck?" Allen replied "that it was the place for gentlemen." The Captain enjoined him not to walk on the same side of the deck that he did. The fleet rendez-voused at the Cove of Cork, and Allen with the other prisoners were generously treated by several merchants, who contributed largely to their relief. They sailed from England Jan. 8th, and from the Cove of Cork the 12th day of February and were taken to Madrid. When they sailed from Madrid Allen was treated cruelly and Captain Symonds seemed in no way anxious to preserve the lives of the rebels, as he called the prisoners, but wished them all dead. As Allen expostulated with the Captain and his men for such treatment; the Captain said he "needed no directions from him how to treat a rebel; that the British would conquer the American rebels, hang the Congress, and such as promoted the rebellion, and you (Allen) in particular, and retake their own prisoners, so that your (Allen's) life is of no consequence in the scale of their policy." Allen replied that if he was safe till they conquered America before they hung him, he should die of old age. The ship in which Allen and the other prisoners were confined cast anchor in the harbor of Cape Fear in North Carolina. They next anchord, the ship Mercury, on which Allen was then confined, near New York, and arrived at Halifax about the middle of June, pinched with hunger, and suffering from inhuman treatment that the Captain refused to alleviate. Allen with the other prisoners were left on board of a sloop six weeks and were not landed at Halifax till the middle of August, and there all of them, thirty-four in number, were locked up in a large room, together, the furniture of which consisted principally of excrement-tubs. They remonstrated against such usage, but to no purpose. Five of the prisoners, including Allen, were legally entitled to parole which they could not obtain. The provisions were better than they had previously been served with, but all grew weaker and weaker on account of sickness contracted from the foulness of the place. On Oct. 12th most of them were ordered on board a man-of-war that was bound for New York.

Allen expected to be treated as cruelly as before, but when he went on deck, he was met by Captain Smith, who gave him his hand and invited him to dine with him, and assured Allen he should be treated as a gentleman, and that he had given orders to the crew to so treat him. This was unexpected. On account of such kindness another side of Allen's character was exhibited. This kind treatment affected him so he could hardly speak and drew tears from his eyes, which all the harsh usage he had met with was unable to produce, but he soon got control of his feelings and expressed his gratitude for the unexpected favors.

A few additional prisoners were taken on board among whom was a Captain Burke. A conspiracy had been concocted by Burke and some of the ship's crew, to kill Captain Smith and take the ship, and the thirty-four thousand pounds Sterling that was theron, into an American port. This Allen and some other prisoners, that was led into the secret, opposed. Allen told them he could not reconcile it to his conscience, and it should not be done, and pointed out the ungratefulness of such an act, and he should guard Captain Smith's life. Nothing more was heard of the conspiracy.

The ship cast anchor at New York and Captain Smith recommended Allen to Admiral Howe and to General Sir William Howe as a gentleman of honor and veracity, and desired that he should be treated as such. He was landed at New York and given his parole, but restricted to the limits of the city. The merciless manner in which the prisoners in the hands of the British at New York were treated, the hellish delight and triumph of the Tories over them, as they were dying by the hundreds by starvation and sickness, the foulness of the places where they were kept, the despair that seemed to be imprinted on their countenances as they begged for a morsel of bread, was too much for Allen to bear in his exhausted condition. Allen regarded General Howe a murderous tyrant. While Allen was detained at New York, General Howe though a British officer offered him the Colonelcy of a regiment of Tories if he turned traitor to his suffering country; they used, as they thought a persuasive argument to induce Allen to accept their offer; they said the country would be soon conquered, and when that should be done he should have a large tract of land either in New

Hampshire or Connecticut. Allen replied, "that if he by faithfullness to the American cause had recommended himself to General Howe, he should be loth, by unfaithfulness to lose the General's good opinion, and besides, he viewed the offer of land to be limited to that which the devil offered Jesus Christ, 'to give him all the kingdoms of the world if he would fall down and worship him;' when at the same time, the damned soul had not one foot of land on earth."

On Jan. 22, 1777, Allen was admitted to parole with other officers and quartered on the westerly part of Long Island, and was treated well till the news came that Burgoyne had retaken Ticonderoga, which made the Britons feel their importance and gave them an insatiable thirst for cruelty. On August 25, 1777, Allen was apprehended, on pretense he had violated his parole, and taken to New York and imprisoned, and denied all food for three days, and suffered otherwise from the inhuman treatment of the enemy and remained their prisoner until the 6th of May, 1778.

It has been claimed that Ethan Allen was destitute of religious principle or faith. Whatever may have been his particular religious belief, it was evident he was a man of action, principle and patriotism, and had a high regard for the rights of his fellow man. He possessed the courage to stand by his convictions in the hour of trial and danger. The poetry composed by him for a monumental inscription for his wife, Mary Brownson Allen, indicated his trust in God. These lines are found on page 29 of this volume.

Ethan, Heman, Zimri, and Ira Allen with Remember Baker constituted the Onion River Land Company, and as such became the most extensive land proprietors in the State, first under the New Hampshire Grants, and subsequently under the State by grants from Vermont. Some of Gov. Thomas Chittenden's letters and public documents were written by Ethan Allen.

It is evident to the reader of all that has been written and published of Ethan Allen, that his public services, after his release from his imprisonment, were far less prominent than before his capture. And the impression has prevailed, to some extent, that he had lost his energy and zeal both for the nation and the State, but this view was a mistake. It is true his patriotism was doubted in the closing months of 1780; that he was arraigned before the General Assembly; and that he resigned his commission as General of the Vermont militia because there was an uneasiness among some of the people on account of his command. He was very indignant that false, ignominious aspersions against him were entertained. He was acquitted of all disloyalty and public confidence was restored to him. The aspersions against him did not serve to dampen his patriotism, and on resigning his commission of general, he said, if the Assembly thought best to give him the command at any time, he would endeavor to serve the State according to his abilities. He served the State afterwards in 1782, on being called upon by the General Assembly and the Governor to suppress the enemies in Windham County, and he met the call promptly. That he was not as prominent in the service of Vermont and the nation as in his earlier days was due not to any change of views towards the State or country, or the decay of his powers, but because the occasions for like and striking services did not again occur. After his arraignment in 1780, he was called into service for the State in 1781, when New York attempted to awe Vermont into subjection to its demands. Allen was one of the few public men who were engaged in the Haldimand correspondence, and took part in it with Ira Allen and Joseph Fay. General Ethan Allen was ready to serve the State with sword or pen to the last day of his life, with all the force of mind and muscle that he ever possessed. He was always a hero.

Allen married for his second wife the daughter of a Colonel in the British army. In August, 1778, the Governor and Council requested Allen to repair to Philadelphia and ascertain in what light the attempted Union of Vermont with a part of New Hampshire was viewed by Congress, which service he performed, and in October, 1778, he reported to the Vermont Legislature that the members of Congress were unanimously opposed to Vermont extending jurisdiction across Connecticut River. On Feb. 16th, 1779, Allen, Jonas Fay, and Paul Spooner, Esquires, were chosen by the House to manage the political affairs of the State at Congress. In March, 1779, Ethan Allen addressed a letter to General Washington, in which, after stating that the enemies' ships and scouting parties were expected down

Lake Champlain to annoy the frontier that was weakly guarded and widely extended, said, "undoubtedly your Excellency will readily conceive that this part of the country has done more than its adequate proportion in the war, and though they are greatly reduced as to materials to maintain standing forces, yet on sudden emergencies the militia is able and willing to face an equal number of the enemy though they should have no other reward but the satisfaction of defeating them." These statements show that his zeal, bravery and patriotism for his country had not abated. In April, 1779, Gov. Chittenden sent Allen to Cumberland County to quell a disturbance that had been created in opposition to a draft for men to re-enforce the military on the border. Col. William Patterson who had been commissioned by Gov. Clinton had raised a regiment of 500 men. Allen with an armed force promptly arrested Patterson and 43 others who were indicted for the part they took in resisting the draft. On June 12th 1779, Allen and Hon. Jonas Fay were directed to wait upon the General Council of America, and recommended to that Honorable Board to do and transact any business that concerned the State of Vermont. This was giving these two men very broad powers. In 1781, Allen was appointed by the Council, with others, a committee to make a draft of the political affairs of the State for publication.

Ethan Allen wrote the *vindication* of the opposition of the inhabitants of Vermont to the Government of New York, and of their right to form an independent State, which was submitted to the impartial *World*. This was the most important document that was written concerning the controversy of Vermont with New York, and the efforts of the Green Mountain Boys to establish the territory called the New Hampshire Grants as an independent jurisdiction. It is too long to be inserted here; it was a protest against the demand of New York to have Congress decide in their favor the controversy on an *ex parte* hearing; it set forth the fact that New York obtained the jurisdiction of the contested territory on an *ex parte* hearing before the King and Council in 1764, contrary to the minds of the settlers under New Hampshire, and that, therefore, such determination so obtained ought to be treated nul and void: that the conduct of New York in the matter was reprehensible; it set forth the measures that were taken by the Grants to modify the decision of the King and Council favorable to the rights of the settlers; it set forth the unwarrantable course of New York to dispossess the settlers of their lands by writs of ejectment and the resistance made by the inhabitants, and how the New Hampshire Grants, west of Connecticut River, declared themselves *a free and independent State*. Ethan Allen also wrote the reply to Gov. Clinton's proclamation that had been issued to induce the Grants, by threats and promises, to become subjects of New York. That proclamation referred to an act of outlawry that had been passed against Ethan Allen and other leading Green Mountain Boys. Allen in his reply, said, "In the lifetime of this act

I was called by the Yorkers an outlaw, and afterwards by the British, was called a rebel; and I humbly conceive that there was as much propriety in the one name as the other; and I verily believe, that the King's commissioners would now be as willing to pardon me for the sin of rebellion, provided I would, afterwards, be subject to Great Britain, as the Legislature of New York, provided I would be subject to New York; and I must confess I had as leave be a subject of the one as the other; and it is well known I have had great experience with them both." Before the proclamation of Gov. Clinton had been issued, New York had granted lands, to New York adherents, that had previously been granted by New Hampshire and Massachusetts Bay, which regranting created great alarm to the people who had taken their title from New Hampshire and Massachusetts Bay, for fear they would loose their lands and their improvements thereon. It had the effect to stir up strong opposition to New York authority. To allay the alarm and opposition to New York, Gov. Clinton stated in his proclamation, in substance, the regrants by New York should be treated as of no effect. If the grants ever had any validity they could not be nullified after people had purchased and took possession of their lands in good faith. If the grants made by New York were not valid, then their offers and overtures were but empty words. Allen exposed the hollowness of their offer in the following language: For the legislative authority of the State of New York, to pretend, as they do in their proclamation, to vacate any grants made by their own authority, in favor of any possession, and to confirm such possessions by nullifying and defeating their own grants, is the hight of folly and stupidity: For the lands being once granted, the property passeth to the grantee who is become the sole proprietor of the same; and he is as independent of that legislative authority which granted it, as any person may be supposed to be, who purchaseth a farm of land of me by deed of conveyance; and it is as much out of the power of that legislature to vacate a grant made by them, or the same authority, in favor of any possessor, as it is out of my power to vacate my deed of conveyance in favor of some second person. It is contrary to common sense to suppose, that the property of the subject is at the arbitrary disposal of the legislature; if it was, they might give a grant to-day, and vacate it to-morrow, and so on, *ad infinitum*." The following shows Allen's activity in the interest of Vermont. Samuel Minott of Brattleboro, the chairman of a committee of the adherents of New York, wrote to Gov. Clinton May 25th, 1779, that, "The Committee of Cumberland (now Windham) County who are now met for the purpose of opposing the authority of the State of Vermont, take this opportunity to inform your Exellency by Express, that Col. Ethan Allen with a number of Green Mountain Boys made his appearance in this County yesterday, well armed and equipped, for the purpose of reducing the loyal inhabitants of this County to submission to the authority of the State of Vermont, and made prisoners of Col. Eleazer Patterson and all of the Militia officers, but one, and a number of other persons. Allen bids defiance to the State of New York, and he and the Green Mountain Boys declare they will establish their state by the sword, and fight all who shall attempt to oppose them. * * * Our situation is truly critical and distressing, we, therefore, most humbly beseech your Excellency to take the most speedy and efficient measures for our relief; otherwise our persons and property must be at the disposal of Ethan Allen, who is more to be dreaded than death with all its terrors."

In October, 1780, Ethan Allen with the approval of the General Assembly entered into an agreement for Vermont, with Maj. Carleton for Gen. Haldimand, in pursuance of which the British force was withdrawn to Canada. On April 12th, 1781, Allen was chosen Brigadier-General again, which office he had previously resigned when inquiry was instituted by the General Assembly on charges made against him by William Hutchins and Simon Hathaway. Allen now declined to accept the office, but with the promise that he would render any service desired of him at any time, although not formally commissioned: that promise he faithfully observed.

The charges that were made against General Ethan Allen were infidelity to the country in connection with the Haldimand correspondence. Allen was very indignant, and while the charges were being read, he declared that the paper contained false and ignominious aspersions against him, and would hear no more of it, and went out of the house.

After the Assembly had heard the testimony of Joseph Fay and Stephen R. Bradley, the charges were withdrawn, and the House by resolution appointed a committee to thank Allen for his good services. The armistice entered into with the British by General Allen and others were not only approved of by the Vermont authorities but was for the benefit of both Vermont and the Confederacy. He betrayed nobody, but served his State. He was a party to a truce which protected Vermont and New York alike. These facts show no stain upon his character as an officer or patriot. Strictly speaking, he owed nothing to the Continental cause, as he was not in the service of Congress, nor was he or his State recognized by it. Congress left Vermont standing alone. Vermont declared herself to be, and in fact was, an independent State; and as such had a right to protect herself from every foe, by any means allowable to a sovereign State. That was Allen's ground, and the ground assumed and asserted by Gov. Chittenden. And as the result proved, it was the true ground. Vermont maintained her independence till she was admitted into the Union.

Allen's loyalty to the Confederacy as well as his magnanimous spirit was shown in his letter to Gov. Clinton of April 14, 1781, in which he tendered his own services, and the services of two other Vermont officers, to New York, to defend that State, against their cruel invaders. This also shows that Gov. Clinton's distrust of Allen's patriotism was unfounded. If we remember the former hostile relations between Allen and Clinton that letter must be deemed extraordinary. On the 11th day of January, 1782, Allen was appointed as one of the Committee to make a draught of the then state of the controversy, to be published. On Sept. 2d, 1782, Allen was commissioned Brigadier General to raise and equip 250 men to march into the County of Windham as a *posse comitatus* for the assistance of the civil authority of that County.

The noted "Catamount-Tavern" house at Bennington was the home of Ethan Allen for several years from 1770, after he came to reside in the New Hampshire Grants, as Vermont was then called. And Allen was sojourning at that house in the spring of 1775. It was from the Council room of that house that he, on May 3d, 1775, issued the order mustering the Green Mountain Boys for the capture of Ticonderoga. It was here in 1778, that David Redding, a traitor and a spy, was tried, convicted and sentenced to be executed by the Green Mountain Boys. Redding was convicted by a jury of six men, though he should have been tried by a jury of twelve men. And many were fearful that the gallows would be cheated of its prey by reason of that fact, and violence was apprehended. Whereupon Allen, who had just returned from his long English captivity, mounted a stump and waiving his hat, exlaimed, "attention the whole!" and then advised the multitude, to depart, peaceably, to their habitations, and return on the day fixed by the Governor and Council, and with an oath said, "you shall see somebody hung at all events, for if Redding is not then hung, I will be hung myself." Redding was retried by a jury of twelve men and hung as predicted by Allen.

In October 1779, Allen was appointed as one of the Committee to form the outlines of the plan to be pursued by the State for defense against the neighboring States in consequence of the acts of Congress. Allen was determined that Vermont should become absolutely independent or be admitted as a State of the American Union; and in no event be subject to New York. In May 1781, Dr. George Smith, who was one of the British commissioners to treat with Vermont, wrote to Gen. Haldimand that he heard Col. Allen declare, "that there was a north pole and a south pole, and should a thunder-gust come from the South, (Congress) they would shut the door opposite that point and open the door facing the North, (Canada).

Allen also wrote the "Concise refutation of the claims of New Hampshire and Massachusetts to the territory of Vermont." It was an able document but too long to be inserted here, and refer the reader to Page 223 of the II. Vol. of the "Governor and Council." Allen again showed his warm attachment to the interests of Vermont and his determination to stand by her against all enemies from whatever quarter they should come in his letter addressed to the President of Congress on March 9, 1781. After justifying his course in arranging for an armistice and an exchange of prisoners with General Haldimand, said, "I am confident that Congress will not dispute my sincere attachment to the cause of my country, though I do not hesitate to say I am fully grounded in opinion that Vermont has an indubitable right to agree on terms of cessation of hostilities with Great Britain, provided the United States persist in rejecting her application for a Union with them: For Vermont of all people, would be the most miserable were she obliged to defend the independence of the United Claiming States, and they at the same time at full liberty to overturn and ruin the independence of Vermont. I am as resolutely determined to defend the independence of Vermont as Congress is that of the United States, and rather than fail, will return with hardy Green Mountain Boys into the desolate caverns of the mountains, and wage war with human nature at large." Reference has been made to the fact that Ethan Allen with other leading Vermonters, took a hand in the correspondence and negotiations with the British in Canada for an armistice and exchange of prisoners for which he and the others were greatly censured. Allen on October 30, 1784, at the request of Gov. Chittenden, addressed to the public a document from which the following extract is taken. "The Foreign Policy of this Government has been demonstrated to be good in the final consequences of it, and the State is in good and respectable condition at present. It only remains that our courts of equity and law do impartial, and that our citizens support the honor and dignity of our laws and unitedly combine to support our liberty and independency."

In 1787, some unjust suspicions had been indulged in that Allen was in some way aiding

Shays's rebellion in Massachusetts. On the 3d of May, 1787, Ethan Allen wrote to Col. Benjamin Simmons of Mass., stating that that State "might depend upon the Vermont Government to aid in quelling the rebellion. Allen also wrote to the Governor of Mass., assuring him that no asylum would be given in the State of Vermont to the insurgents of the State of Mass." In December 1780, Ethan Allen applied to Gov. Trumbull of Connecticut in behalf of Vermont, for powder with which to ward off an expected invasion from Canada and the Governor ordered two tons of powder to be sent to the Green Mountain Boys from the powder mill of Elderkin and Wales of that State. This fact shows that while Allen and others in Vermont, from October 1780, until 1783, were trying to protect the State from the British army in Canada by diplomacy, they also relied upon the effects of powder. And they had it on hand for use.

Ethan Allen died in Burlington, Vt., February 12th, A. D. 1789, and was buried near the site of his monument in Green Mountain Cemetery. No portrait of Allen has ever been found. Allen was commissioned as a Brigadier-General by Vermont and engaged in the Revolutionary war, but was in that sense only a Brigadier-General in the American Army. The several statues of him are unlike and are said not to be perfect representations. The statues at Montpelier, Vt., and at the national capital at Washington, D. C., were produced by the same sculptor. It was a long time after the first move was made to erect a monument to his memory before the efforts were crowned with success. At Montpelier in Council on October 17th, 1831, it was resolved that a committee be appointed to inquire into the expediency of making an appropriation for the purpose of erecting a monument to the memory of Ethan Allen, late Brigadier-General in the American Army, and report by bill or otherwise.

The Legislature November 14th, 1855, appropriated a sum not exceeding two thousand dollars to erect a monument at the burial place of Ethan Allen, but it was finally placed at the State House at Montpelier. The preamble to the act appropriating the money, was as follows: viz, "Whereas, the courage, the perseverance, the sagacity, and the virtue of Ethan Allen zealously and constantly exercised in upholding the rights and liberties of the people of the New Hampshire Grants, and his successful efforts in establishing the sovereignty of the State of Vermont, against the active opposition of New Hampshire and New York, the wavering neutrality of the Federal government, and the artful overtures of the agents of the British Crown, have justly rendered his name the foremost, in the early history of this State, and entitle it to the grateful and reverent remembrance of the citizens thereof." The monument and statue erected at the place of his burial were completed, unveiled, and presented July 4th, 1873, with appropriate exercises. The monument is of Barre granite. The base of the pedestal is eight feet square on the ground and consists of two steps of granite, on which rests a die of solid granite six feet square. Above the pedestal rises a Tuscan shaft of granite, four and a half feet in diameter and forty-two feet high. Upon its capital on a base bearing the word "Ticonderoga," stands a heroic statue of Ethan Allen, eight feet four inches high. The expense of the statue was about $2,700, and was raised by subscription. Larkin G. Mead was the sculptor of this statue.

The Honorable John N. Pomeroy of Burlington, Vt., in his address at the ceremonies of the unveiling this statue on July 4th, 1873, said, "Long may it stand over the sacred ashes of the patriot soldier—the ornament of this beautiful spot on the banks of the Winooski appropriately backed by the Green Mountains on the East, and boldly facing the Adirondacks on the West—in view of that rural retreat where at the age of fifty-two years he died, and of that beautiful and historic Lake which ninety-seven years ago bore him and his Green Mountain Boys to the bold assault upon Ticonderoga, and which washes its interesting ruins. Yes, sir, long may it stand on its granite pedestal, through its coming centuries, to bear testimony to the high appreciation of a grateful people of one, who, with an ever active and dauntless spirit, by the pen and voice as well as the sword, warred against the most desperate and powerful enemies successfully, and largely contributed to the establishment of a State and the Independence of a Nation! And when time and storms shall crumble this stately column and statue, as crumble they must, and the antiquarian of the future shall explore the ruins and develope the contents of the leaden casket they enclosed, may it be divulged to a free and noble people, who shall still recognize this *Glorious Anniversary*, and cherish the memory of Ethan Allen.

In Governor Julius Converse's response, he said, "As an assurance of the just appreciation with which this honored gift is received, in the name of the State I promise that the same shall be vigilantly guarded and tenderly cherished as long as the marble shall endure, or deeds of noble daring shall find admirers amongst the brave and the good."

In the days of Ethan Allen, despotic power and oppresion were seen and felt on every hand. His very soul rebelled against every tyrannical act of whatever sort. And when the news of England's first attempts, with force of arms at Lexington and Bunker Hill, to enslave America, came to his ears, it electrified his mind, and he was ready and fully determined to cast in his lot in the interest of American independence. The welfare of the world and the American cause needed men full of the spirit of liberty, and who possessed the dauntless courage to oppose the Kings and Potentates of earth in their mad career to trample on the rights of mankind. The world needed such men as Ethan Allen to roll back the tide of slavery, injustice, oppression, and despotic barbarism, that the nations of the earth might move on under the banner of the free, and to a higher state of civilization. Ethan Allen stood in the front rank of those who made it possible to establish the independence of Vermont as a separate jurisdiction and the free *American Nation*.

CHAPTER XV.

THE TRIAL OF STEPHEN AND JESSE BOORN FOR THE ALLEGED MURDER OF RUSSEL COLVIN.

In the year 1819, Stephen and Jesse Boorn were arrested and tried in Bennington County, Vermont, for the alleged murder of Russel Colvin on May 10, 1812, at Manchester.

It appears that Stephen and Jesse Boorn and Russel Colvin had a quarrel May 10th, 1812, at Manchester, Vt., resulting in Colvin leaving the State, and was not heard from till after Stephen and Jesse Boorn had been tried and convicted of his alleged murder. The legal proceedings in the case and the evidence on which a conviction of the respondents was found, so far as I have been able to obtain it, was as follows: viz. "Lewis Colvin testified that, grandfather was gone to the street. Grandmother sent me to Mr. Sacket's. I did not return till night, as I went to Matterson's to carry meat. I next saw Stephen and Jesse at night down at the house—heard nothing from them about Russel's absence—heard Stephen say that on the day of the quarrel, Russel ran away to the mountain, and I did not hear Russel's name mentioned by them for a year. My mother had been gone over the mountain for some time. On the day of the quarrel, John was ploughing over the ridge, and when I ran home from the field, John was at home bating the team. I did not tell John of the quarrel—do not know the reason.

Lewis Colvin cross examined by Mr. Skinner. I told this story just before snow went off, one Sunday night, to Mr. Pratt and Mr. Sheldon. Sall, never told me to tell this story—do not remember that Stephen killed the woodchuck the day Russel went off, nor anything about it. Do not know where Jesse lived at that time. He did not live at Briggs' at that time. John was ploughing on the flat this side of the lot where the boys were at work; do not remember where Rufus (a younger brother) was at the time. A month after the quarrel, heard mentioned in the family of Russel's running off—Stephen and Jesse were not present. Stephen told me he would kill me if I told of his striking Russel. This was at the door the day after the quarrel. Lewis then said it was two days after.

Sallie Colvin. Better than four years ago Mr. Hitchcock told me I could not swear my child on any person if my husband was living. I went to my father's—stood in the stoop—Stephen told me I could swear the child, for Russel was dead and he knew it; and Jesse said I could swear it, but would not. When I returned from over the mountain, about five days after the disappearance of my husband, I asked Lewis where Russel was; he answered, gone to hell. I heard nothing at my father's what had become of my husband.

William Wyman. About three or four weeks before Colvin went off, Stephen came to my house and asked me if his father was obliged to support

Colvin's young ones. I told him yes. Stephen asked if it was not hard, and further said if there was no one else to put a stop to it, he would, and he said it with an oath.

William Farnsworth. In conversation with Stephen, about two months ago, I questioned him about killing, cooking and eating the woodchuck, and if he was at home then, and told him that his parents had denied that it was so; he however said that it was so, and that his parents had sworn themselves to the devil, and that their condition was worse than his own. I told Stephen that Johnson had stated that he (Stephen,) Jesse, Russel and the boy were together picking up stones the day Russel went off, and that his father and mother had denied it, and stated that he and Jesse were not then at home. Stephen replied that it made no odds what his father and mother had sworn to, but that what Tom Johnson had sworn to was true. I advised him to confess the whole facts which he knew.

Silas Merrill, (a fellow prisoner and in chains,) stated, that in June last, Jesse's father came to the prison, and spoke to Jesse—after the old man went away, Jesse appeared much afflicted—we went to bed and to sleep—Jesse waked up, and shook me, and wanted that I should wake up—he was frightened about something that had come into the window, and was on the bed behind him—he stated he wanted to tell me something, we got up and he went on to tell me, he said it was true that he was up in the lot together with Stephen, Russel Colvin and his son, picking up stones as Mr. Johnson had testified—that Stephen struck Colvin with a club and brought him to the ground—that Colvin's boy run, that Colvin got up, and Stephen gave him a second blow above his ear and broke his skull—that the blood gushed out—that his father came up, and asked if he was dead—they told him no, he then went off—soon after he came again and asked if he was dead, they told him no, and he again went off—soon after, the old man came the third time and asked if he was dead, they told him no—the old man said, *damn him*—Then he, Jesse, took him by the legs, Stephen by the shoulders, and the old man round the body, and carried him to the old cellar hole where the old man cut his throat, with a small pen-knife of Stephen's,—that they buried him in the cellar between daylight and dark, that he stood out one side and kept watch—that a jack-knife was found which he knew was Russel's, that he had often borrowed it to cut fish-poles—two or three days after, Stephen had Colvin's shoes on—that he, Jesse, spoke to Stephen and told him that Sal. would know the shoes—that he saw no more of them--the old man gave Stephen $100, and Stephen promised $25 of it to him. After Jesse was put into another room, when we were permitted to see each other, Jesse told me that he had informed Stephen of having told me the whole affair—Stephen then came into the room—I asked him if he did take the life of Colvin. He said he did not take the main life of Colvin, he said no more at that time. A week or ten days after, Stephen and I went up into the court room together—Stephen then said he had agreed with Jesse to take the whole business upon himself, and had made a confession which would only make manslaughter of it—I told him what Jesse had confessed and he said it was true. Jesse told me, that in February, 18 months or more after Colvin was buried, there came a thaw—that he and Stephen took up the body, secured the bones and remains in a basket and pulled up a plank in a place where they kept sheep, and put the bones under the floor—that the next spring the barn was burnt—that they took the bones and pounded them up and put them into a deep hole in the river—that the skull bone was burnt so that it crumbled to pieces, that his father scratched up some pieces and put them into a hollow birch stump near the road.

WITNESS CROSS EXAMINED BY MR. SKINNER.— Jesse, when he confessed the affair, did not say the body was removed anywhere till they carried it off as stated—that Jesse said Esq. Pratt was gone to talk with his wife, but she knew nothing about it.—Jesse wished me not to tell anything of what he said to me—I first told Mr. Pratt of Jesse's statement, if I recollect right—nobody was present in the court-room when Stephen told me as before mentioned—that Jesse one Sunday, when we were on the bed together told me he wished me to keep council, and that he understood that his wife had said something about keeping watch. I understood from Jesse that Russel struck Stephen first—that they had been *jawing* all the time the fore part of the day.

Mr. Attorney offers a written confession signed

by Stephen Boorn, dated August 27th, 1819; but it appearing that some promises of favor had been made to him previous to the confession being made, it was rejected by the court.

WILLIAM FARNSWORTH was produced to prove what Stephen told him when he and Stephen were alone, about his being present when Russel was killed. He was objected to by respondent's counsel because it was subsequent to the proposition made by Esq. Raymond; and Mr. Skinner offered to prove other proposals and promises made to the prisoners, at other times, before the conversation now offered to be proved.

The Court decided that the witness, Farnsworth, should be examined, and on preliminary examination, the witness stated that neither he, nor anybody else to his knowledge had done any thing directly or indirectly to influence the said Stephen to the talk he was now about to communicate.

The witness states—That about two or three weeks after the written confession, Stephen told me he killed Russel Colvin, that there was a quarrel, and that Russel struck at him, that he struck Russel and killed him, that he put him into the bushes, that he buried him and dug him up, put the remains under the barn which was burnt, the bones were taken up and put into the river, just above the deep hole, that he scraped up the remains and put them into a stump, that he knew the nails which were found were Colvin's, that no person was present, that he perpetrated the whole business himself. I asked him about the jack-knife;

he said it was Russel's, he knew it, as soon as he saw it. I told him the case looked dark, he replied, that if Jesse had kept his guts in they should have done well enough, that he put the pieces of bones under the stump through a hole between the roots and stamped the dirt down.—He said he wished he had back that paper, I asked him what paper: he said "Hav'ent you seen a paper I wrote?"

Here Mr. Skinner stated, that as Mr. Farnsworth had, contrary to his expectations, been allowed thus to testify, he now in behalf of the prisoners, called for the written confession, which was read as follows, viz.—

"May the tenth, 1812, I, about 9 or 10 o'clock, went down to David Glazier's bridge, and fished down below uncle Nathaniel Boorn's, and then went up across their farms, where Russel and Lewis was, being the nighest way, and set down and began to talk, and Russel told me how many dollars benefit he had been to father, and I told him he was a damned fool, and he was mad and jumped up, and we sat close together, and I told him to set down, you little tory, and there was a piece of a beech limb about two feet long, and he catched it up and struck at my head as I sat down and I jumped up and it struck me on one shoulder, and I catched it out of his hand and struck him a back-handed blow, I being on the north side of him, and there was a knot on it about one inch long. As I struck him I did think I hit him on his back, and he stooped down and that knot was broken off sharp, and it hit him on the back of the neck, close in his hair, and it went in about a half of an inch on that great cord, and he fell down, and then I told the boy to go down and come up with his uncle John, and he asked me if I had killed Russel—I told him no, but he must not tell that we struck one another. And I told him when we got away down, Russel was gone away, and I went back and he was dead, and then I went and took him and put him in the corner of the fence by the cellar-hole, and put briers over him and went home and went down to the barn and got some boards, and when it was dark I went down and took a hoe and boards, and dug a grave as well as I could, and took out of his pocket a little barlow knife, with about half of a blade, and cut some bushes, and put on his face, and the boards and put in the grave, & put him in four boards, on the bottom and on the top, and the other on the sides, and then covered him up and went home crying along, but I want afraid as I know on. And when I lived at William Boorn's I planted some potatoes, and when I dug them I went there and something I thought had been there, and I took up his bones and put them in a basket, and took the boards and put them on my potatoe hole, and then it was night, took the basket and my hoe and went down and pulled a plank in the stable floor, and then dug a hole, and then covered him up, and went in the house and told them I had done with the basket and took back the shovel, and covered up my potatoes that evening, and then when I lived under the west mountain, Lewis came and told me that father's barn was burnt up, the next day or the next but one, I came down and went to the barn and there was a few bones, and when they was at dinner I told them I did not want my dinner, and went and took them, and there want only a few of the biggest of the bones, and threw them in the river above Wyman's, and then went back, and it was done quic ktoo, and then was hungry by that time, and then went home, and the next Sunday I came down after money to pay the boot that I gave to boot between oxens, and went out there and scraped up the little things that was under the stump there, and told them I was going to fishing, and went, and there was a hole, and I dropped them in and kicked over the stuff, and that is the first any body knew it, either friends or foes, even my wife. All these I acknowlege before the world.

STEPHEN BOORN.

"Manchester, Aug. 27, 1819."

It appeared from the testimony of a number of respectable witnesses, that a jack-knife and a button were found at the old cellar-hole, which belonged to said Colvin immediately previous to his disappearance—that a number of bones and two nails were found in a hollow stump, one of which was supposed to be a thumb nail, but the other nail and the bones were so decayed that it was not ascertained whether they were animal or human bones—that some bones were found at the cellar-hole which were not human bones—that the respondents had said that Russel had gone to hell, and that they had put him where potatoes would not freeze; and that they had made various statements concerning the transaction, sometimes stating that they were present at the time of Colvin's disappearing, sometimes that they were at Pawlet, Rupert, Sandgate, and various other places.

The jury found both the respondents *guilty*, and they were sentenced to be executed on the 28th January, 1820.

Soon after the trial ended, a petition was sent to the Legislature, then sitting at Montpelier, for *pardon* or *commutation* of their punishment. The Hon. Judge Chase laid the facts before the Legislature, by their request, in a form of a report, and on the 15th of November, the house adopted the following resolution:—

"*Resolved*, That the prayer of Stephen and Jesse Boorn be so far granted, as to commute the punishment of death, for that of imprisonment for life, in the State's Prison at hard labor, in the case of the said Jesse Boorn, and that he have leave to bring in a bill accordingly; and that it is inexpedient to grant any relief to the said Stephen." On the question, *Shall the first clause of the resolution be adopted*, the yeas were 104—nays 31. On the second clause, yeas 94—nays 42. A bill was subsequently passed comporting with the first clause of the above resolution.

Stephen Boorn, on hearing that the Legislature had not granted him any relief, caused a notice to be published in the *Rutland Herald*, of the following import:—

"MURDER.—Printers of Newspapers throughout the United States, are desired to publish that Stephen Boorn, of Manchester, in Vermont, is sentenced to be executed for the murder of Russel Colvin, who has been absent about seven years. Any person who can give information of said Colvin, may save the life of the innocent by making immediate communication. Colvin is about five feet five inches high, light complexion, light hair, blue eyes, about forty years of age.

"Manchester, Vt. Nov. 26, 1819."

What can be suposed were the feelings of the public on seeing the foregoing advertisement? Could any person believe that Colvin was alive, after having heard the confessions of the two prisoners, that they had murdered him, buried him, dug up his bones, buried them under the barn, the barn afterwards being burned, and the bones taken up again and thrown into the river, Colvin's hat, button and knife found, Stephen with Colvin's shoes on, and Colvin not heard of for more than seven years? But after all, it turns out that Colvin is still in "the land of the living," although various opinions were formed as to the correctness of the following letter published in the New-York Post.

Shrewsbury, Monmouth, N. J. Dec. 6.
"To the Editor of the N. Y. Evening Post.

"Sir—Having read in your paper of Nov. 26th last, of the conviction and sentence of Stephen and Jesse Boorn, of Manchester, Vermont, charged with the murder of Russel Colvin, and from facts which have fallen within my own knowledge, and not knowing what facts may have been disclosed on their trial, and wishing to serve the cause of humanity, I would state as follows, which may be relied on: Some years past, (I think between five and ten) a stranger made his appearance in this county, and being inquired of, said his name was Russel Colvin (which name he answers to at this time)—that he came from Manchester, Vermont—he appeared to be in a state of mental derangement, but at times gave considerable account of himself—his connections, acquaintances, &c. He mentions the name of Clarissa, Rufus, &c. Among his relations he has mentioned the Boorns above—Jesse, as Judge, (I think) &c. &c. He is a man rather small in stature—round favored, speaks very fast, and has two scars on his head, and appears to be between 30 and 40 years of age. There is no doubt but that he came from Vermont, from the mention that he has made of a number of places and persons there, and probably is the person supposed to have been murdered. He is now living here, but so completely insane, as not to be able to give satisfactory account of himself, but the connexions of Russel Colvin might know by seeing him. If you think proper to give this a place in your columns, it may possibly lead to a discovery that may save the lives of innocent men—if so, you will have the pleasure, as well as myself of having served the cause of humanity. If you give this an insertion in your paper, pray be so good as to request the different editors of newspapers in New-York and Vermont, to give it a place in theirs.

"I am, Sir, with sentiments of regard, yours, &c.
"TABER CHADWICK."

On the promulgation of the above letter in New York, the members of the corporation of the city sent a Mr. Whelpley, of that city, who was formerly acquainted with said Colvin in Vermont, to

New-Jersey to ascertain the fact. Mr. Whelpley, being satisfied that it was the same Colvin who was supposed to have been murdered, he was conducted to Manchester, through New-York, Albany and Troy, at which places the streets were literally filled with spectators to get a peep at the murdered Colvin! On the 22d day of December, 1819, a large assembly of people from various towns adjoining, had convened at Manchester to behold the entrance of Colvin into the town, in order to see the *dead man*, and hear his story! His entrance was announced by the firing of cannon, and Stephen Boorn was immediately released from prison, and his chains, to behold his old acquaintance!

Russel Colvin came to the house of William Polhemus, in Dover, Monmouth county, New-Jersey, in March or April, 1813, somewhat deranged and has lived there since until his removal as above stated; and after staying in Manchester a day or two, he returned back to New-Jersey. He did not give any particular account of the quarrel mentioned in the trial, nor would he own his wife, from which circumstances some have supposed that he was not the man supposed to have been murdered, but some other person every way resembling the said Colvin; and I must confess, that if there had been no stronger proof of the return of Russel Colvin to Manchester than that every person in Manchester formerly acquainted with him, knew him to be the same Colvin, I should have my doubts; but on inquiring of the people of Manchester, and ascertaining that the man returned for Russel Colvin, would call the people who he was formerly acquainted with by their names and their titles, such as *Esq.*, *Capt.*, *uncle*, &c. my doubts are removed, and I am in the full belief of the said Russel Colvin having returned to Manchester as stated.

Various are the opinions relating to this mysterious affair, but one thing is certain—that is, that Stephen Boorn, Jesse Boorn and Russel Colvin had a quarrel as stated by Thomas Johnson, and the Boorns' confessions, and I think also that Colvin received a bad wound from Stephen, and that Russel went off without his hat and shoes unknown to Stephen or Jesse, and not being heard of for a number of years, Stephen and Jesse were no doubt of the opinion that Colvin had died of the wounds received from them. After they were examined and committed for trial, knowing they had told different stories about the transaction, and Colvin not being heard of, and others advising them to confess, they were induced to make the confessions and in such a way as to make Colvin the first aggressor, and if possible save themselves from the gallows.

CHAPTER XVI.

THE TOWN OF JERICHO.

The town of Jericho in the County of Chittenden was one of the one hundred and twenty-nine towns that were granted by Benning Wentworth, the Governor of New Hampshire, when that State claimed jurisdiction over the territory now called Vermont. The town is in lat. 44°—27′, and long. 4,° 4′. The 129 towns were all granted between Jan. 2nd, 1749, and Nov. 4th, 1764. The grant for Bennington bears date on the 3d day of January, 1749, it being the first town granted. Jericho was granted the 7th day of June, 1763. The grant was in the words, figures and names following:

JERICHO.

*2—33   *Province of New-Hampshire.

Jerico   GEORGE THE THIRD,

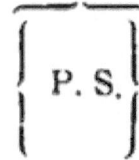

By the Grace of God, of Great-Britain, France and Ireland, KING, Defender of the Faith &c.

To all Persons to whom these Presents shall come.

Greeting.

KNOW ye, that We of Our special Grace, certain Knowledge, and meer Motion, for the due Encouragement of settling a *New Plantation* within our said Province, by and with the Advice of our Trusty and Well-beloved BENNING WENTWORTH, Esq; Our Governor and Commander in Chief of

Our said Province of NEW-HAMPSHIRE in NEW-ENGLAND, and of our COUNCIL of the said Province; HAVE upon the Conditions and Reservations herein after made, given and granted, and by these Presents, for us, our Heirs, and Successors, do give and grant in equal Shares, unto Our loving Subjects, Inhabitants of Our said Province of NEW HAMPSHIRE, and Our other Governments, and to their Heirs and Assigns for ever, whose names are entered on this Grant, to be divided to and amongst them into Seventy two equal Shares, all that Tract or Parcel of Land situate, lying and being within our said Province of NEW-HAMPSHIRE, containing by Admeasurement, 23040 Acres, which Tract is to contain Six Miles square, and no more; out of which an Allowance is to be made for High Ways and unimprovable Lands by Rocks, Ponds, Mountains and Rivers. One Thousand and Forty Acres free, according to a Plan and Survey thereof made by Our said Governor's Order, and returned into the Secretary's Office, and hereunto annexed, butted and bounded as follows, *Viz.* Beginning at the Southerly or South Easterly Corner of Essex at the Northerly side of Onion or French River (so called) from thence Easterly up said River so far as to make Six Miles on a straight Line, allowing the same to be Perpendicular with the South Easterly Line of said Essex from thence Northerly a Parralell Line with the south Easterly line of said Essex six Miles from thence Westerly about six Miles to the North Easterly corner of said Essex, from thence southerly by the Easterly Line of said Essex Six Miles to the place begun at

—And that the same be, and hereby is Incorporated into a Township by the Name of Jerico And the Inhabitants that do or shall hereafter inhabit the said Township, are hereby declared to be Enfranchized with and Intitled to all and every the Priviledges and Immunities that other Towns within Our Province by Law Exercise and Enjoy: And further, that the said Town as soon as there shall be Fifty Families resident and settled thereon, shall have the Liberty of holding *Two Fairs*, one of which shall be held on the

And the other on the
annually, which Fairs are not to continue longer than the respective
following the said   and that as soon as the said Town shall consist of Fifty Families, a Market may be *opened and kept one or more Days in each   *2—434 Week, as may be thought most advantagious to the Inhabitants. Also, that the first Meeting for the Choice of Town Officers, agreable to the Laws of our said Province, shall be held on the 14th July next which said Meeting shall be Notified by Mr. John Burling who is hereby also appointed the Moderator of the said first meeting, which he is to Notify and Govern agreable to the Laws and Customs of our said Province; and that the annual Meeting for ever hereafter for the Choice of such Officers for the said Town, shall be on the second Tuesday of *March* annually, To HAVE and to HOLD the said Tract of Land as above expressed, together with all Priviliges and Appurtenances, to them and their respective Heirs

and Assigns forever, upon the following Conditions, viz.

I. That every Grantee, his Heirs or Assigns shall plant and cultivate five Acres of Land within the Term of five Years for every fifty Acres contained in his or their Share or Proportion of Land in said Township, and continue to improve and settle the same by additional Cultivations, on Penalty of the Forfeiture of his Grant or Share in the said Township, and of its reverting to Us, our Heirs and Successors, to be by Us or Them Regranted to such of Our Subjects as shall effectually settle and cultivate the same.

II. That all white and other Pine Trees within the said Township, fit for Masting Our Royal Navy, be carefully preserved for that Use, and none to be cut or felled without Our special License for so doing first had and obtained, upon the Penalty of the Forfeiture of the Right of such Grantee, his Heirs and Assigns, to Us, our Heirs and Successors, as well as being subject the Penalty of any Act or Acts of Parliament that now are, or hereafter shall be Enacted.

III. That before any Division of the Land be made to and among the Grantees, a Tract of Land as near the Centre of the said Township as the Land will admit of, shall be reserved and marked out for Town Lots, one of which shall be alloted to each Grantee of the Contents of one Acre.

IV. Yielding and paying therefor to Us, our Heirs and Successors for the Space of ten Years, to be computed from the Date hereof, the Rent of one Ear of Indian Corn only, on the twenty-fifth Day of *December* annually, if lawfully demanded, the first payment to be made on the twenty-fifth Day of *December*, 1763.

V. Every Proprietor, Settler or Inhabitant, shall yield and pay unto Us, our Heirs and Successors yearly, and every Year forever, from and after the Expiration of ten Years from the abovesaid twenty-fifth Day of DECEMBER, namely, on the twenty-fifth Day of DECEMBER, which will be in the Year of our Lord 1773 *One shilling* Proclamation Money for every Hundred Acres he so owns, settles or possesses, and so in Proportion for a greater or lesser tract of the said Land; which Money shall be paid by the respective Persons abovesaid, their Heirs or Assigns, in our *Council Chamber in Portsmouth* or to such Officer or Officers as shall be appointed to receive the same; and this to be in Lieu of all other Rents and Services whatsoever.

In Testimony whereof we have caused the Seal of our said Province to be hereunto affixed. Witness BENNING WENTWORTH, Esq; Our Governor and Commander in Chief of Our said Province, the Seventh Day of June In the Year of our LORD CHRIST, One Thousand Seven Hundred and Sixty three And in the Third Year of Our Reign.

By HIS EXCELLENCY's Command,
With Advice of COUNCIL,
  P T Atkinson Junr Sec^{ry}
 Pro^v New Hamp^r June 7th 1763
 Recorded According to the Original Charter under the Prov^e Seal
    P T Atkinson Junr Sec^{ry}

*2--435 *The Names of the Grantees of Jerico (Viz)

Edwd Burling	James Burling
Thos Burling	Walter Burling
Saml Burling	Benja Burling
John Sackett	James Sackett Junr
John Sackett Junr	Danl Wiggins
John Wiggins	Danl Wiggins Junr
Willm Wiggins	Benja Wiggins
Willm Latham	Danl Latham
Lancaster Burling	Amos Dodge
Amos Dodge Junr	Arthur Jarvis
James Jarvis	James Jarvis Junr
Charles Jarvis	Benja Bill
Philip Brasher	Abrm Brasher
Willm D Peyster Junr	Morris Earle
Barnard De Forcest	John Bates
Amos Underhill Junr	David Underhill
Soloman Underhill	Edmd Underhill
Saml Laurence	James Laurence
Thos Grenell	Thos Grenell Junr
William Mercier	John Dyer Mercier
John Burling	Philip Burling
John Bowne	John Vermilye
Nichs H Bogart	John Martine
Jereah Martine	John Guerinaux
Peter Tetard	Saml Gillat
Charles Davis	Stephen Davis
John Davis	James Davis
James McCreedy	John Cornell of Flushing
Henry Matthews	Saml Averil
Collo Saml Barr	Joseph Blanchard
Dr John Hale	Benja Jarvis
Thos Grenell Senr;	

Hon John Temple, Theo: Atkinson, Mk H^g Wentworth Esqrs.

His EXCELLENCY Benning Wentworth Esqr a Tract of Land to Contain Five Hundred Acres as marked B—W—in the Plan which is to be Accounted two of the within Shares, One whole share for the Incorporated Society for the Propagation of the Gospel in Foreign Parts, One Share for a Glebe for the Church of England as by Law Establish'd, One Share for the First settled Minister of the Gospel, & One Share for the benefit of a School in said Town—

Province of New Hamp^r June 7th 1763

Recorded according to the Back of the Original Charter of Jericho under the Pro^v Seal

P T Atkinson Jun Sec^{ry}

The town contained 23,040 acres. By an Act of the Legislature, Richmond was incorporated Oct. 27th, 1794, and a part of Jericho, together with a part of Williston, and a part of Huntington (then called New Huntington) were taken to make that town.

The town is well watered with springs and brooks. The Onion or Winooski River (in the early history of Vermont called the French River) washes the southwestern boundary. Brown's river enters the town at the northeast from Underhill and runs through the town into Essex. Lee River also takes its rise in the town of Underhill, entering Jericho in the east part, and running through the town the distance of six miles, and unites with Brown's River at the village of Jericho in the west part of the town. Mill Brook enters the town rom Bolton, and runs into Onion River about half-way from Richmond to Essex. Jericho is a good farming town, and well adapted to raising most kinds of grain and grasses.

In the early days of Jericho there were but few families that had come to settle there to fell the forest and to establish homes for themselves. Those that first came were poor and had to struggle with poverty, and hardships incident to a pioneer life, and were exposed to cruel treatment from the British and hostile Indians, and were required to be watchful to guard against capture by the enemy. At first there were a few families who settled in the south part of the town near Onion River, and a family by the name of Joseph Brown settled on Brown's River near Underhill in 1774. On Oct. 16, 1780, hostile Indians from Canada, inspired and aided by the British, made their way to and burnt the village of Royalton, and on their return the party divided on Onion River near Bolton, one division going down the river to Lake Champlain and made their way back to Canada, while the other division passed over through Jericho to said family of Browns on Brown's River. Before the Indians had found the residence of the Brown family, a man by the name of Gibson who had been hospitably entertained by Brown for some time, while hunting in that section, fell into the hands of the Indians. He told the Indians if they would let him go, he would lead them where they could get a whole family. The Indians agreed to this and were led by Gibson to the house of Brown; six savages entered the house and took prisoners Mr. Brown and his wife and two children, (not their own,) who were living with them at the time. A man by the name of Old residing with Brown, seeing the Indians enter, jumped from a window and escaped to the family of Roderick Messenger living in the south part of the town near Onion River. At the time the Indians reached the house Brown's two boys, Charles and Joseph, of 14 and 12 years of age respectively, were not at home. When the two boys returned home at night they were also taken prisoners by the Indians laying in wait for them. The Indians after securing their prisoners, killed the cattle, sheep and hogs belonging to Mr. Brown, set the house on fire and started for Montreal. The prisoners suffered much on their journey through the woods, from fatigue and hunger. On their arrival at St. Johns, they were sold to British officers at eight dollars per head, and by them retained as prisoners nearly three years and kept at hard labor as servants for their masters, and were allowed but miserable fare. The said sons, Joseph and Charles, fled from the British service and imprisonment in the spring of 1783, and returned to their Jericho home, where their father and mother joined them when they were released upon the declaration of peace between Great Britain and the United States.

The said Charles, the eldest boy that was captured, was the father of Zina Brown, formerly a Methodist minister, and Luther Brown who formerly lived in the brick house near the cemetery a little east of the village of Underhill, and the other boy, Joseph, was the grandfather of Henry M. Brown, who now lives near the place where the two boys were captured.

The first three settlers, and who came from the western part of Massachusetts, were the said Joseph Brown, Senior, Roderick Messenger already referred to, and Azariah Rood, who settled in town in 1774.

The town was organized March 22, 1786, at a meeting warned by John Fassette, Judge of the Supreme Court. At this meeting James Farnsworth was chosen Moderator; Lewis Chapin, Clerk; Peter McArthur, Constable. At another meeting held June 13th, 1786, Azariah Rood, Joseph Hall and Jedediah Lane were chosen Selectmen. Jedediah Lane was the first Representative of the town to the General Assembly and was elected Nov. 29, 1786.

Among the early settlers were David T. Stone, who came to town about 1791, from Connecticut, Gaius Pease and George Brutts came to town about the same time and all settled on Lee River. The following, a well authenticated incident, is related of these three men who believed in exact justice. One Casey, who lived in the same neighborhood, for some offence took his son to the woods at night, and after a dreadful whipping left him tied to a tree until his screams brought the neighbors to his relief in the early morning. Notice was given of the transaction to the executors of the law, in this case, who appeared at the abode of Casey, the next night, and with the "beech seal" and rawhide well laid on sought to change the disposition of Casey.

Among the early settlers were John Lyman, the father of John, (who was Clerk of the town for many years,) and Daniel who lived in Jericho for many years and till their death after the death of their father; David and Jedediah Field who came to Jericho from Guilford, Conn., about 1797, Martin Chittenden, Nathaniel Bostwick, John Lee, Caleb Nash, Benjamin Day, Polli C. Packard, Jesse Gloyd, Jesse Thompson, James Marsh, Isaac Benham, Oliver Lowrey, Truman Barney, Truman Galusha, Nathaniel Pliny, Lemuel Blackman, Elias Bartlett, Hosea Spaulding and Timothy Bliss.

One of the first roads that was built through Jericho, was built, as it was a custom in those days in a direct line over high hills, ran from what is now called Underhill Flatts to Onion River, over the hill and by the now farm house of Eugene Herrick, and crossed Lee River near where W. R. Macomber now lives, and from there over the hill and by where Arthur K. Morse now resides, to Onion River.

It may be of some local interest to record where persons who were for a long time citizens of the town, resided. It will not be my purpose to be definite as to the time when such person's residence commenced or when they removed or died; nor will it be practicable for the writer, to state the residence of the inhabitants before 1857, when he became a citizen of the town, but will state the residence of the persons hereafter named from about the year 1857 to about 1870. On the road leading from Jericho to Onion River, Daniel Lyman and his son Charles H., owned and lived on the farm where Mrs. E. L. Sargent now resides, and Horace Babcock a little east of the same road on land now owned by Wert Brigham. David Hutchinson lived on the farm where his son James H. Hutchinson now lives; Orin Crane resided on the next farm to the south. Orley Thompson owned and lived upon the farm a little east from said road, that is now owned by Hosea Wright.

On the road running up Onion River Rufus Bishop lived on the place where Daniel B. Bishop now lives, and the said Daniel B. resided on his farm a little farther towards Richmond. Leet A. Bishop resided a long time on the farm now occupied by E. C. Fay, and until he removed to Williston. George Goodrich lived on the road leading from the Leet A. Bishop place to Jericho Center, on the farm now owned and occupied by Edgar L. Barber. On the cross road leading from the said Leet A. Bishop place to the road leading from Jericho Center to Richmond there resided Sylvester and Cyrus Tarbox on the farm where the survivor Cyrus now lives; and about one-half mile to the east of said Tarbox farm resided Solomon Powell on a farm which he afterwards sold and removed therefrom.

On the road running from Richmond to Jericho Center Jesse Gloyd has resided many years near Richmond line, where he and his son now live. About half a mile north from the last named place Dea. Ezra Elliott resided on the farm where George E. Cunningham now resides. Lewis Marsh resided for many years a little north of the Elliott farm, and Harvey Ford lived on the north bank of Mill Brook as you go north on said road. Subal Palmer lived at the top of the hill a few rods north of the Ford place and kept spruce beer for sale, and for a sign indicating what article he had to sell, he had placed over his door, "Spruss Bier." A little further towards the Center Henry Borrowdale lived on his large farm, where S. W. Hoyt now lives. At the forks of the road where the Mill Brook road connects with the road to Richmond John T. Clapp lived many years, and till he removed to Jericho Corners. A little to the north of the Clapp place where the road is lined with handsome maple trees, there resided Dana Bicknell, where B. G. Brown now resides. Said Bicknell afterwards removed to where his children, Dustin and Emma now live. On the same street Josiah Townsend formerly resided. Russell French resided in the brick house north of the Bicknell place, where his son Warren F. French now lives.

On the Mill Brook road there lived Rollin M. Clapp, A. S. Wood, Lyman Hall, and William Nealy. There lived on the East hill on the road leading across said brook, Harvey Field on the farm where his grandson Robert Field now lives. Silas J. Haskins, Ansel, Daniel, Zenas, and Horace Nash lived at Nashville.

Martin Howe, Theodocia and Lavina Monroe, and Harry Hoskins lived on the road running from Nashville to Lee River. There lived on the road leading from Nashville to West Bolton Judge Andrew Warner on the farm now occupied by Charles and Willie Bentley. Hubbel B. Smith lived at the end of a spur of a road where Newell Story now lives. Further east on the main road leading to Bolton there lived Chauncey Abbott. Benjamin B. Hatch lived on the farm where Moses Leary and his son now live; Billings Stroud lived on the same road near Bolton line. On the road leading towards Jonesville there lived Chesman Johnson and John McAndlass. Nathan Smith lived at the end of the spur of road leading north from near the Moses Leary place.

South from Jericho Center near the Cemetery Hoyt M. Chapin lived, and on the same road running round to the Richmond road there lived Henry Gibbs and Nathan Richardson. Nathan Benham lived on the farm where his son-in-law, H. H. Hall, now resides. On the road running north-easterly from the Common there lived William Bartlett; and Norman Wight lived at the north end of that road. James Morse lived and carried on mercantile business at the south side of the Common until he moved on to his farm, where Arthur K. Morse now lives. Elias Bartlett lived a little north of the Common, on the road leading to Jericho village. Joel B. Bartlett lived at the west side of the Common near the store where George Styles has since resided. E. H. Lane was for a long time a merchant, doing business on the west side of the Common. Hosea Spaulding lived in the red house north of the village on the road towards Jericho, where Wells Lee now owns, and John Chambers lived at the corner of the road a little north of the said Spaulding place; Martin Bartlett, the land surveyor, owned and lived on the farm now owned by Isaac C. Stone.

William Johnson, Hira A. Percival, Phillip Carrol and Bryan Reddy lived on the Plains on the south road leading from Jericho to Jericho Center, and Alexander Miller lived east of the Plains on the hill where Henry Smith now resides. Charles Hilton lived on the hill on the road leading from the said Miller place to Onion River where Carl Schillhammer now lives, and where W. R. Macomber formerly lived. Vincent Varney lived on the road leading from the said Hilton place to Jericho Center on the farm where Sarah Varney and Jed Varney now reside. On the road from there to Onion River there lived James Morse. John Smith; and Gordon Smith lived where he now lives. On the road leading from the said Miller place to Jericho Center Everet W. Johnson lived a little east of said Miller place, and James Graham resided on the farm where Oliver H. Brown now lives.

Allen Balch owned and lived on the farm where W. W. Ring now lives on the Lee River road leading up said river from Jericho village; Milton Ford lived where Matthew J. Tierney resides; Addison M. Ford lived where he now does; T. Chittenden Galusha resided where John Schillhammer now lives. Henry B. Percival lived on the farm where W. I. Byington now lives; Lyman Stimson lived on the farm now owned by Sidney S. Thomson, and carried on the wheelwright and blacksmith business. Robert Gibson lived and carried on the shoe and boot making and repair business for many years and until he died, a little east of the Stimson place near the bridge. Asa Church lived at the corner of the roads where the Lee River road crosses the road leading to Underhill.

Lucius L. Lane lived up the river on the farm where L. H. Chapin now resides, and Reuben Lee lived on the farm now occupied by his son-in-law, Luther M. Howe. Silas Ransom lived on the farm now occupied by B. B Mattimore; Cyrus Lane lived on the farm now owned and occupied by Martin V. Willard and son George. Ezra Kinney lived near the school house. Antoine Laflash lived where Frank E. Kinney now does; Hiram Stone lived on the farm where James Morse now resides. Simeon Pease, Benjamin Joy and Thomas Choate lived on the road running from Lee River near said Hiram Stone farm to Underhill Center. Said Pease lived where Ezra J. Brown now lives. On the Lee River road, Leonard Pease lived on the farm now known as the McGinnis farm.

Nehemiah Prouty lived in the two story house adjoining the Leonard Pease farm. David Benson lived where his widow resides, and Edgar Barney owned the saw-mill and lived on the premises there situated, where J. E. Burrows now resides. There lived on the upper road running from Lee River towards Underhill Center Isaac Smith and P. B. Smith his son; Stephen Hale lived on a farm on the same road leading to West Bolton, where John McGee now lives. Benial McGee, a litegous man, lived in the north-east corner of the town. James Martin lived where F. N. Fuller now lives, and on the same road F. A. Fuller, D. W. Doncaster lived for many years. Alva Pease lived on the farm where his son, Frank W. Pease, now resides; Leon Gauvin lived in the brick house on the same road, and Oatis Church lived on the farm next to Bolton line.

On the road running from Lee River to Underhill Flatts (so called) Ezra Church lived on the farm where Asa Church now lives; Cyrus Packard lived where his son Harrison now resides, and Edmund Martin lived on his farm situated on the road leading from the Packard farm easterly to Lee River.

Homer Rawson lived where he now resides, on the corner of the roads, one leading northerly on to the Cilley hill (so-called.) Dr. Jesse Thompson lived where James McLane now lives, and C. M. Spaulding lived where Clark R. Varney resides, and Henry Oakes lived where Albert Cilley since lived till he died. Uzziel S. Whitcomb lived where James Hanley now lives, and Hiram Martin lived on the farm where Nelson A. Prior now resides, and Oliver Lowrey in the next house to the east of the Martin place, while Albert Lowrey owned and occupied the farm where his son, O. J. Lowrey, now lives, and George P. Howe lived on the farm now owned by Ira Hawley; Arthur L. Castle lived for many years and till he died, on the farm now owned by Irving A. Irish, and Selah Babcock a few rods to the east, adjoining the Castle farm. Lucius S. Barney lived on the farm now owned by his son, Truman B. Barney; and Hiram B. Day on the farm now owned by Elmer G. Irish.

Joseph Brown resided on the farm where his son Henry Brown now lives, on the road leading to Jericho Center; and Albert Gleason lived on the farm now owned by his son, I. R. Gleason. Rextus Orr lived on the middle road running south from the said Hiram B. Day farm, and on the same road, about a mile to the south, Newell Marsh lived, on the farm that was afterwards owned by Martin H. Packard, and now owned by M. B. Small. Abijah Whitton and his son, John P. Whitton, lived on the first farm on the road leading south from the said Albert Lowrey farm; Rollin M. Townsend lived where Loren Jackson now lives, on the same road; and Harvey Booth lived on the farm where his son, Hawley C. Booth, resides; while Hiram Booth lived on the farm where William Schillhammer resides. Julius H. Hapgood lived on the farm now owned by S. A. Hale on the Race-way road.

At the Flatts village, Charles Hubbell lived near the covered bridge that spans Brown's River; and Edward S. Whitcomb, Senior, owned the farm and store situated where C. H. Hayden is carrying on the mercantile business. Robert Jackson lived on the farm now owned by Frank S. Jackson on the road leading to Underhill Center; and Luther Brown owned and lived in the brick house on the same road. The Arthur "Bostwick House," afterwards the "Dixon House," that was run as a hotel and summer boarding house for many years, stood on the road leading north through the main part of the village, a few rods north-westerly from said Whitcomb store building. L. M. Dixon lived where E. S. Whitcomb now resides; Julius H. Bostwick owned and lived upon the premises where Samuel A. Hale lives; Isaac C. Bostwick lived at the corner of the said village road and the Raceway road; and Joseph Kingsbury lived on the opposite corner on the farm where Walter E. Russell and his son John now reside. Amos Eastman lived in the next house north, nearly opposite of the Episcopal church. Samuel B. Bliss lived on the premises where his son Edwin Bliss resides, and carried on the blacksmith business there for many years; and George Claflin on the place on the opposite side of the road. Stephen S. Brown, formerly an eminent lawyer, resided westerly from the Claflin place, at the end of a spur of a road. Dr. A. F. Burdick lived many years where he now does, nearly opposite the Methodist church.

Benajah C. Buxton lived on the saw mill premises on the south bank of Brown's River, on the road leading from where Homer Rawson lives to the "Cilley Hill," and Patrick Russell on the opposite side of Brown's River, on the premises where Julia E. Moulton now resides. George B. Oakes owned the farm where Mrs. Henry L. Lane now lives; and Andrew J. Cilley lived on the farm where George White now resides. Spencer Cilley lived on the first farm on said "Cilley Hill" (so-called); and Walter E. Russell owned and occupied the next farm north till he moved on to the Kingsbury farm at Underhill Flatts (so-called); and George W. Smith lived for many years, and till his death, where his son-in-law, Henry T. White, now resides.

At the village of Jericho, sometimes called Jericho Corners, Rollin M. Galusha resided in the brick house below the bridge; and Horatio B. Barney lived in the brick house below the "Tavern House" that was kept for many years by his brother, Martin C. Barney. Solomon Papineau lived where Joseph Bissonett now lives. George B. Oakes lived on the corner where E. B. Williams now resides; David Fish lived for many years where Charles E. Percival now lives; and Erastus Field, on the opposite side of the street. Anson Field, Sr., lived at the corner of the road opposite of the said George B. Oakes' place. Sylvanus Blodgett lived on the same premises where the Lucius Irish house now stands, and his son R. S. Blodgett a few rods further east; Orlin Rood lived for many years where his son, D. E. Rood, resides. Dea. Truman Galusha lived in the brick house on the hill where H. N. Percival now resides. R. Loomis Galusha lived on said Truman Galusha place, after the death of his father Truman, till his death.

The writer lived for many years above the Barney "Tavern House," on the opposite side of the street; and Ferdinand Beach lived on the west side of the street as the street rises the hill. J. H. Hutchinson lived at the top of the hill west of the school house. Luther Prouty occupied the brick house and premises on the opposite side of the street from the school house where Horace S. Wood now resides. Joel Davis lived in the house west of the Methodist church, which house Calvin Morse afterwards owned and lived in, and is where H. A. Percival now lives. Dr. George Howe lived, before 1857, on the same street, in the house now owned by Anson Field; and Dr. Dennison Bliss lived on the south side of the street where Warren Fellows now resides. Anson Field lived where L. F. Wilbur now resides.

John Oakes resided on the farm now owned by Glenn Booth, and William E. Oakes resided where Frank Howe now lives; and Nathan Porter lived where Mrs. M. B. Atchinson now lives, it being one of the oldest houses in the village. Simon Davis and Henry M. Field, his son-in-law, lived where Anson Field now does, on the street running north from the main street in the village; Joseph Jocko lived at the north end of the bridge, on the east side of said road; while Hiram B. Fish lived in the next house north from the Jocko place. John Fairchild lived on the opposite side of the road, adjoining the saw-mill premises.

The Baptist and the Methodist churches now occupied by those denominations respectively were built in the year 1858.

There are two places in Jericho with the buildings thereon that have an interesting history that should receive more than a passing notice: viz., the Academy at Jericho Center and the Brick Church at the Village of Jericho.

At Jericho Center the Academy building and the land where it stands were conveyed by deed by Lewis Chapin on the 6th day of September, A. D., 1825, in words and figures following: viz.:—

"Know all men by these Presents that I Lewis Chapin of Jericho do by these presents give grant, convey and confirm unto the owners and proprietors of the building called the Baptist Meeting House and select School Room, the ground on it—the spot to contain 40 feet on the road and forty feet back—being forty feet on each of the four lines. To have and to hold the above granted and bargained premises to them," etc.

Said deed was received for record by John Lyman, Jr., Town Clerk, and recorded in Vol. 4, on Page 500 of the land records of Jericho. On October 28th, 1828, the Legislature of Vermont passed an Act of incorporation, by which Harvey Smith, Nathaniel Blackman, Wm. P. Richardson, Simon Bicknell, Hosea Spaulding, Simeon Parmelee, Septimeus Robinson, and Seth Cole, and their associates and successors, were constituted a body politic and corporate, the Trustees and Members of Jericho Academy, with powers to hold property, real and personal, including a library.

At the Centennial anniversary of the organization of the First Congregational Church of Jericho in 1891, Professor Joseph S. Cilley, who was educated at said Academy when the school there was having its palmy days, prepared and read at the anniversary a paper, which he gave me permission, before he deceased, to have appear in this book. The paper was as follows, Viz.:

"There are, in the lives of us all, occasions of special interest and of great importance. Seasons of success and failure, of victory and defeat; times of gladness and of sorrow; days of exceeding brightness and the deepest darkness; hours of the purest delight and of the deepest grief.

Nor are these times, days and hours ended when passed; they exist in memory forever, way marks in the journey of life over which we often pass in review to find return of joy or renewal of grief. This is a day especially calling for such review. One hundred years in the life of the First Cong. Church in Jericho end to-day. Most of those here assembled will find their review of life limited by much less than half the century, but others there are whose early recollections extend time much farther gone than that. Of that number I am one, and I am glad to live over again in memory, for a day, my early life in Jericho, my union with this Church in those boyhood days, and my pleasant hours spent as student in your academy, concerning which Institution I was invited to speak to-day.

So to live again in my early home, with early friends, and amid the sports and delights of boyhood days, is joy indeed, though lessened much by the thought that most of the things that then were, now are not.

In very early life Jericho was my home for two or three years, and again, years intervening, I was here a large share of the time for years in attendance at the Academy. And as I think of those bright days, I sympathize most fully with Holmes, as he exclaims:

> "O, for one hour of youthful joy,
> Give back my twentieth Spring,
> I'd rather laugh a bright haired boy,
> Than reign a gray beard king."

But my recollections of the Academy go back of my connection with it. I well remember its Principal, Simeon Bicknell, who took charge of the school in the spring of 1827, I think. I remember him as my first teacher in Vermont, in a district school in that part of Jericho vulgarly called Beartown. The next spring after that he became Principal of the Academy, and remained so about five years.

Mr. Bicknell was a good man, a fine scholar, an excellent teacher, a Christian gentleman. So said the people, so said his pupils, and his praise was no less upon their tongues in after years than then. Under his administration Jericho Academy stood first, or among the first schools of the State, of its kind.

Scholars came in large numbers from far and near, many of whom stood high as students and afterwards attained eminence as men in the different pursuits of life, or as women in the noble works of her sex.

Those were the days of glory for the Academy and for the town of Jericho. Nor did that glory, though dimmed, fade entirely upon the departure of Mr. Bicknell. For several years the School flourished and prospered greatly in the hands of others.

I do not know the name of the immediate successor of Mr. Bicknell, but am sure that Eleazer J. Marsh soon followed him as principal, and that he remained a year or two. Mr. Marsh was my first teacher in the Academy, and to him I owe much of the delight I have since found in study, and for whatever success, little though it be, I have had in my life work. He was a noble man and a good teacher, respected and beloved by his pupils. Under his instruction I learned to read most of all, and I have since acted in accordance with my view, that when one has learned to read, he may further educate himself, if he will.

John Boynton, my second teacher, succeeded Mr. Marsh. He was the superior of Mr. Marsh in some respects, and inferior in none. Under him the Academy flourished. The people approved and his pupils rejoiced in his instruction and his counsel. He was a brilliant genial, kind hearted, *manly man*. He was courteous to all, but especially kind in manner to the poor and ignorant as shown in his daily intercourse with the people. He despised empty show and vain pretense, but honored solid worth whether in rich or humble garb. Dear, good man, long since he passed from earth away to rest, I trust in the presence of the God to whom with his pupils he offered his morning prayer.

My third and last teacher at the Academy, was James T. Foster, a kind, pleasant man, and a good teacher, though hardly the equal of either Mr. Boynton, or Mr. Marsh.

After him there was but little of permanence in instruction at the Academy, and the interest of former days began to decline. There were many teachers, one after another, for several years, but no special success attended the administration of any.

I was here during the summer of 1839, while a Rev. Mr. Kingsbury was principal of the school. He was a good man, no doubt, and I presume was competent to instruct, but he had no power to control. Simply an apology for a teacher, he ought to have apologized to all concerned for engaging as such, as ought every one who is in the position of a teacher and yet has no power of discipline, *no vim*.

To lack of this, in most of those engaged as teachers in subsequent years, (though other things tended the same way,) was due the steady decline of interest and prosperity in Jericho Academy. So positive was that decline that the return of Mr. Bicknell, the first able Principal, failed to restore its ancient fame. Though he was still the same able and efficient teacher and in a measure successful, the decline continued, after his short stay, and death followed.

The building still remains but its halls echo not the steps of the student as once they did. Humble in its origin, never pretentious, and now plain in appearance as at first, but for those educated therein, it stands a reminder of pleasant hours, months, and years of joyous student life.

Incidents in my early life here, and especially of my school, so throng upon my memory that I can not dismiss them all, without a word of joyous remembrance or of sad recollection. My remembrance of those days is very fresh and clear.

To the days of my school life here I refer now with special interest. It was on this wise: it was my fortune to be the son of a poor man; upon my importunity, he said to me, you may have your time and attend school, if you wish, having your home here whenever you desire it, but you must pay your own bills at school.

I was soon on my way here, rejoicing in the privilege given me. On my way, as I was just starting out in life for myself, I thought it well to take an inventory of stock. Doing so, I found a decent suit of clothes, books sufficient for present need, and down deep in my pocket my cash deposit, 25 cents, an old American quarter. That was my outfit. How I was to succeed I did not know, but I had faith and hope. I had already learned that this Jericho was not the place for one to fall among thieves, but I knew that I must find a good Samaritan to take me in, and I found him in the person of Mr. Nathaniel Blackman, who said he would board me for one dollar per week, and I might pay him when I could. And I found another in the Preceptor of the Academy, who also took me in on trust. The year was one of great prosperity for me. Considerable progress was made in study; the winter was spent in teaching; in the spring my bills were all paid; and I had 300 per cent on my cash deposit, so that I then had a full round dollar, and that I paid for a second hand Latin Dictionary; and then, pennyless, I again went on my way rejoicing. Nor was I alone in the struggle with poverty. Others there were reliant alone upon themselves. Among these I remember Paraclet Sheldon, who became an eminent teacher; Charles C. Parker, afterwards an able and successful minister of the gospel, and Burr Maynard now an eminent lawyer in Detroit. Others of this class were successful in the struggle, and among them a very dear class mate, Lester Warren, now an able and respected clergyman. There were noble ladies in this class who struggled hard for victory and gained it. But by far the larger number of students had help in their course, and by their scholarly attainments and virtuous action they well repaid parental care and friendly aid. Mr. Chairman, there were scholars in the days of that Academy, made so by hard study.

How their names stand out in memory. George Lee Lyman, George and James Blackman, Lucius and Edgar Lane, Emerson Chapin, George Bliss; and from away, were John A. Kasson and Luke P. Poland, men of national reputation, and dearer still do I remember as school mates, Whipple Earl and Torrey E. Wales. Nor are the ladies forgotten, Lucinda Bartlett, Irene Blackman, Hannah Richardson, Marcia Howe, Valencia and Minerva Lane, Esther G. Smith and many more of whom I can not speak now, live in memory with you as well as me. There was not a dishonored name among all I have mentioned or with whom I was associated in the school, so far as I know.

But, ah me! Where are the glad, joyous, hopeful and happy ones that thronged the Academy in those well remembered days? Silence would respond to the roll call of most of their names. But very few live in this vicinity. Some are far away, yet useful and happy, I trust, but most of them live only in the memory of the few who survive. The noble men and women who lived in these homes, fifty, sixty, seventy years ago, now rest yonder in their silent, windowless places of rest. The support of school and of the church, nobly borne by them, now rests upon their children who are themselves fast becoming old men and women. May this support so essential to the prosperity, happiness and eternal welfare of the people, never fail the good old town of Jericho.

Jericho Academy, like many others, stands today silent and alone, but those prepared therein for College, for teaching, for business, or for study of the professions, can never look upon it but with reverence and gratitude for the good there received, and will never think of it but with pride in its ancient fame, and sorrow for its present desolation."

The old Brick Church at Jericho Corners, which has been so handsomely repaired and furnished, and rededicated to the service of God, has been subject to many changes and has quite a history. The house was built in 1824 and 1825, on the land of Dr. George Howe, by an organized association called the "Brick Meeting House Society of Jericho," under an "act of the Legislature for the support of the Gospel," passed October 26th, 1798; that said Howe by deed conveyed said house and the green or common on which it stands to Oliver Lowry, Luther Prouty and Wm. A. Prentiss, April 3d, 1834, in trust to be used for religious worship, with a condition that it should revert to said Dr. Howe and his heirs if the owners and proprietors of the house should neglect to occupy the same for the purpose for which it was granted. Dr. Howe died in 1857, testate, leaving his property to his wife, who survived him. The Second Congregational and Baptist churches occupied the house for public worship each on alternate Sabbaths from 1826 down to 1858. In 1858 the Baptist church and society built a house of their own and abandoned the "Old Brick Church." The Second Congregational church at that time was weak, but they continued to occupy the house for religious worship till 1865, when, by reason of their inability to support preaching, it was voted to suspend meetings, and no meetings were afterwards held in it. No care was taken of the house by anybody and the windows were soon all broken out and it appeared as though it was truly forsaken, and most of the people thought the conditions of the deed had not been kept and that it had reverted to the widow of Dr. Howe. At that time the village was in need of a school house, and, as the walls of the Old Brick Church were sound, the school district took measures to acquire a deed of Mrs. Howe of the Old Brick Church and common, to be used for school purposes, and appointed a committee to remove the pews from the house and fit it up for a school house—which work the committee proceeded to do. But before they had proceeded far in their work, those who were opposed to converting the church into a school house, and believed that the Second Congregational church had not abandoned the house but merely suspended religious meetings for the time being, brought their bill in Chancery against the school district and its committee, enjoining them from converting the building into a school house. After a long litigation the Supreme Court decided that the house had not reverted, and said that "it could not be assumed but that a time of strength and prosperity will follow their time of weakness." And time has shown the wisdom and correctness of their decision. After the title of the property had been thus settled, one of the original owners of a pew brought suit against the school district committee to recover the value of his pew, and after another long litigation the Supreme Court decided that inasmuch as the owner of a pew is only entitled to the right of sitting, and the house was in no condition to be occupied for religious services, his recovery must be limited to one cent damages and one cent costs. The title having become settled by these suits, the house stood in the midst of the beautiful village an unsightly object and a disgrace to the people, till November, A. D. 1876.

In 1874 and 1875, the state of things which the Supreme court thought might come to pass in respect to the condition of the church, was realized. The Second Congregational church in 1874, was reorganized and quite a large number have been added. In the year 1876 the church felt as though they must have a house of their own in which to worship, and during that year the church, with those who felt an interest in the "Old Brick Church" and common, at the expense of three thousand dollars made it a beautiful edifice. The audience and vestry rooms were tastily finished and furnished. This house was rededicated by the Second Congregational church on the 19th of December, 1877, M. H. Buckham, President of the Vermont University, preached the re-dedication sermon from the text found in Acts II. 42, and the dedicatory prayer was made by Rev. Edwin Wheelock, of Cambridge."

The history of the litigation referred to may be found in two reported cases; viz, Howe and others vs. School District No 3 in Jericho, 43 Vt. Law Reports on Page 282; and Howe vs. Stevens and others 46 Vt. on Page 262.

In the year 1894 or 1895, the writer prepared

for the press, and there was published in the Chittenden Reporter, a paper printed at Jericho, the following: Viz,

The town of Jericho was created by grant from Benning Wentworth, Gov. of New Hampshire, its charter being dated June 7, 1763. The township then consisted of 23,040 acres, but in 1794 about 5,000 acres was taken by an act of the Legislature to form, in part, the town of Richmond.

Most of the land of the town is well adapted to agricultural purposes. There are no swamps creating miasma to render the town an unhealthy place in which to live. Proverbially it has been a healthy town in which to reside. Like most rural districts of Vermont, it has suffered in consequence of some of its enterprising citizens emigrating to the West, and many removing to the larger centers of population. Such changes have been our loss, but a gain to the communities to which they removed.

But it is in reference to its present prosperity and the advantages that all new comers will reap by becoming its actual residents, that I wish to speak. In the year 1874, the town bonded to the amount of $24,000 in aid of the construction of the B. & L. Railroad. The last of these bonds were paid the present year, and the town is nearly free from debt. Our railroad accommodations are now first-class. The people in the north-easterly part of the town are accommodated by the Underhill depot, which is within ten rods of the line of the town; the south part of the town is accommodated by the depot at Richmond; the south-westerly part by the depot at North Williston, and the people of the whole town as well as the people of West Bolton and the eastern part of Essex, are well accommodated by the depot at Jericho.

There are more than 75 dairies in the town, ranging from 6 to 50 cows each, and more than 25 dairies of more than 15 cows each. There are four creameries in different parts of the town. There are three postoffices in town, located at Nashville, Jericho Center, and Jericho. There are three villages. The village of Underhill Flatts, (so called) the larger part of which being in Jericho, is a prosperous village. On the Jericho side of the line are four stores, a steam saw mill, a tin shop, two physicians, and an Episcopal and a Methodist church. The village at the Center has two stores, a blacksmith shop, and a Congregational church, in front of which is a handsome green park with shade trees.

The village of Jericho, sometimes called Jericho Corners, is the principal village of the town, situated on Brown's River, on which there are several good mill privileges, some of which are improved and others where manufacturing industries might be greatly extended. At this village there are now two stores, three blacksmith shops, one harness shop, a paint shop, two house painters, a carriage painter, a lawyer and two physicians, one of the best grist mills in New England, where flour is manufactured by the roller process, a pump manufactory, a saw mill, a manufactory for butter and cheese boxes, a manufactury for all sorts of wooden ware, a large tin shop, two millinery shops and a good hotel. There are also two weekly papers printed here, and offices where a large amount of press work is done. The village has first-class schools, run under the town system. Prof. J. S. Cilley resides here, who fits students to enter college. The village is pleasantly located, the streets are handsome, the buildings and residences are kept in good repair. There are three churches—Congregational, Baptist, and Methodist—and a school house hall that can be used for meetings and entertainments. The gospel is dispensed here by ministers of four different beliefs, Congregational, Baptist, Methodist, and Episcopalian. There is a Good Templar's organization, a Literary and Scientific Club that meets once in two weeks, and a Lecture Course has been provided for. With such facilities, time here will be pleasantly and profitably spent.

As a place of residence or for those who desire to engage in agriculture or manufacturing industries, Jericho is an inviting place. Its excellent farming lands, pleasant villages, good schools, pleasant surroundings, low taxes, its undeveloped water power that can be utilized for manufacturing purposes, and the fact that it is easy of access by railroad, furnishes great inducement for energetic people to come hither.

Many prominent and professional men have practised and resided in the town of Jericho, among whom were Jacob Maeck an able lawyer, the Honorable David A. Smalley, who was not only a prominent lawyer and an eloquent advocate, but became Judge of the District Court of the United

States for the District of Vermont, which office he held for many years. Hon. Asahel Peck, who was Judge of the Supreme Court of Vermont, was also a resident of Jericho when he afterward held the office of Governor of Vermont. It would be a long list of names to mention all of the men and women who have been citizens of Jericho, who have been successful in business life and in teaching, and prominent in the professions and as statesmen. Many left their native State and became useful citizens in some other of the United States and the world, to make a name for themselves and to bless mankind.

CHAPTER XVII.

MEMBERS OF THE WINDSOR CONVENTION, COUNCIL OF SAFETY, GOVERNORS AND SENATORS.

Members of the Windsor Convention, Council of Safety, Governors and Senators.

The members of the adjourned session of the Windsor Convention, convened at Windsor June 4th, 1777, (at which the name of the State was changed from New Connecticut to Vermont, and at which it was resolved to form a Constitution for the State) were as follows: Viz.—

Capt. Joseph Bowker, Pres.
Mr. Simeon Hathaway,
Dr. Jonas Fay, *Secretary*,
Mr. Gideon Olin,
Mr. Abel Benedict,
Mr. Eli Brownson,
Mr. Thomas Bull,
Mr. Moses Robinson, 2d,
Captain William Fitch,
Mr. Caleb Smith,
Mr. Jesse Churchill,
Capt. Ebenezer Allen,
Mr. Whitefield Foot,
Mr. Stephen Place,
Nathan Clark, Esq.,
Mr. John Burnham, Jun.
Major Jeremiah Clark,
Capt. Ebenezer Willoughby.
Mr. Joseph Bradley,
Mr. Martin Powell,
Mr. Cephas Kent,
Dr. Gaius Smith,
Capt. Jonathan Willard,
Capt. Zebediah Dewey,
Capt. William Gage,
Benjamin Spencer, Esq.
Mr. Joseph Smith,
Mr. John Sutherland,

Capt. Jonathan Fasset,
Mr. Gamaliel Painter,
Capt. Ira Allen,
Mr. William Mellen,
Col. Benjamin Carpenter,
Mr. Israel Smith,
Mr. Dennis Lockland,
Mr. Joshua Webb,
Mr. Jabez Sargeant,
Capt. William Utley,
Capt. William Curtis,
Capt. William Gallop,
Mr. Stephen Tilden,
Mr. John Throop,
Mr. Asa Whitcomb,
Col. Peter Olcott,
Mr. Jacob Burton,
Mr. Daniel Gilbert,
Mr. Frederic Smith,
Dr. Bildad Andrus,
Mr. John G. D. Bailey,
Mr. Amaziah Woodworth,
Capt. Josiah Powers,
Capt. Heman Allen,
Col. Thomas Chittenden,
Dr. William Hill,
Capt. John Barney,
Mr. John Dyer,
Nathaniel Robinson, Esq.
Dr. Reuben Jones,
Capt. John Coffein,
Mr. Ebenezer Hoisington,
Major Joel Matthews,
Mr. Benjamin Emmons,
Col. Joseph Marsh,
John W. Dana, Esq.,
Mr. Asa Chandler,
Major Thomas Moredock,
Joel Marsh, Esq.,
Mr. Abner Chamberlin,
Mr. Amos Woodworth,
Mr. Benjamin Baldwin,
Capt. Robert Johnson,
Capt. Jeremiah Powers.

MEMBERS OF THE COUNCIL OF SAFETY.

The persons who composed the original Council of Safety of 1778 under the Constitution were: Viz,

1. Thomas Chittenden, Governor.
2. Ira Allen, State Treasurer and Councillor.
3. Nathan Clark, Speaker of the General Assembly.
4. Joseph Fay, Secretary of the Gov. and Council.

5. Jonas Fay,
6. Jeremiah Clark,
7. Benjamin Carpenter,
8. Paul Spooner,
9. Jacob Bayley,
10. Moses Robinson,
11. Heman Allen,
12. Matthew Lyon, Dep. Sec'y of Gov. and Council.

GOVERNORS OF VERMONT WITH THEIR TERMS OF SERVICE, FROM 1778 TO 1898.

Names of Governors.	Commencement of Service.	Expiration of Service.
Thomas Chittenden,	Feb. 1778,	Oct. 1789.
Moses Robinson,	Oct. 1789,	" 1790.
Thomas Chittenden,[1]	" 1790,	" 1797.
Paul Brigham,[2]	Aug. 1797,	" 1797.
Isaac Tichenor,	Oct. 1797,	" 1807.
Israel Smith,	" 1807,	" 1808.
Isaac Tichenor,	Oct. 1808,	" 1809.
Jonas Galusha,	" 1809,	" 1813.
Martin Chittenden,	" 1813,	" 1815.
Jonas Galusha,	" 1815,	" 1820.
Richard Skinner,	" 1820,	" 1823.
Cornelius P. Van Ness,	" 1823,	" 1826.
Ezra Butler,	" 1826,	" 1828.
Samuel C. Crafts,	" 1828,	" 1831.
William A. Palmer,	" 1831,	" 1835.
Silas H. Jennison,[3]	" 1835,	" 1836.
" "	" 1836,	" 1841.
Charles Paine,	" 1841,	" 1843.
John Mattocks	" 1843,	" 1844.
William Slade,	" 1844,	" 1846.

Horace Eaton,	Oct. 1846,	Oct. 1848.
Carlos Coolidge,	" 1848,	" 1850.
Charles K. Williams,	" 1850,	" 1852.
Erastus Fairbanks,	" 1852,	" 1853.
John S. Robinson,	" 1853,	" 1854.
Stephen Royce,	" 1854,	" 1856.
Ryland Fletcher,	" 1856,	" 1858.
Hiland Hall,	" 1858,	" 1860.
Erastus Fairbanks,	" 1860,	" 1861.
Frederick Holbrook,	" 1861,	" 1863.
J. Gregory Smith,	" 1863,	" 1865.
Paul Dillingham,	" 1865,	" 1867,
John B. Page,	" 1867,	" 1869.
Peter T. Washburn,[4]	" 1869,	" 1870.
George W. Hendee,[5]	" 1870,	" 1870.
John W. Stewart,	" 1870,	" 1872.
Julius Converse,	" 1872,	" 1874.
Asahel Peck,	" 1874,	" 1876.
Horace Fairbanks	" 1876,	" 1878.
Redfield Proctor,	" 1878,	" 1880.
Roswell Farnham,	" 1880,	" 1882.
John L. Barstow,	" 1882,	" 1884.
Samuel E. Pingree,	" 1884,	" 1886.
E. J. Ormsbee,	" 1886,	" 1888.
William P. Dillingham,	" 1888,	" 1890.
Carroll S. Page,	" 1890,	" 1892.
Levi K. Fuller,	" 1892,	" 1894.
Urban A. Woodbury,	" 1894,	" 1896.
Josiah Grout,	" 1896,	" 1898.
Edward C. Smith,	" 1898,	" 1900.

1. Thomas Chittenden died in office August 25th, 1797.
2. Paul Brigham, Lieutenant-Governor and Governor from August 25th 1797 to October 16, 1797.
3. Silas H. Jennison, Lieutenant-Governor, and Governor by reason of no election by the people.
4. Peter T. Washburn died in office February 7th, 1870.
5. George W. Hendee, Lieutenant-Governor, was Governor from February 7th, 1870, to October, 1870, by reason of the death of Governor Peter T. Washburn.

UNITED STATES SENATORS FROM VERMONT, SHOWING THEIR TERM OF OFFICE.

Elections took place in October.

Moses Robinson,	1791–1796.
Isaac Tichenor, for the unexpired term of Moses Robinson resigned,	1796–1797
Nathaniel Chipman,	1797–1803.
Israel Smith,	1803–1807.
Jona. Robinson, for the unexpired term of Isaac Smith resigned,	1807–1809.
Jona. Robinson, for six years,	1809–1815.
Isaac Tichenor,	1815–1821.
Horatio Seymour,	1821–1833.

Stephen R. Bradley,	1791–1795.
Elijah Paine,	1795–1801.
" "	1801–1801.
Stephen R. Bradley, for the unexpired term of Elijah Paine resigned,	1801–1807.
Stephen R. Bradly, for six years,	1807–1813.
Dudley Chase,	1813–1817.
James Fisk, for the unexpired term of Dudley Chase resigned,	1817–1818.
Wm. A. Palmer, for the unexpired term of James Fisk resigned,	1818–1819.
Wm. A. Palmer, for six years.	1819–1825.
Dudley Chase, from	1825–1831.
Horatio Seymour, "	1821–1833.
Samuel Prentiss, "	1831–1842.
Benjamin Swift, "	1833–1839.
Samuel S. Phelps, "	1839–1851.
Samuel C. Crafts, "	1842–1843.

William Upham,	"	1843–1853.
Solomon Foot,	"	1851–1866.
Samuel S. Phelps,	"	1853–1854.
Lawrence Brainerd,	"	1854–1855.
Jacob Collamer,	"	1855–1865.
Luke P. Poland, [1]	"	1865–1867.
George F. Edmunds, [2]	"	1866–1891.
Justin S. Morrill, [3]	"	1867–1898.
Redfield Proctor,	"	1891–
Jonathan Ross, [3]	"	1899–

1. Luke P. Poland was appointed by the Governor to fill the vacancy occasioned by the decease of Jacob Collamer.
2. George F. Edmunds was appointed by the Governor to fill the vacancy occasioned by the death of Solomon Foot.
3. Jonathan Ross was appointed by the Governor to fill the vacancy occasioned by the death of Justin S. Morrill, who died Dec. 1898. Jonathan Ross received his appointment Jan. 11th 1899.

CHAPTER XVIII.

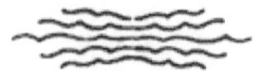

LIST OF JUDGES OF THE SUPREME COURT FROM THE YEAR 1778, TO THE YEAR 1899, AND SHOWING THEIR TERM OF OFFICE.

The Judges of the Supreme Court were elected annually by the Legislature in joint Assembly, that commenced its session in October, and their term of service commenced as soon as they were elected until the Statute provided that their term of service should commence the 1st of December following their election. In the year 1870 the biennial system of elections was adopted, and from that time their term of office continued two years. It will be understood that the names given were assistant judges, except those who are designated as Chief Judge. And all of the Judges are *ex-officio* Chancellors of the Court of Chancery.

From the year 1857, to 1870, the full bench consisted of a Chief Judge and five Assistant Judges, and after the year 1870, the full bench consisted of a Chief Judge and six Assistant Judges.

When vacancies occur by death, resignation or otherwise they may be filled by appointment by the Governor. Until the year 1849, the Judges of the Supreme Court were also the Chief Judges of the County Court, but in the year 1849, the system was changed and three Judges were elected annually that constituted the full bench in the Supreme Court, and whose duties were confined to that Court; and another set of Judges were elected annually, to serve as Chief Judges in the County Courts of the State, and their duties were confined to that Court. This system for both the Supreme and County Courts was continued till the year 1857, when the State returned to the present system, where all of the Chief Judges of the County Courts are also Judges of the Supreme Court.

During the time the Judges of the Supreme Court consisted of three Judges, who were relieved from the duty of holding County Courts, the Counties of the State were divided into four Judicial Circuits. The first Circuit consisted of Bennington, Rutland and Addison Counties:—the second, Windham, Windsor and Orange Counties:— the third, Chittenden, Franklin, Lamoille and Grand Isle Counties:—the fourth, Washington, Caledonia, Orleans and Essex Counties. And each Circuit had a Judge who was elected by the Legislature, and who was the Chief Judge of the County Court in the several Counties composing his Circuit. The following were the Judges who were elected and served as Chief Judges of the County Courts in the four Circuits during the time that that system continued, although all of them were not in office at the same time: Viz, Robert Pierpoint, Jacob Collamer, Asahel Peck, Luke P. Poland, Abel Underwood, John Pierpoint, James Barrett, A. O. Aldis, Milo L. Bennett and Wm. C. Kittredge.

All the Judges of the Supreme Court, except the

Chief Judge, are denominated Assistant Judges, as 1st, 2nd, 3d, 4th, 5th, and 6th, as the number might be, and take their position in the order in which their names appear, respectively, in the list of Judges. The occasion of vacancies that occured from time to time, and appointments made by the Governor to fill vacancies are stated in notes at the end of the list. By the act of Legislature of 1870, the official term of service of the Judges commenced December 1st, following their election.

It has been the practice, that when a vacancy occurs in the list of Judges, to promote those who stand below the place made vacant and let the new appointee grace the lowest position.

Elected Oct., 1778,—
Moses Robinson, Ch. J.
John Shepardson,
John Fassett, Jun.
Thomas Chandler,
John Throop.

October, 1780,—
Moses Robinson, Ch. J.
Paul Spooner,
John Fassett, Jun.,
Increase Moseley,
John Throop.

October, 1779,—
Moses Robinson, Ch. J.
John Shepardson,
John Fassett, Jun.,
John Throop,
Paul Spooner.

Oct., 1781 to Feb., 1782.
Elisha Payne, Ch. J.
Paul Spooner,
John Fassett Jun.,
Simeon Olcott,*
Jonas Fay.

From Feb. to Oct. 1782,[a]
Moses Robinson, Ch. J.
Paul Spooner,
John Fassette, Jr.,
John Throop,
Jonas Fay.

October, 1782,—
Moses Robinson, Ch. J.
Paul Spooner,
Jonas Fay,
John Fasset, Jun.
Peter Olcott.

October, 1783,—
Moses Robinson, Ch. J.
Paul Spooner,
John Fassett,
Peter Olcott,
Thomas Porter.

October, 1784,—
Paul Spooner, Ch. J.
John Fasset,
Nathaniel Niles,
Thomas Porter,
Peter Olcott.

October, 1785,—
Moses Robinson, Ch. J.
Paul Spooner,
Nathaniel Niles,
John Fassett,
Thomas Porter.

October, 1786,—
Moses Robinson, Ch. J.
Paul Spooner,
Nathaniel Niles,
Nathaniel Chipman,
Luke Knowlton.

October, 1787,—
Moses Robinson, Ch. J.
Nathaniel Niles,
Paul Spooner.

October, 1788,—
Moses Robinson, Ch. J.
Paul Spooner,
Stephen R. Bradley.

Oct., 1789 and 1790,—
Nathaniel Chipman Ch. J.
Noah Smith,
Samuel Knight.

Oct. 1791, 1792 and 1793,—
Samuel Knight, Ch. J.
Elijah Paine,
Isaac Tichenor.

Oct., 1794 and 1795,—
Isaac Tichenor, Ch. J.
Lot Hall,
Enoch Woodbridge.

October, 1796,—
Nathaniel Chipman Ch. J.
Lot Hall,
Enoch Woodbridge.

October, 1797,—
Israel Smith, Ch. J.
Enoch Woodbridge,
Lot Hall.

Oct., 1798, 1799 and 1800.
Enoch Woodbridge, Ch. J.
Lot Hall,
Noah Smith.

Oct., 1801 and 1802,—
Jonathan Robinson Ch. J.
Royal Tyler,
Stephen Jacob

Oct., 1803, 1804, 1805 and 1806,—
Jonathan Robinson Ch. J.
Royal Tyler,
Theophilus Harrington.

Oct., 1807 and 1808,—
Royal Tyler, Ch. J.
Theophilus Harrington,
Jonas Galusha.

Oct., 1809, 1810, 1811 and 1812,—
Royal Tyler, Ch. J.
Theophilus Harrington.
David Fay,

Oct., 1813 and 1814,—
Nathaniel Chipman Ch. J.
Daniel Farrand,
Jonathan H. Hubbard.

October, 1815,—
Asa Aldis, Ch. J.
Richard Skinner,
James Fisk.

October, 1816,—
Richard Skinner, Ch. J.
James Fisk,
William A. Palmer.

Oct., 1817, 1818, 1819 and 1820,—
Dudley Chase, Ch. J.
Joel Doolittle,
William Brayton.

October, 1821,—
C. P. Van Ness, Ch. J.
Joel Doolittle,
William Brayton.

October, 1822,—
C. P. Van Ness, Ch. J.
Joel Doolittle,
Charles K. Williams.

Oct., 1823,—
Richard Skinner, Ch. J.
Charles K. Williams,
Asa Aikens.

Oct. 1824,—
Richard Skinner, Ch. J.
Joel Doolittle,
Asa Aikens.

OF VERMONT.   341

The last list of Judges were elected October 1824, and their term ended October, 1825.

The list of Vermont State Judges that have served the State since the year, 1825, with the *expiration* of their terms of service respectively are given below. The elections took place in October previous to the years hereafter named: Viz,

1826 and 1827,—
Richard Skinner, Ch. J.
Samuel Prentiss,
Titus Hutchinson,
Stephen Royce, Jr.

1828,—
Richard Skinner, Ch. J.
Samuel Prentiss,
Titus Hutchinson,
Bates Turner.

1829,—
Richard Skinner, Ch. J.
Samuel Prentiss,
Titus Hutchinson,
Bates Turner,
Ephraim Paddock.

1830,—
Samuel Prentiss, Ch. J.
Titus Hutchinson,
Charles K. Williams,
Stephen Royce, Jun.,
Ephraim Paddock.

1831,—
Titus Hutchinson, Ch. J.
Charles K. Williams,
Stephen Royce, Jr.,
Ephraim Paddock,
John C. Thompson.[1]

1832 and 1833,—
Titus Hutchinson, Ch. J.
Charles K. Williams,
Stephen Royce, Jr.,
Nicholas Baylies,
Samuel S. Phelps.

1834 and 1835,—
Charles K. Williams Ch. J.
Stephen Royce,
Samuel S. Phelps,
Jacob Collamer,
John Mattocks.

1836, 1837 and, 1838,—
Charles K. Williams, Ch. J.
Stephen Royce,
Samuel S. Phelps,
Jacob Collamer,
Isaac F. Redfield.

1839, 1840 1841 and 1842.
Charles K. Williams, Ch. J.
Stephen Royce,
Jacob Collamer,
Isaac F. Redfield,
Milo L. Bennett.

1843, 1844 and 1845,—
Charles K. Williams, Ch. J.
Stephen Royce,
Isaac F. Redfield,
Milo L. Bennett,
William Hibbard.

1846,—
Charles K. Williams, Ch. J.
Stephen Royce,
Isaac F. Redfield,
Milo L. Bennett,
Daniel Kellogg.

1847 and 1848,—
Stephen Royce, Ch. J.
Isaac F. Redfield,
Milo L. Bennett,
Daniel Kellogg,
Hiland Hall,
Charles Davis.

1849 and 1850,—
Stephen Royce, Ch. J.
Isaac F. Redfield,
Milo L. Bennett,
Daniel Kellogg,
Hiland Hall,
Luke P. Poland.

1851,—
Stephen Royce, Ch. J.
Isaac F. Redfield,
Daniel Kellogg.

1852,—
Stephen Royce, Ch. J.
Isaac F. Redfield,
Pierpoint Isham.

1853, 1854, 1855, 1856 and 1857,—
Isaac F. Redfield, Ch. J.
Pierpoint Isham,
Milo L. Bennett.

1858 and 1859,—
Isaac F. Redfield, Ch. J
Milo L. Bennett,
Luke P. Poland,
Asa O. Aldis,
John Pierpoint,
James Barrett.

1860,—
Isaac F. Redfield, Ch. J.
Luke P. Poland,
Asa O. Aldis,
John Pierpoint,
James Barrett,
Loyal C. Kellogg.

1861, 1862, 1863, 1864
and 1865,—
Luke P. Poland, Ch. J. [2]
Asa O. Aldis,
John Pierpoint,
James Barrett,
Loyal C. Kellogg,
Asahel Peck.

1866 and 1867,—
John Pierpoint, Ch. J. [3]
James Barrett,
Loyal C. Kellogg,
Asahel Peck,
William C. Wilson,
Benjamin H. Steele. [3]

1868 and 1869,—
John Pierpoint, Ch. J.
James Barrett,
Asahel Peck,
William C. Wilson,
Benjamin H. Steele,
John Prout.

1870,—
John Pierpoint, Ch. J.
James Barrett,
Asahel Peck,
William C. Wilson,
Benjamin H. Steele,
Hoyt H. Wheeler.

1871,—
John Pierpoint, Ch. J.
James Barrett,
Asahel Peck,
Hoyt H. Wheeler,
Homer E. Royce,
Timothy P. Redfield,
Jonathan Ross.

1872, 1873, and
1874,
John Pierpoint, Ch. J.
James Barrett,
Asahel Peck, [4]
Hoyt H. Wheeler,
Homer E. Royce,
Timothy P. Redfield,
Jonathan Ross.

1875 and 1876,—
John Pierpoint, Ch. J.
James Barrett,
Hoyt H. Wheeler,
Homer E. Royce,
Timothy P. Redfield,
Jonathan Ross,
H. Henry Powers.

1877,—
John Pierpoint, Ch. J.
James Barrett,
Hoyt H. Wheeler, [5]
Homer E. Royce,
Timothy P. Redfield,
Jonathan Ross,
H. Henry Powers,
Walter C. Dunton. [6]

1878,—
John Pierpoint, Ch. J.
James Barrett,
Homer E. Royce,
Timothy P. Redfield,
Jonathan Ross,
H. Henry Powers,
Walter C. Dunton.

1879,—
John Pierpoint, Ch. J.
James Barrett,
Homer E. Royce,
Timothy P. Redfield,
Jonathan Ross,
Walter C. Dunton, [7]
Wheelock G. Veazey. [8]

1880,—
John Pierpoint, Ch. J.
James Barrett,
Homer E. Royce,
Timothy P. Redfield,
Jonathan Ross,
H. Henry Powers,
Wheelock G. Veazey.

1881,—
John Pierpoint, Ch. J.
Homer E. Royce,
Timothy P. Redfield,
Jonathan Ross,
H. Henry Powers,
Wheelock G. Veazey,
Russell S. Taft.

1882,—
John Pierpoint, Ch. J. [9]
Homer E. Royce, [10]
Timothy P. Redfield,
Jonathan Ross,
H. Henry Powers,
Wheelock G. Veazey,
Russell S. Taft,
John W. Rowell. [11]

1883 and 1884,—
Homer E. Royce, Ch. J.
Timothy P. Redfield, [12]
Jonathan Ross,
H. Henry Powers,
Wheelock G. Veazey,
Russell S. Taft,
John W. Rowell.

1885,—
Homer E. Royce, Ch. J.
Jonathan Ross,
H. Henry Powers,
Wheelock G. Veazey,
Russell S. Taft,
John W. Rowell,
William H. Walker.

1886,—
Homer E. Royce, Ch. J.
Jonathan Ross,
H. Henry Powers,
Wheelock G. Veazey,
Russell S. Taft,
John W. Rowell,
William H. Walker.

1887,—
Homer E. Royce, Ch. J.
Jonathan Ross,
H. Henry Powers,
Wheelock G. Veazey,
Russell S. Taft,
John W. Rowell,
William H. Walker, [13]
James M. Tyler, [13]

1888 and 1889,—
Homer E. Royce, Ch. J.
Jonathan Ross,
H. Henry Powers,
Wheelock G. Veazey,
Russell S. Taft,
John W. Rowell,
James M. Tyler.

1890,—
Homer E. Royce, Ch. J. [14]
Jonathan Ross,
H. Henry Powers, [14]
Wheelock G. Veazey, [15]
Russell S. Taft,
John W. Rowell,
James M. Tyler,
Loveland Munson. [15]

From Dec., 1st 1890, to Dec. 1st 1898 inclusive the Judges of the Supreme Court were as follows: Viz,
Jonathan Ross, Ch. J.
Russell Taft,
John W. Rowell,
James M. Tyler,
Loveland Munson,
Henry R. Start.
Laforest H. Thompson.

The Judges after Dec., 1st 1898 were :
Jonathan Ross, Ch. J. [16]
Russell S. Taft, [17]
John W. Rowell,

EARLY HISTORY

James M. Tyler,
Loveland Munson,
Laforest H. Thompson.
Henry R. Start,
John H. Watson. [18]

---

* Simeon Olcott resigned Feb. 13, 1782 and Samuel Fletcher was elected but declined to accept, and John Throop was elected: and probably Elisha Payne resigned at the same time as his name does not appear as Judge of the Court after Feb. 13, 1782.

The list of Judges for 1781-1782 in Slade's State Papers is inaccurate. See Governor and Council, Vol. II. pp. 116, 117.

a The change in the list of Judges in Feb., 1782, was owing to the dissolution of the eastern and western Unions at that time.

1. John C. Thompson deceased in June. 1831.
2. Luke P. Poland held the position of Chief Judge till Dec., 1865, when he resigned, and was appointed by the Governor United States Senator.
3. John Pierpoint was appointed Chief Judge Dec. 1st, 1865, to fill the vacancy occasioned by the resignation of Luke P. Poland, and Benjamin H. Steele was appointed Judge in Dec., 1865 to fill the vacancy occasioned by the resignation of Luke P. Poland, Ch. J. and the promotion of John Pierpoint to the Chief Judgeship.
4. Asahel Peck resigned August 31st, 1874, and was elected Governor Sept. 1st of the same year.
5. Hoyt H. Wheeler resigned March 31st 1877, having been appointed Judge of the District Court of the United States for the District of Vermont.
6. Walter C. Dunton was appointed Judge April 13th, 1877, to fill the vacancy occasioned by the resignation of Hoyt H. Wheeler.
7. Walter C. Dunton resigned October 27th, 1879.
8. Wheelock G. Veazey was appointed Judge to fill the vacancy occasioned by the resignation of Walter C. Dunton.
9. John Pierpoint Chief Judge, died January 7th, 1882.
10. Homer E. Royce appointed Chief Judge January 10th, 1882, to fill the vacancy occasioned by the decease of John Pierpoint.
11. John W. Rowell was appointed Judge January 10th, 1882.
12. Timothy P. Redfield in 1884 declined re-election.
13. James M. Tyler was appointed Judge Sept. 16th, 1887, to fill the vacancy caused by the resignation of William H. Walker.
14. Homer E. Royce Chief Judge and H. Henry Powers Judge declined re-election at the end of their official year in 1890.
15. Loveland Munson was appointed Judge to fill the vacancy caused by the resignation of Wheelock G. Veazey.
16. Jonathan Ross Chief Judge resigned January 11th, 1899, and was appointed the same day, by the Governor, United States Senator for Vermont.
17. Russell S. Taft was appointed by the Governor Chief Judge on January 19th, 1899, to fill the vacancy occasioned by the resignation of Jonathan Ross, Chief Judge.
18. John H. Watson was appointed Judge by the Governor January 19th, 1899, to fill the vacancy occasioned by the resignation of Jonathan Ross as Chief Judge and the promotion of Russell S. Taft to the Chief Judgeship and the promotion of the other Judges.

WIT AND HUMOR.

SELECTED.

HOW WITTY LAWYERS SCORE POINTS.

Judge Poland, of Vermont, was the last of the Congressmen who dressed in the old Whig uniform of "buff and blue"—a buff vest and a blue coat with brass buttons, and a white neckerchief—such as Daniel Webster used to wear when he addressed the Senate or the Supreme Court.

The Judge, who was an excellent lawyer, was once presiding at the trial of a long and intricate case. With him sat two side-judges—the office in those days was not infrequently occupied by men who knew little and thought less. During the trial one of them was heard whispering to a friend "The Chief Justice agrees with me in my opinion of the law in this case and will charge the jury just as I should." Judge Poland also heard the remark, and smiled. Several years before that he not only smiled but laughed heartily at some remarks made by a brother lawyer.

He and Joshua Sawyer were opposing counsel in a case of assault and battery. Sawyer had drawn a prolix declaration in which the assault appeared much worse than the witnesses represented it. Commenting on this difference, Poland told the jury that the declaration reminded him of an incident in his own practice.

"Years ago," said he, "I began a suit of this character in favor of Asa Barnard against Maj. Hyde, who inflicted corporal punishment upon my client for the trivial offense of telling him he was a great liar. Barnard asserted that the Major had struck him a blow on the head with a heavy cane, and he came to me to obtain redress. I framed a declaration in ten counts, setting forth the beating, bruising, wounding and evil entreating with all the tautological nonsense I could command. In the last count I recited that Barnard's life was greatly despaired of.

"I read the declaration to my client in a voice almost as sympathetic as that in which my brother Sawyer read his declaration to you, gentlemen. I noticed the tears were coursing down my client's furrowed cheeks in rivulets. I asked him the cause of his grief. With sobbing utterance he answered, 'I didn't know it was half so bad before.'"

Court and jury laughed at this humorous suggestion that Sawyer's evidence did not sustain Sawyer's declaration, and many thought that witty as he was he would be unable to turn the laugh from him. He made a long speech, and as he was about to close, said, as if Poland's humorous remark had just occurred to him:

"Gentlemen, you appeared to be much delighted when the learned counsel related an incident of his own practice. I confess I was not amused. My old friend Barnard has told me the story many times, but with this difference: He said he did weep when Poland read a long paper to him; but that paper was not Poland's declaration, but his bill!"

The retort upset everybody. Even the grave Judge laughed, and no one enjoyed the reply more than Poland himself.

On the prosecution of a negro for stealing a dog with a collar on, when a demurrer to the indictment was sustained because it was not larceny to steal a dog, the prosecution claimed that he also stole the collar that was on the dog, but the defense claimed that the negro took the dog only and the dog took the collar. The prisoner was finally discharged. 3 Cent. L. J. 554.

Justice Brewer's Estimate of Lawyers.

"While it is cheap wit for many to say sneering things of our profession, yet, if you strike from Anglo-Saxon history the thoughts and deeds of her lawyers you rob it of more than half its glory. Blot from American society to-day the lawyer with all the work that he does and all the power that he exerts, and you leave society as dry and shifting as the sands that sweep over Sahara. For the mystic force that binds our civilization together and makes possible its successes and glories in the law, and they who minister at its shrine and keep alive its sacred fires, are you and I and that vast multitude of our co-workers who boast no higher title than that of lawyer."

Her Judgment Sustained.—In a divorce case where there was evidence that the wife called her husband "an old fool," the court says, "The record sustains the wife's judgment." And on another point also her conclusion was affirmed. She told him she would have been foolish to have married a man of his age who had no money, and the court says, "Again we think her judgment was correct."

"I make whisky," said the moonshiner, "to make shoes for my little children." The judge seemed touched, for he had children of his own. "I sympathize with you," he said, "and I am going to send you to the Ohio Penitentiary, where you can follow the shoe business for two years."

An Impossible Possibility.—The foreman of a jury in a recent murder trial reported: "The probability, or even possibility, of this jury ever agreeing is impossible in my opinion."

A BAD HABIT.—That suicide is a "pernicious habit that obviously tends to shorten life" is the defense set up by a life insurance company in a recent action on a policy which expressly excluded liability for such reprehensible habits. It must be conceded that suicide if it becomes habitual would have the tendency described.

WEEPING IN COURT.—We, some time ago, drew attention to a Kentucky case which decided that counsel might legally shed tears in court. In France, however, it seems that an attorney may not do so, on account of which rule a French disciple of Blackstone was induced to try a new expedient, which unhappily proved ineffective. It appears that he had instructed his client to weep every time he struck the desk with his hand, but forgot and struck the desk at the wrong moment. She promptly fell to sobbing and crying. "What is the matter with you?" asked the judge. "Well, he told me to cry as often as he struck the table." "Gentlemen of the jury," cried the unabashed lawyer, "let me ask you how you can reconcile the idea of crime in connection with such candor and simplicity."

KINSHIP OF HOG AND BACON.—The following is related by Lord Bacon of his father, Sir Nicholas. When the latter was appointed judge on the Northern Circuit, "he was by one of the malefactors mightily importuned for to save his life; which when nothing he said did avail, he at length desired his mercy on account of kindred. 'Prithee, said my lord judge, 'how came that in? 'Why, if it please you, my lord, your name is Bacon and mine is Hog; and in all ages Hog and Bacon have been so near kindred that they are not to be separated.' 'Ay, but,' replied Judge Bacon, 'you and I cannot be kindred except you be hanged; for Hog is not Bacon until it be well hanged.'"

How Lawyers are like Lies.—In a very witty address by Jesse Holdon before the Chicago Credit Men's Association (published in "The American Lawyer" for September), he said of lawyers: "Like the boy's version of the text about lying, they may be an abomination unto the Lord, but they are an ever present help in time of trouble, as all of you know by actual experience."

Lied to His Attorney.—A German on trial many years ago in western Ohio for maliciously cutting a neighbor's cow had so convinced his attorney of his innocence that, although the evidence against him was totally insufficient to convict him, his attorney, in order to give him the completest vindication, placed his client on the stand and asked him point blank, "Did you cut the cow?" The effect was startling. With blanched face and quivering lips, the accused starred in agony at the court and stammered, "Mein Gott, shudge, I can't tell you a lie. I know I shall go in de hell if I do. I cut dot cow."

Moonshine Courts Didn't Count.—A witness in a North Carolina state court was asked on cross-examination if he did not testify in a former trial directly contrary to what he had just sworn to. He replied, with evident unconcern, "I did, sir." Lawyer. "You did. Well, which was the truth and which was the lie?" Witness. "What I told the first time was a lie, and what I say now is the truth." Lawyer. "And aren't you ashamed to confess that you perjured yourself in a court of justice?" Witness. "Why, no, sir, that first time was only the Federal court."

Mrs. Peck—Suppose that you and I were all alone upon a desert island, what is the first thing that you would do?" Henry (impulsively)—Try to get away.

His Character All Right Yet.—The following cross-examination of a witness in a court in western North Carolina is sent us as an actual occurrence:

Dist. Atty. "Now, Mr. Blinkins, you swear before this court and jury that you know the defendant's reputation in the community in which he lives and that he is generally reputed an upright peaceable, law-abiding citizen?"

Witness. "Yes, sir."

Dist. Atty. "Now, Mr. Blinkins, don't you know that Lafe Huggins has never done anything but loaf around and drink moonshine whiskey and fight?"

Witness. "Yes, sir."

Dist. Atty. "And don't you know that he abuses and beats his wife terribly?"

Witness. "Yes, sir.

Dist. Atty. "And don't you know that he broke up the Pigeon River camp meeting last winter and whipped the circuit rider?"

Witness. "Yes, sir."

Dist. Atty. And don't you know that he kicked his old father down the steps and out of the yard and nearly killed him?"

Witness. "Yes, sir."

Dist. Atty. And don't you know that he was convicted in this very court three years ago of maliciously shooting Deacon Smith's hogs?"

Witness. "Yes, sir."

Dist. Atty. "And don't you know that he was once accused of stealing a horse, and that the owner of the horse and the principal witness for the prosecution were killed just before the trial was to be had?"

Witness. "Yes, sir."

Dist. Atty. "And don't you know that his neighbors all know these things?"

Witness. "Yes, sir."

Dist. Atty. Then how can you sit there and

swear that this defendant's reputation is good in the community in which he lives?"

Witness. "Why, mister, a man has to do a heap wuss things than that to lose his character in our neighborhood."

A Correct Judgment.—In Buffalo many years ago, when Judge Stryker was on the common pleas bench, there was an elderly lawyer named Root who sometimes appeared in court when he had taken a drop too much. On one of these occasions he persisted in interrupting the court with irrelevant remarks. Every time he was ordered to sit down he obeyed but soon popped up again. Finally the exasperated judge exclaimed: "Sit down, Mr. Root, and stay there. You are drunk." "I will cheerfully obey your honor," said the offender, "inasmuch as it is the first correct judgment rendered by the court this term."

Judge—Did you see the beginning of this trouble? Witness—I did, your honor. It occurred five years ago. Judge—Why, how is that? Witness—It began when the minister pronounced them man and wife.

Holding It under Advisement.—A Missouri justice of the peace at the close of a case announced with great dignity: "I will hold this case under advisement until next Monday morning, at which time I will render judgment for the plaintiff."

Where the Law is.—An attorney writes: "The opinion of our supreme court in the case is not instructive, and was evidently written by a judge who wished to affirm a judgment clearly unsupported by both law and facts, but in our briefs you will find the law."

A well-known judge, noted for his tendency to explain things to juries, expressed in a recent case his own ideas with such force that he was surprised the jurors thought of leaving the box. They did leave, however, and were out for hours. Inquiring the trouble, the judge was told one of the twelve was standing out against the eleven. He summoned the jury and rebuked the recalcitrant sharply. "Your honor," said the juror, "may I say a word?" "Yes, sir," said the indignant judge; "what have you to say?" "Well, what I wanted to say is, I'm the only fellow that's on your side."

One of the older members of the Cincinnati bar was once pleading a case before Judge Sage, and had talked incessantly for two hours. Suddenly and unexpectedly, the long-winded man stopped short and coughed. "I should like a glass of water," said he to the court attendant; and the man disappeared to get it for him. For a moment there was a long-drawn sigh from the listeners; and then Judge Sage leaned forward to the friend who tells the story, and whispered, "Why don't you tell your friend, Alfred, that it is against the law to run a windmill with water?"

As Affidavits Usually Be.—An attorney who filed pretended affidavits to which he affixed his official jurat as notary public when the signers had never been sworn, but merely admitted the signing, excused himself by asserting that this was "the usual manner of administering oaths in such cases;" but he was not able to convince the court of that fact.

A unique formula for swearing to an affidavit adopted by a well-known attorney whose characteristic nasal solemnity made it effective, was this: "I swear that this affidavit is as true as affidavits usually be."

Where a small dog was away from home *decolette*, although the statute required a collar, and was killed by a large dog, and the defense was that the killing was lawful because of the want of a collar, it was held by the court that the big dog was not *de jure* or *de facto* a police officer or constable, and was not shown to have examined the records to see whether or not the little dog had been licensed to travel without a collar. Heisrodt v. Hackett (Mich.) 3 Cent. L. J. 479.

IN PURSUANCE OF THE CODE.—In an affidavit taken before a Mississippi justice of the peace, on which a conviction for assault and battery was sustained, the affiant declared that the accused "did wilfully assault and strike him with a deadly weapon, to wit, 'a tobacco box,' in pursuance of chapter 29 of the Annotated Code of 1892, against the peace and dignity of the state of Mississippi."

Senator Walcott, Mr. Reed,—the famous T. B.,—and Mr. Choate were spending a cosey evening together at Senator Walcott's home. "I have never smoked a cigar, I have never played a game of poker, and I have never attended a horse-race in my life," said Mr. Choate in the course of the conversation. Senator Walcott looked pathetically at the Speaker of the House. "I wish I could say that," he remarked. "You can," said Mr. Reed : "Choate did."

An officer in the army, seated at the table d'hote, of an hotel, looking significantly at a clergyman opposite, said : "If I had a son who was an idiot I would make him a clergyman." "Evidently your father was not of that opinion," quietly responded the clergyman.

A professor of Trinity College, Dublin, overhearing an undergraduate using profane oaths, rushed at him, exclaiming, "Are you aware, sir, that you are imperilling your immortal soul, and what is worse, incurring a fine of five shillings?"

Curiously worded advertisements are common in the London papers. One paper offered a prize for the best collection of such announcements, and the following is the result :—

"A lady wants to sell her piano, as she is going abroad in a strong iron frame."

"For Sale : A pianoforte, the property of a musician with carved legs."

"Wanted : A room for two gentlemen about thirty feet long and twenty feet broad."

"Lost : A collie dog by a man on Saturday evening answering to Jim with a brass collar round his neck and muzzle."

"Wanted : By a respectable girl, her passage to New York ; willing to take care of children and a good sailor."

"Mr. Brown, furrier, begs to announce that he will make up gowns, capes, etc., for ladies out of their own skins."

"Wanted : An organist and a boy to blow the same."

"Wanted : A boy to be partly outside and partly behind the counter."

"To be disposed of, a mail phaeton, the property of a gentleman with movable headpiece as good as new."

"Well, father," exclaimed the prodigal son, as he made his appearance again at the family fireside, "are you ready to kill the fatted calf?" "No," replied the old man grimly, I think I'll let you live."

"No," said Senator Sorghum, with emphasis, "I can't talk for publication to-day." "But Senator, in all the years of our acquaintance, this is the first time you ever declined to let me quote you." "I don't want you not to quote me. I want you to say I decline to be interviewed. This is confidential; I've concluded it's time for me to act as if I'd got to be so important that I dare not talk for fear of giving something big away."

An exchange says a gentleman invited some friends to dinner; and, as the colored servant entered the room, he accidentally dropped a platter which held a turkey. "My friends," said the gentleman, in a most impressive tone, "never in my life have I witnessed an event so fraught with disaster in the various nations of the globe. In this calamity we see the downfall of Turkey, the upsetting of Greece, the destruction of China, and the humiliation of Africa."

The founder of one of our agricultural colleges, who was more noted for having the interest of the public at heart than for aptness of expression in speech, was once called to be chairman of a meeting convened to consider the necessity of procuring ground for a new cemetery. "Gentlemen," said he, "I suppose you all know that there has got to be a new cemetery, and now we are anxious to know how many of you are ready to go into it!"

The dude was making the girl dead tired by his long and vapid talk on the advancement of women. "Don't you ever wish you were a man?" he asked as a kind of clincher. "No," she responded in the sweetest, most womanly way. "Do you?"

"Owing to unforeseen circumstances," announced an Australian paper not long ago, "our last issue did not appear."

"Annual bargain sale now going on Don't go anywhere else to be cheated," is the rather dubious manner in which a New York furniture dealer worded his announcement.

"When I was first married," says Rev. Dr. Lorimer, pastor of Tremont Temple, Boston, "I had my strict ideas about Sunday observance. Mrs. Lorimer had a colored 'aunty' for cook ; and on the first Saturday after she came I went into the kitchen, and told her I did not want any Sunday work, so she could prepare all meals for that day beforehand. She didn't say one word while I was talking. Then she looked up, and pointing to the door, exclaimed, 'Now look hyar, Marse George, you jest go in dar and 'tend to your Christianity, and leave me 'tend to mah kitchen!' I went ; and, as near as I can remember, she had hot dinners Sundays as long as she stayed with us."

"What is the meaning of the saying 'The king can do no wrong'?" "I think it must be a sort of insanity plea—a theory that most monarchs are *non compos mentis*, or pretty near it."

Irascible Lieutenant (down engine-room tube) —Is there a blithering idiot at the end of this tube? *Voice from the engine-room.*—Not at this end, sir.

"It's a standing rule in my church," said one clergyman to another, "for the sexton to wake up any man that he may see asleep." "I think," returned the other, "that it would be much better for the sexton, whenever any man goes to sleep under your preaching, to wake you up."

LAWYER: "I have my opinion of you." Citizen: "Well, you can keep it. The last opinion I got from you cost me $150."

A Boston Sunday-school teacher lately gave her class a rather graphic description of how Eve was created from the rib of Adam. "Mamma," said the youngest member of the class that evening, pressing his hand to his side, "I'm afraid I'm going to have a wife."

Gilboy—I understand that Judge Marrymore is breaking up housekeeping.
Gadman—That can't be; he's very busy these days deciding divorce cases.
Gilboy—Well, isn't that what I said?

Kind Neighbor (accompanied by a large mastiff, to a little girl very much afraid of him): "He's a good dog, he never hurts any one. Don't you see how he's wagging his tail?" Little Girl (still shrinking back): "Yes, I see; but that isn't the end I'm afraid of."

"Are you a native of this town?" asked a traveller of a resident of a sleepy little Southern hamlet. "Am I a what?" "Are you a native of the town?" "*Hey?*" "I asked if you were a native of this place?" At that moment his wife, tall and sallow and gaunt, appeared at the open door of the cabin, and, taking her pipe from between her teeth, said acridly: " 'Aint' ye got no sense, Jim? He means wuz ye livin' here when you was born, or wuz ye born before you begun livin' here. Now answer him."

Mistress (to Norah)—What must be the condition of a person in order to be buried in consecrated ground? Norah (in great surprise)—Dead, mum!

Governess—Come Ethel; it's time for good little girls to be in bed. Ethel—Yeth, Miss Morgan; but you know I have been naughty to-day.

While Col. Gillam, with the Middle Tennessee Regiment, was occupying Nashville he stationed sentries in the principal streets. One day an Irishman, who, not long enlisted, was put on duty, kept a sharp watch. Presently, a citizen came along. "Halt! Who goes there"? "A citizen," was the response. "Advance, and give the countersign." "I have not the countersign," replied the indignant citizen. "And the demand for it at this time and place is unusual." Well, begorrah! Ye dont pass this way until ye say, 'Bunker Hill'!" The citizen appreciating the situation, smiled and advanced to the sentry, and cautiously whispered the magic words. "Right! Pass on!" And the wide-awake sentinel resumed his beat.

"My boy Johnny has such a cheerful disposition." "Yes?" "Oh, yes. When I make him wash his neck, instead of grumbling, he just says he's glad he is not a giraffe."

"We bought a lawn mower at the Montague auction." "Well, that was all right, wasn't it?" "All right? Maria says it is our old one which they borrowed and never returned."

PERFECTLY HARMLESS. DIX—I once knew a young man who smoked fifty cigarettes daily without any particular harm resulting therefrom. HIX—Is it possible! DIX—Yes; and the only noticeable effect was the death of the smoker.

THE DUPE—Tell me the worst! THE DOCTOR (gloomily)—You will soon be up and around.

A girl sued a man for breach of promise, and proved him such a scoundrel that the jury decided that she ought to pay him something for not marrying her.

FIRST ARTIST—Well, old man, how's business? SECOND ARTIST—Oh, splendid! Got a commission from a millionaire. Wants his children painted very badly." FIRST ARTIST (pleasantly)—Well, my boy, you're the very man for the job.

A new post-office was established in a small village away out West, and a native of the soil was appointed postmaster. After a while complaints were made that no mail was sent out from the new office, and an inspector was sent to inquire into the matter. He called upon the postmaster, and, stating the cause of his visit, asked why no mail had been sent out.

The postmaster pointed to a big and nearly empty mail-bag hanging up in a corner, and said:

"Well, I ain't sent it out 'cause the bag ain't nowheres nigh full yet!"

During a discussion at a meeting of the Trinity College Historical Society upon the slight consideration attached to life by uncivilized nations, a speaker mentioned the extraordinary circumstance that in China if a man were condemned to death he could easily hire a substitute to die for him; "and" the debater went on, "I believe many poor fellows get their living by acting as substitutes in that way!"

MISS DE STYLE—Oh, major! Did you ever go to a military ball? OLD VETERAN—No, my dear young lady; in those days I had a military ball come to me. It nearly took my leg off.

LITTLE BOB—I could walk the rope just as well as the man in the circus, if it wasn't for one thing. LITTLE WILLIE—What is that? LITTLE BOB—I'd fall off.

REVERSE ACTION.—*The Elderly Matron*—You shouldn't mind the baby crying a little. It strengthens his lungs.

THE YOUNGER MATRON—Oh, no doubt; but it weaken's his father's religion.

MISTRESS (to servant)—Did you tell those ladies at the door that I was not at home ? SERVANT—Yis, mum. MISTRESS—What did they say ? SERVANT—"How fortinit !"

GOOD SENSE—The court, in the case of Marshall vs. State, 59 Ga. 156, said "To be too drunk to form the intent to kill, one must be too drunk to form the intent to shoot."

MRS. JONES—Why don't you do something to support yourself ?

THE TRAMP—I wuz t'inkin', madam, of startin' one of dem endless chains of letters contributing to me relief.

SHE—"Sometimes you appear really manly, and sometimes you are absolutely effeminate. How do you account for it ?" HE—"I suppose it is hereditary. Half of my ancestors were males and the other half females.'

www.ingramcontent.com/pod-product-compliance
Lightning Source LLC
Chambersburg PA
CBHW020305240426
43673CB00039B/707